MOOSE JAW

MOOSE JAW

PEOPLE • PLACES • HISTORY

John Larsen and Maurice Richard Libby

COTEAU BOOKS
WWW.COTEAUBOOKS.COM

Editor for the press, Geoffrey Ursell.
Edited by Dave Margoshes.

Cover images – Top: "Temple Gardens Mineral Spa," © Danny Boyer
Bottom: CPR station, about 1912, Moose Jaw, Saskatchewan,
Courtesy Moose Jaw Public Library Archives.

Cover and book design by Duncan Campbell.
Printed and bound in Canada by Houghton-Boston, Saskatoon.

National Library of Canada Cataloguing in Publication Data

Larsen, John, 1965-
Moose Jaw

ISBN 1-55050-163-1

1. Moose Jaw (Sask.) – History. I. Libby, Maurice, 1951- II. Title.
FC3549.M6L37 2001   971.24'4   C2001-910354-9
F1074.5.M66L37 2001

1 2 3 4 5 6 7 8 9 10

401-2206 Dewdney Ave.
Regina, Saskatchewan
Canada   S4R 1H3

AVAILABLE IN THE US FROM
General Distrubution Services
4500 Witmer Industrial Estates
Niagara Falls, NY, USA 14305-1386

The publisher gratefully acknowledges the financial assistance of the Saskatchewan Arts Board, the Canada Council for the Arts, the Government of Canada through the Book Publishing Industry Development Program (BPIDP), and the City of Regina Arts Commission, for its publishing program.

"A little city that lived big dreams."

– *Pamela Wallin*

4. The Effects of War

5. Boom and Bust

6. March to the Millennium

I lovingly dedicate this book to memory of my Grandmother Nessie —
and to my Mother Sheilagh — for their passionate pursuit of life,
and to my wife Denise, for her tremendous love and encouragement.
— JOHN LARSEN

This book is dedicated to my family — Harvey, Ruby,
and Michael — who made me what I am,
and to Laura, who helped me find what that was.
— MAURICE RICHARD LIBBY

Foreword

Maurice Richard Libby and John Larsen

Moose Jaw native Rick Hancock, in a short film made in the early 1990s, argues that the future of the city cannot be found in its past, that history has little role in determining the city's success for the future. We disagree vehemently! It is exactly the traditions and principles of Moose Jaw's past – to create something out of nothing, to stay when others have left, and to reinvent rather than capitulate – that will ensure its future.

The revival of Moose Jaw is fully underway. The Temple Gardens Mineral Spa has had national press coverage, numerous television and radio programs have turned their attention to the city, new industry and building continues to enhance the economy, a progressive and original tourism program draws thousands of visitors annually, and a fresh agreement to train military pilots from around the globe will provide increased national attention for "The Friendly City."

During the early stages of writing this book, the great Canadian prairie writer W.O. Mitchell died. No other author has so firmly put Saskatchewan on the literary map; no other writer has so accurately captured that nebulous but pervasive power of the prairie mindset. His memory and legacy inspired us. Life in Saskatchewan in general, and Moose Jaw in particular, is one of conviction, dedication, pride, and raw honesty. We hope that the efforts and results of that unique prairie mindset, to some degree, are captured in the following pages.

Moose Jaw is exactly like almost every small town in North America; but it is unlike anywhere else in the world, with its own unique mythology.

The history of Moose Jaw is the story of its times. Boom, bust, good times, bad times: everything that happened, happened here, sometimes less, sometimes more. Moose Jaw is the place everyone has heard of, and now many more are coming to see.

Welcome to Moose Jaw!

– John Larsen & Maurice Richard Libby, August 2001

The Most Canadian of Cities

Peter Gzowski

In the spring of 1957, I was just finishing my year as editor of the University of Toronto's daily newspaper, *The Varsity* and the future looked bright. But since (a) my income from *The Varsity* was about to run out, and (b) I had failed to attend any lectures while I was editing it, I was not going to graduate with the rest of my class, I figured I'd better get a job. A man named Ron Brownridge, the managing editor of the Moose Jaw *Times-Herald* came to see me and ask whether I'd like to take a crack at being the city editor of his paper – well, Roy Thompson's, but Ron was running it. I said sure, and a few weeks later, when most of my friends were heading off for Europe or other capitals of the exotic world, I took a train across Canada to the city with the funny name.

It was as wise a thing as I have ever done. From my first trip – on which I sat next to an Englishman who told me he thought the land we were passing through was "the biggest expanse of bugger all" he'd ever seen in his life – to the people I met and the stories I saw unfold, from the awareness of the real history that I came to realize was everywhere around me (or even under my feet), to the sense of place and of belonging that stayed with me ever since, the education I had thought had finished at university took its most important road.

I did not even begin to absorb the lessons Moose Jaw offered me: lessons of politics, heritage, and community, of a feel for the landscape and its place in the way things worked. I wish I'd had a version of this book to look at then.

But something was planted. Forty years later, when it was time to stage the last-ever edition of *Morningside,* the CBC Radio program that had become the culmination of my long career in writing and broadcasting, I knew we would have to do it from Moose Jaw, the most Canadian of cities, where so much of what I'd learned about the country had first set in.

Peter Gzowski

BEGINNINGS

Building a Town

A Traditional Waypoint

The formal establishment of Moose Jaw was the direct result of the arrival of the Canadian Pacific Railway in 1882.

However, long before railway speculators and survey crews pitched their tents along the shallow banks of the Wakamow Valley, the location of Moose Jaw had been a traditional waypoint for frontier travellers, including the white adventurers, traders, and settlers who would transform the area.

Henry Kelsey of the Hudson's Bay Company is thought to have been the first European in the area, as early as 1690. Traders of "the company," forging west from Fort Qu'Appelle to Fort Walsh, would often pitch camp at what was known then simply as "the turn in the creek," the point at which the Moose Jaw River flowed from a north-west to a north-east location. "The turn" was the most practical place to cross the river. The Trans-Canada Highway today overlies the route, known as the Fort Walsh Trail.

At this bend in the river, early settler Paul Xavier built a one-room 3.5 x 5-metre log cabin in 1865 which he proudly named the Denomie Hotel. With a dirt floor, parched buffalo hides for windows and a single fire for heating and cooking, the Denomie Hotel was, far beyond any intention by Xavier, the embryo of a future city. The cabin was often used by traders of the Hudson's Bay

Opposite page: Breaking the prairie sod with a team of oxen. A Lewis Rice photograph.

A crowd outside Buffalo Store on a very warm December 28, 1888, in a very warm winter.

John Palliser and James Hector about 1860, shortly after their return from their Western sojourn.

Company in checking wintering posts at Old Wives Lake and Wood Mountain.

Before the first squatters began to seize land along the Moose Jaw River, before the Canadian dream of a national railway was set in motion in 1871 with passage of the National Railways Act, and before the building of the Denomie Hotel, the land had been formally surveyed by the noted Irish explorer and wilderness traveller, John Palliser. On assignment to survey the western frontier for the British government, Palliser found little of redemption in the area around Moose Jaw. In his diary on September 15, 1857, Palliser noted his impressions of the area between Regina and Moose Jaw:

"Off at 4:30 a.m., and halted for breakfast at 10 o'clock beside a small lake; from this we had an extensive view of the prairie coteau, extending away to the north-west. Our Indian guide, the peace-maker, to whom we had given the name of Nichiwa, or friend, counselled us to cut wood and bring it along in our carts, as he said it was the last we should see today; there is no more wood except in the valleys of the rivers. Our course was due west, and as far as the eye can reach nothing but desolate plains meet the view."

When John Macoun surveyed the area some twenty-three years later, his impressions were remarkably more positive. Finding an abundance of resources including fish, water, brush, natural shelter and wild animals, Macoun recommended the area to the power brokers of the CPR. The editorial pages of the inaugural edition of the *Moose Jaw News* on May 4, 1883, described the area as "the prettiest town site on the Canadian Pacific Railway. Moose Jaw is beautifully located...the soil is a rich clay loam which, for agricultural purposes, cannot be surpassed in the territories."

Even the weather seemed to cooperate with the idea of large-scale settlement: a photo taken in the winter of 1888 shows a crew of the CPR posed outdoors without jackets. In an interview, former Moose Jaw sheriff John Rutherford claimed that "the fall of 1888 was one of the most remarkable ever experienced in the west, and on New Year's Day 1889 we played a game of baseball."

From Inland Sea to Seas of Grass

Far from the rolling wheat fields and windswept prairie that typify the geography of Moose Jaw today, the area of southern Saskatchewan was, millions of years ago, the home of a tropical rainforest and volcanic mountains. When a series of glacial ice ages ended some fifteen thousand years ago, the last great ice sheet retreated from the Saskatchewan landscape and left in its place the scenic Qu'Appelle Valley, the buried skeletons of extinct dinosaurs, and a huge inland sea, Lake Agassiz, which covered most of modern day Ontario, Manitoba, Saskatchewan, North Dakota, and Minnesota.

As Lake Agassiz emptied into the Hudson Bay ten thousand years ago, it left behind an abundance of clay silt which served as fertilizer for Saskatchewan's future farmland. With temperatures continuing to rise, grasslands developed, buffalo and other animals migrated onto the plains, and humans began their earliest patterns of settlement. Limestone etchings from southern Saskatchewan's petroglyph caves, dating back seventeen hundred years, depict Plains Indians, bears and buffalo. And archaeological findings in south central Saskatchewan point to the establishment of early communities some ten thousand years ago.

It is from these early ancestors that various native tribes are believed to have sprung. The land was, Palliser's views notwithstanding, not inhospitable at all. The Cree, the Blackfoot, the Assiniboine, and the Sioux had passed through and thrived here for thousands of years.

CPR employees and townsmen at the CPR Station on that same warm December 28, 1888.

It was a good place. Great thundering herds of buffalo passed by on their migrations. From horizon to horizon the massive beasts would churn up the soil, clouds of dust rising high into the summer air. Three streams – the Moose Jaw River and Thunder and Spring Creeks – provided water in the hot dry summers, valleys that gave shelter from the bitter winds of winter, and food in the hard, cold times, when the deer sought shelter in those same valleys.

With the arrival of traders from the Hudson's Bay Company, traditional ways of life for the Indians on Canada's western plains began a rapid, and sorrowful, transformation. In just over one century, from King George's proclamation of 1763 announcing that no Indians would be dispossessed of their natural land, to the near destruction of traditional native ways of life by the mid-1880s, a culture which had taken thousands of years to develop had systematically and callously been devastated. The lure of tobacco, the effects of alcohol, the appeal of convenience goods, and the outright lies of government conspired to cripple a proud and complex heritage.

It is impossible to point to a single factor directly causing this social destruction, but certainly the arrival of

A Sioux teepee at Moose Jaw about 1890.

the railway accentuated and accelerated the process. The never-ending tracks of steel, built on a man-made berm some 18 metres wide by 1.25 metres high, permanently altered the migratory pattern of the buffalo and encouraged their massive overhunting by whites, resulting initially in hunger, and eventually, in outright starvation for First Nations people. Even before the arrival of the railway, in the period from 1871

Railroad construction in the 1880s. Railway ties are being unloaded at the end of the track.

to 1875, white hunters killed an estimated ten million buffalo, taking with them only the hides, and leaving the carcasses to rot on the plains.

Relations between First Nations people and European settlers slowly deteriorated throughout the 1870s. A pivotal turning point was the Cyprus Hills massacre of 1878 when thirty-six Assiniboine were murdered by a small group of American hunters, an event that speeded the formation and dispatch west of the Royal North West Mounted Police. The Mounties, while ostensibly the protectors of the Indians, also ensured their subjugation.

A few years later, while laying tracks through to Moose Jaw, a CPR crew was stopped in its construction by a group on Indians, led by the Cree Chief Piapot. RNWMP officers disbanded the gathering. The demonstration speaks loudly to the discontent and frustration among Indians in the early days of Moose Jaw.

As popular historian Pierre Berton has pointed out, the railway symbolized the end of a way of life for the plains First Nations. In the space of half a dozen years, the Blackfoot and Cree were transformed from members of independent nations roaming freely across the prairies hunting buffalo and other wild game to half-starved inhabitants of prison-like reserves totally dependent upon government for food, shelter, and clothing.

It was the beginning of a very difficult period for the prairie First Nations. Within a decade of the arrival of the CPR, the sea of grass that had sustained the buffalo – and, through them, the First Nations – had been replaced by seas of wheat, the foundation of the settler economy.

A Harsh and Elemental Land

From Winnipeg to the Rocky Mountains, the prairie seemed to go on forever. It was flat. It stretched out like a table top to the ends of your imagination. It was unbroken and virginal. The only thing that disturbed the infinite line of the horizon was the tall prairie grass undulating in the ceaseless wind. It was so flat and featureless you would feel a lonely, empty ache in the pit of your stomach, made only worse by the sky – that painfully blue and endless canopy. It made you feel small, dwarfed by God and

Breaking the prairie sod with a tractor.

submerged in the infinity of His works.

To the pioneers used to the rolling hills and ancient forests of England, or the protected fiords of the northern lands, or the heartbreakingly green rolling hills of Ireland, it was almost beyond imagining. Even the rocky and inhospitable highlands of Scotland seemed almost cosy next to this terrible expanse, where it was easy to believe that you could just go on and on until you fell off the edge of the world.

In the summer, the sun blazed, searing the ground and roasting it to a bright gold. The daytime heat sucked the moisture from the skin and the energy from every living creature. When the wind died down, the mosquitoes swarmed like living storm clouds, trying the patience of the strongest man and driving animals to distraction and even to madness.

In the winter, the glare of that same sun on the snow could blind the eyes of the unwary stranger. Temperatures dropped so low that the mercury seemed to freeze in the thermometer. The wind – that ceaseless maddening wind – cut across the endless plain in all seasons, and many grew to hate the

sound, that howling, whining, keening sound that would sometimes go on for days, weeks, even months on end.

But still, there was something about this harsh and elemental land. It was fertile, there was no question of that. The grass in places grew a metre or more high, and where it grew, people thought, given enough care, and if the living skies were generous, you could grow wheat. Anywhere that could support those immense herds of buffalo could surely support modest herds of cattle.

The Future Townsite

Although people of the First Nations and, later, Metis hunters and white traders had been erecting tipis and hide tents for many years on its prairies and in its valleys, the first semi-permanent buildings weren't erected in what is now southern Saskatchewan until the arrival of European settlers from Eastern Canada in the late 1870s and early 1880s. First they put up sod huts, then log cabins, and finally buildings of cut wood and stone. These builders meant to stay.

Mr. Laird, with mosquito netting on his hat, Major Snyder, and James H. Ross.

James H. Ross with his wife Barbara and an unidentified woman
(possibly the bride's mother) around the time of their wedding in 1886.

As the CPR stretched across the prairie, a small group of opportunistic land speculators and businessmen were at the forefront of the earliest township developments. These were the men who, for a calculated chance at financial success, braved the scarcities and rigours of the endless prairie. If they were in the right place, at the right time, they stood to gain huge profit from the wealth and social recognition accompanying the spread of the CPR. These were "the movers and shakers" of the early west, the men who claimed the profitable land, established entertainment and business venues, and assumed the first posts in a new political and judicial order.

In the case of Moose Jaw, the man who made it all start was explorer J.H. Ross, once a city councillor from London, Ontario, who would be Moose Jaw's first mayor and later a member of the Senate.

Many of those who first settled in the fledgling towns of the new west were employed by the CPR, most notably as advance surveyors or supply runners from the newest end-of-line point. As part of a CPR supply crew, Henry Battell arrived in Moose Jaw on May 24, 1882, and noted with surprise that his crew were not the first white people there. Four months earlier, Ross and some associates, including his brother Fred and their friend Hector Sutherland, had already laid claim to some of the choice locations in the future townsite. They had arrived at the future location of Moose Jaw almost a year earlier, in July of 1881.

"There was nothing here at the time," Ross would recall later, "excepting a camp site at the river crossing of the old Hudson Bay trail from Fort Qu'Appelle to Fort Walsh."

After their initial survey of the region, the Ross party returned east, collected more belongings, and left again for Moose Jaw in early winter. Their arrival was a dramatic moment.

It's brutally cold. The January wind cuts James Ross's face with a stinging bite, swirls viciously around his body, pulls at the neck and arms of his buffalo fur jacket, and blows shards of hardened snow into his cheek and forehead.

"This better be right," says Fred Ross, huddled at his brother's back.

"It's right," replies James, his voice rising. He turns enthusiastically to the group of half-dozen men standing around him. Framed against a sheet of white, looking almost unhuman wrapped in his multilayered clothing and covered in black blowing fur, James Ross surveys the lonely land. His sparkling eyes, made watery by the driving wind, are large in his weathered face.

"Believe it or not gentlemen, but this is where we stood last summer." He points to a sunken, winding creek bend. "This is where the water ran." He looks to a small grove of trees growing in isolation, and then turns his face upward, squinting at the harsh winter sun. "This, gentlemen, I assure you, is where the rail will come, where the people will come, where the money will come. And we are here now. Let us put this journey, and our pasts behind us. Let us look to tomorrow."

His right foot, wrapped in a heavy mukluk, stomps the hardened snow while his left arm cuts a wide arch toward the horizon. His eyes settle on the group of adventurers.

"By God, gentlemen, this is our home."

Building a Town

Land sectioning in the territories was divided on a system of quarter sections, with baselines established every twenty-four miles (thirty-nine kilometres) from the US border. Ross and his brother settled on the fourth baseline north, and procured the first real estate in Moose Jaw on what is now the area north of Caribou street and east of Main street, including the Hillcrest golf course.

Within months, settlement soared. William Burton and John Waddell moved to Moose Jaw from Fort Qu'Appelle in April, Henry Battell arrived in May and quickly purchased eight sections, and settlers poured in from as far east as Ontario and the Maritimes. Other future developers of the town, most notably R.K. Thompson, E.N. Hopkins, and F.W. Green, established farm property at the going rate of $2.50 per acre in the seventy-seven-kilometre belt along the CPR, of which half was rebated by the government if the land was developed and cropped within three years. For an initial pay down of only fifty cents per acre, land was plentiful. Anyone with a mind for business could smell the fragrant winds of opportunity in those early months of Moose Jaw. Within three decades, city land would appreciate from $1.25 to as much as $500 per acre, according to some accounts.

The railway was the stimulus, no question, but the earliest stages of township development began before the arrival of the CPR. Tents stood as hotels, with hanging blankets serving as walls. Before the arrival of imported brick, or the provision of local brick, most buildings were ramshackle wooden fire hazards. More substantial structures, both houses and businesses, were constructed of stone and clay, with roofs comprised of hay and wooden poles.

So proud was Moose Jaw of its initial growth that the May 11, 1883, inaugural edition of the *Moose Jaw News* proclaimed that "settlers should understand that everything required for a pioneer life is obtainable in Moose Jaw."

Of course, the vast majority of immigrants to the new area were more interested in the rugged life of homesteading. Many of the new settlers came with little more than the clothes on their backs, a limited amount of start-up cash, and the dreams of a new tomorrow. They endured blizzards, spring thaw washouts, summer droughts, farming and construction accidents, loneliness, bankruptcy —

A sod house and unidentified family of homesteaders north or northwest of the city about 1900.

even starvation. It was no wonder that the bright lights of the city attracted them. When they needed supplies, or relaxation, it was to Moose Jaw that they came.

Some of the newcomers managed to mix town and country.

Tom McWilliams arrived in the area in 1884. Originally homesteading near Moose Jaw, he soon discovered the potential value of the clay deposits near Claybank, and relocated his homestead in order to gain legal possession of the clay.

McWilliams' grandson Bill, a lifelong Moose Javian, recalls that his father Sam, then only a boy, was left to tend the new homestead while Tom McWilliams and his wife turned their attention to the new economic developments in Moose Jaw.

"My grandfather bought some cows, took my dad out when he was thirteen," Bill McWilliams recalls. "They cut some rails in the bush to make corrals, went and got a load of lumber from Moose Jaw, went down and made a one-room shack, and left my dad there to fend for himself and look after the animals."

The closest neighbour was sixteen kilometres away. As McWilliams' father tried to survive, literally, on the Claybank homestead, his grandparents ran the Queen's Hotel boarding house in Moose Jaw. "This was a railway town and there was an awful lot of men looking for a place to eat and sleep, and my grandfather gave them room and board while they worked with the CPR."

Eventually, Tom McWilliams' intuition paid off and the clay deposits at Claybank became the source of one of the most successful businesses in Saskatchewan. The silt deposits of the great Lake Agassiz would eventually make bricks which were used in much of Moose Jaw's construction, most notably the building of the Bellamy Block and the Capitol Theatre.

A riding party at the Moose Hotel. The ladies are mounted sidesaddle.

What's in a name?

Often cited as one of the most unusual place names in Canada, if not in the world, the true origin of Moose Jaw's name is difficult to determine. Many interpretations abound, some possible but not plausible, some outright concoctions of the imagination made only marginally believable by the strength of their voice through generations.

Perhaps one of the most enduring, and certainly most dramatic accounts of the naming of Moose Jaw is that of an early settler who was passing through the area in the mid-1850s when his Red River cart suffered a broken wheel. Without recourse to the use of trees, the lone traveller eventually came across a pile of bones left from hunts and, in a moment of inspired ingenuity, used the jawbone of a moose to fix his wagon.

The *Moose Jaw Times*, in its September 20, 1907, edition, relates a slightly different version when referring to the travels of the partially blind Earl of Dunsmore, who also suffered from a broken wagon wheel. "At this site he mended the wheel of his Red River cart with the jawbone of a moose he had shot and the Red Indian scouts called it 'the place where the one-eyed white chief mended his cart with the jaw bone of a moose.'"

Long-time Moose Jaw resident Lawrence "Moon" Mullins has yet another account of the city's name origin:

"The way my Dad said it happened was that they were moving cattle and they'd move them so far from the last point and they'd come to a post with a moose jaw on it, and they were told that when they came to the moose jaw they had to turn left – there were two trails, one to the north and one going west – they'd go left and come out south of Mortlach where the springs were. They could water the cattle there and then move on up."

MOOSEJAW.

The Future Great Central City of the North-West.

The Prettiest Townsite on the Canadian Pacific Railway.

MOOSEJAW is beautifully located on a high table-land which extends for many miles in all directions, and consequently it has the advantage of good natural drainage. Situated at the confluence of Moosejaw River and Thunder Creek, the country to the north rises gradually for many miles, and to the south the land is beautiful rolling prairie. The soil is a rich clay loam which, for agricultural purposes cannot be surpassed in the Territories, and is especially adapted for market-gardening. The surrounding country is interspersed here and there with beautiful lakes and intersected with running streams.

Several wells have been sunk by settlers near the city, and abundant water procured at 17 to 20 feet from the surface.

The coal fields of the South Saskatchewan are being rapidly developed and coal will be delivered in Moosejaw at low rates within a month, when the C. P. R. has reached that River. Plenty of wood is obtainable at Buffalo Lake on the north, at Wood Mountain on the south, and along the Moosejaw River.

An idea of the importance of this point may be gained from the fact that the Northwest Land Company have made Moosejaw the head... ... of their lands,

It is unlikely that any accounts referring to the mending of carts by moose bones or the posting of skeletal directional beacons are accurate. Long before the visits of one-eyed earls or the regular movement of cattle in the region, the area had already been identified as Moose Jaw. In his initial survey report of 1857, noted in both print and on a lithographed map, John Palliser refers to the area as "Moose Jaw Bone Creek."

The simplest explanation for the name is the most likely, that it originates from the Cree word pronounced *moosegaw,* meaning "warm breezes."

Official Status

Much of Moose Jaw's earliest history can be captured from the pages of its original newspaper, the *News*. According to the May 4, 1883, inaugural edition of the paper:

"Two months ago the settlement of Moose Jaw was distinguishable from the boundless prairie only by its natural beauty and two buildings. Today it contains upwards of one hundred buildings, many of which are handsome and substantial structures."

The Cemeteries

Death took a moratorium in Moose Jaw for a year. But, of course, it couldn't last.

In 1883, a work crew was moving a house on Main Street. It was a routine job on a normal day and everything was as it should be – until disaster struck. The moving chain broke, its heavy steel links striking like a massive deadly snake. One of the crewmen fell to the ground screaming in pain. His leg was crushed beyond repair and he died shortly thereafter, becoming a dubious footnote to Moose Jaw's history – he was the first person to die in the town since it was established the previous year.

With no cemetery, this created a problem – where to put him?

The pillars of the community decided to put a cemetery across the river about a quarter mile east of the future location of the Moose Jaw College (later St. Anthony's Home) between the CPR tracks and the trails that would become the Trans-Canada Highway. Since the only way across the river was via the CPR bridge, the funeral party took the train.

In 1890, a new and more convenient cemetery was built at Ninth Avenue and Caribou Street East. It contained room for fifty-five hundred plots, with a chapel added in 1911. In an unusually ecumenical gesture for the time, the Moose Jaw Cemetery was not segregated by race, religion, or ethnic group. It remains the resting-place for many diverse people, including the first Chinese child born in the city, the first victim of an unsolved homicide, and thousands of pioneers. It continued to be used for many decades, but by the early 1920s all the plots had been sold and a new cemetery was needed.

The new cemetery was built in the northwest corner of the city and opened in 1922. It was a little less tolerant than its predecessor, being segregated by religion, ethnicity, and race until 1976. In 1989, a private cemetery was built just outside the city west of 9th Avenue SW.

In 1956, British American Oil, which owned the large refinery by the river, bought the first cemetery and obtained permission to move the residents to the Moose Jaw Cemetery. Although records are not clear, somewhere between fifteen and thirty bodies were removed. The process was difficult because the bodies were not laid out geometrically and were unmarked except for an outline of stones. It was further exacerbated by the fact that no records were ever kept of who was laid to rest there.

Some evidence was found to indicate that the cemetery, although it was officially closed when the Moose Jaw Cemetery was built, might have been used by passing wagon trains in the 1890s. It has been suggested that some of the large number of bodies resulting from the influenza epidemic of 1918, when hundreds of people died in the Moose Jaw area, were buried there.

Researchers in 1958 advertised for information about the residents of the old cemetery but received no reply, and the identities remain a mystery.

In 1999, Moose Jaw Cemetery was designated a heritage site.

Moose Jaw, the paper said, was "the end of passenger traffic west, with a floating population between two thousand and three thousand. The sound of hammers was heard from daylight until dark."

The town's growth was reflected in the provision of a variety of public services. The first church service was held in March, 1883, in a railway shack. Years later, the local paper recalled that "in 1883 a Mr. Winnet had a few chairs and tables under a tent and during the summer a Mr. Clark from Toronto preached in the first crude church. There were planks for seats, which were very uncomfortable. Mr. Clark said that if we should try and raise some money, he would pay half the money for some chairs and I thought this was too good an offer to let go." That year also saw construction of the first cemetery and the establishment of a fire brigade.

A huge step in consolidating the importance of Moose Jaw as a viable business and social centre was the transfer of CPR roundhouse timbers from Regina to Moose Jaw. Within the first year, Moose Jaw had merchants dealing in groceries, dry goods, flour and feed, clothing, hardware, agricul-tural supplies, bakery, pharmaceutical supplies, furniture, blacksmith, and barber services. Professionals such as archi-tects, doctors, and lawyers were also setting up shops. Moose Jaw further offered the first dental x-ray service west of Winnipeg. The town was already the seat of a dozen hotels and restaurants, including the Brunswick, the Ottawa, and the Occidental.

The only aspect of Moose Jaw's earliest development that did not keep apace of public expectation was the establishment of a post office, which wasn't built until the summer of 1884, on 2nd Avenue and High Street West. The first telegraph service, between Moose Jaw and Wood Mountain, fol-lowed in 1885.

As one visitor wrote to the *News*, on May 4, 1883: "I have not, in all my peregrinations through the Northwest, been so favourably impressed with a town site as I have with that of Moose Jaw." The letter was signed simply as "A Citizen of the World."

Others were not as impressed. As late as 1890, with Moose Jaw by then an influential social and commercial force, mounted policeman John Donkin could find little to redeem this prairie town. As he wrote in the *News*:

"Moose Jaw lies in a hollow of the prairie, the population is five hundred and there is the usual scattering of hotels and stores standing at regular intervals upon the unromantic flat. Ugly, square objects all of them, with-out the slightest pretence of architec-tural beauty. A prairie town is a more depressing object than a burnt forest."

The majority of Moose Jaw's earli-est residents did not share Donkin's opinion. From a sprawling village of canvas tents and impromptu wooden huts, Moose Jaw grew to gain official status as a town on February 13, 1884. In years to come, one of Moose Jaw's most prominent mayors, Louis "Scoop" Lewry, would proudly claim that "the dreams and plans of the pioneer settlers who foresaw a city on a barren prairie site are now being fully realised."

It wasn't long before residents sought to convert the town from a mere location of amenities to an aes-thetically pleasing living environment complete with all the social fibres that bind a town together. In September, 1884, the Moose Jaw Agricultural Board planted the city's first trees along Main Street, and school classes began, in a

Opposite: One hundred and fifty students and teachers in front of Victoria School in 1907 (in the original photograph).

room of the Simpson's store, moving a year later to the Brunswick Hotel and a section of a pool hall (partitioned by a hanging curtain). Teachers were often volunteers and student attendance was irregular. In 1886, classes were moved to Moose Hall, and the following year to a room above a tinsmith shop in the Scott Block. Not until the opening of Victoria School in 1898, did Moose Jaw provide a permanent home for education. It was the first multi-room school in the territory. In its first incarnation, it had four classrooms, two of them used for high school classes.

Ribbons of Steel

It could well be argued that if it wasn't for the Canadian Pacific Railway, there would be no Moose Jaw. For it was on the arms of the great national railway that many a new town was born, economies set in motion, and societies raised. So, had the CPR not existed, or had it taken another route, there's a good chance there would have been no European settlement along the banks of the Moose Jaw River, and the people who settled there would have put down roots in some other town.

As plans were made for the national railroad mandated by Prime Minister John A. MacDonald in the mid-nineteenth century, the main point of discussion was which route to follow across the West. There was strong argument for taking the northern Yellowhead route, linking previously established settlements in Saskatoon and Edmonton.

In 1857, British surveyor John Pal-liser had found the southern region — a triangle running between present day Winnipeg, Calgary, and Saskatoon — too arid for settlement. But CPR surveyor John Macoun saw wisdom in running the rail line across a straighter southern route. The prospect of establishing a line close to the American border, secured by a noncompetition agreement with other railways, was appealing to CPR managers. By cutting into the new southern territory, the railway would serve as a lifeline to new business and social centres, would yield profits from settlement contracts, and would stave off

A special CPR homesteader train, using a Minneapolis, St. Paul, and Sault Line coach, about 1900.

competitive U.S. railway interests.

An ambitious construction schedule called for an average of five and a half kilometres of track being laid per day. Omer Lavallee, former historian of the CPR, claims that on one single day – August 29, 1882 – 6,513 metres of track were spiked into place just east of Moose Jaw between Pense and Belle Plaine – a little more than four miles. The setting of track around Moose Jaw was no easy task. Along the bald prairie, water was scarce, and what water could be found had high alkaline levels, rendering it unsuitable for locomotive boilers; the earth was harder than in Central Canada, making horse-drawn scrapers inoperable; and supply lines were weakened over the increasing distance between supply depots.

But on September 6, 1882, a construction rig first entered Moose Jaw on freshly laid track, and on December 10 of that same year the first passenger train – "Old 103" – pulled into town. The arrival of the CPR thus marked the unofficial birth of the community that became Moose Jaw.

Only six months later, being extended at a phenomenal rate of five and a half kilometres per day, the CPR had already reached Calgary. The railway was radically altering the West, and Moose Jaw – with its roundhouse, coal shed, eight separate side-tracks, and supervisor's office – was at the heart of it.

No sooner had the CPR run its tracks across the prairie than other railway companies began to consider the business advantages of running north-south lines. Soon, a series of north-south tracks were established by the Souris and Rocky Mountain Railway that allowed settlers to access the CPR main line. The CPR itself also recognised the need for expansion, and in 1890 established a line between Regina and Prince Albert. The next year, a line was built from Calgary to Edmonton in the north, and this was quickly followed by a line from Calgary to Fort MacLeod in the south. In 1899, the Canadian National Railway was established, extending services throughout Saskatchewan beginning in 1905.

All of this activity had an impact on Moose Jaw, but one of the biggest developments to effect the city's growth was the arrival of the Soo Line on September 18, 1893. Serving as the major artery between the eastern United States and western Canada, the Mountaineer train ran between Moose Jaw and Chicago, intersecting Minneapolis, in a scant thirty-six hours.

The arrival of the Soo Line was a social and economic coup for Moose Jaw. American travellers, with wide experience and thick wallets, soon poured into town, eager for a glimpse of Canada's untamed West. Moose Jaw was picked as the terminus of the Soo Line because of its excellent railway facilities, and its growing reputation as a vibrant social centre. The arrival of the Soo only helped catapult Moose Jaw to new heights, and it set the stage for the infamy which the city would inherit as a result of booze trafficking along the Soo some two decades later.

Opposite: CPR employees with a locomotive ("Old 80") at the roundhouse in 1894.

Red Lights and Empty Bottles

It has often been said that Moose Jaw became Regina's red light district. Regina, as a government town, quickly developed a prim and proper reputation. Moose Jaw, a mere hour's train ride away, was, from the beginning, much more hurly-burly. The CPR itself had a lot to do with it, with the throngs of women who catered to the working men of the early west following the same course as the ever-lengthening railway.

In his book, *Red Lights on the Prairie,* a clear account of prostitution on Canada's new frontier, James Grey claims that up to a hundred common bawdy houses were kept in Moose Jaw during the summer months during the 1880s. With the nearly complete absence of traditional family structures, the company of women for the exchange of money became the norm. It was a social situation which the law neither encouraged nor invoked too much authority to suppress.

The judicial attitude of tolerance toward the skin trade continued for many years, and eventually led to the growth of Moose Jaw's infamy during the Roaring Twenties, a decade rampant with the vices of prostitution, gambling and illicit alcohol sales. A report submitted by an agent of the Central Detective Service of Canada in 1913 points to the police attitude of indifference, which began some three decades earlier. "I located a hooker in

Walter Johnson, Chief of Police, about 1906.

room 105, Hotel Empress, late Sunday night, registering from Winnipeg; learned that she came here learning that there was good money in Moose Jaw, and that you could square it with police if you lived quietly in the hotels."

Beyond the issue of prostitution, Moose Jaw and all of Saskatchewan rode the on-again, off-again roller coaster of prohibition – in all its various forms – for years. As early as 1875, the North West Territories Act prohibited the importation, sale or possession of alcohol except that approved by permit issued through the Lieutenant Governor, giving that office tremendous social and political leverage. Such a law did little to stifle alcohol consumption, but merely slowed the process of acquiring the spirits. Eventually, somebody would know someone with a connection to the proverbial tap and a drunken crowd could be found. According to Grey, whiskey was the

Top left: River Street looking west about 1910. On the right side are many of the hotels that made the street famous.

Top right: The infamous Annie Hoburg's Railroad Restaurant, with a crowd that includes four Sioux.

fuel that kept the political machine humming. Control of alcohol was subsequently spread into the hands of senior railway officials, who withheld it from construction crews in the interests of faster development.

Until 1924, when Prohibition finally ended in Canada, the fortunes of alcohol rose and fell in Saskatchewan, but the various government restrictions did little to quench Moose Jaw's thirst. Many early news articles reported the activities of Moose Jaw's Annie Hoburg, who continually defied the laws. Employing the most unique methods of illicitly smuggling booze throughout Saskatchewan, Hoburg was once caught transporting whiskey in a baby carriage, and had a petticoat designed which would support specially-built bags of liquor.

Like the illegal drugs of today, the prohibition of alcohol created opportunities for abuse of police power. In Moose Jaw, Walter Johnson, who was appointed police chief in 1905, became notorious, though little was ever proved against him. A 1913 Central Detective Service of Canada investigation into illegal police activity in Moose Jaw stated that "the proprietor of the Elmo

The CPR Dining Hall in 1891. The diners include Dr. Duncan Forgie, Dr. Turnbull, Jim Calder, Nellie Doran, Joe and Frank Daley, and Jasey Lily.

Road Room said he had the privilege of running games in his pool room from Chief Johnson; he has a slot machine there which he said was arranged through the sergeant." The report later goes on to advise that Chief Johnson's "rake off the grifters at the fair three years ago was $50 a (gambling/prostitution) joint, and there were upwards of forty joints doing business." But no action was taken on the report.

An Oasis of Civilization

Within a year of the CPR forging its way through Moose Jaw, the town had already grown to acquire considerable regional social and economic influence. As early as 1884, Timothy Eaton, the nation's foremost catalogue retailer, had pinpointed the town as a promising new market. Merchants from eastern Canada travelled west in search of new economic opportunity; among them was Walter Joyner. Trained as a tailor with the Ontario garment factory of Alphonse Lorraine, Joyner established what would prove to be one of the most enduring private businesses in Moose Jaw. Joyner's Men's wear would keep its doors open for nearly a century.

Perhaps the biggest single factor contributing to the economic vitality of Moose Jaw in the early years was the transfer in 1883 of the CPR divisional point from Regina to Moose Jaw. With the move came an enhanced financial fortune. Trains now had to pass through

Moose Jaw for connections either east or west. Thousands of passengers pumped money through the CPR diner, stayed in local hotels, enjoyed local entertainment, and purchased local goods. The Railroad Restaurant on Main Street announced "Meals All Hours." The Occidental Hotel, also on Main, proudly proclaimed that it offered visitors "Good, Clean Beds," while the Wilson and Co. store on High Street advertised "Fancy Goods and Reading Matter." There was little not to be had in Moose Jaw in the early years.

By 1888, the Moose Jaw Board of

Trade was founded and was soon involved in a campaign to advertise the town as the source of high quality international grain. A quarter of a century later, the board of trade could proudly proclaim that Moose Jaw was the "buckle of the greatest wheat belt in the world."

In fact, the route of the CPR, the influx of settlers, and the growth of Moose Jaw would not have been possible if it weren't for the opportunities afforded by agriculture. The farming business gave birth to Moose Jaw, and has sustained the city ever since.

A harvest scene on Ben Thomson's farm at Boharm. In 34 days they threshed 70,000 bushels of wheat; 2,868 on their best day.

The town was, in many respects, a service depot for the numerous farming communities that sprung up around it, with all the amenities required by a new settler. The first mill for wheat and oats was constructed in 1900, and was operated by Donald McLean. Within a few short years, small farming hamlets such as Boharm, Cobourg, Buffalo Lake, Eastview, Pasqua, and Petrolia were established around Moose Jaw. As early as 1884, the Moose Jaw Agricultural Society was established, and later in the year it held the first annual agricultural fair, complete with ox races along Main Street.

A street parade celebrating Queen Victoria's Diamond Jubilee on June 22, 1897.

Up in Smoke

The year 1891 marked a turning point for Moose Jaw. It was a year of destruction, but, ironically, it was also the beginning of an unprecedented period of growth. On Dec. 14, the still wet-behind-the-ears town suffered what has come to be known as "the great fire." It was a calamity that destroyed nearly half of Main Street and brought to an abrupt end the chorus of raucous laughter and good cheer that had flowed through town for nearly a decade.

Like so much else in the early days of Moose Jaw, booze was involved, with the blame for the fire falling on the drunken shoulders of George Waterfield, a lodger at Jackman's Hotel.

Bill McWilliams' father was an attendant at the Jackman's. Here's how Bill describes what happened as passed down through family lore:

"This guy came back from River Street and went upstairs and Dad went up shortly afterwards. He was drunk and was galloping around with a kerosene lamp, and Dad tried to get it away from him, and of course he said he could see where that was going to be disastrous. So he tried talking him into putting it down on the table, and hoped he'd go to sleep. Well, he did, but not till after he had dumped the lamp somewhere and started the fire. There was no hope, there was no fire department; just no hope at all."

Destruction by the fire was rapid and deadly. The proprietor of the hotel died trying unsuccessfully to save his daughter from the flames. Three other

The City Hotel, at 54 River Street West, opened in 1905.

residents of the hotel also perished. With only a rudimentary bucket brigade to tend the flames as a volunteer fireguard, spread of the fire was beyond control. Within a couple of hours, the flames had consumed nearly all the wooden structures along the west side of Main Street. A bakery was purposely destroyed to prevent the ravages of the fire from spreading further. By the following morning, ten of

eleven structures on the east side of Main Street had been burned to the ground and a full six of eight buildings had been razed on the west side. In total, seventeen businesses and St. John the Baptist Anglican Church were lost. As the *Regina Leader* reported the following morning:

"Within half an hour, with the aid of a strong south-west wind which was blowing at the time, and before the inhabitants could be well roused from their slumbers, nearly the whole south side of Main Street was in flames. The chemical engine was brought into requisition as quickly as possible but owing to the fire having made such headway it was impossible owing to the intense heat to get near enough the fire for the chemicals were all but exhausted. How-

ever, good execution was done with the water pail system in keeping the fire from crossing River Street, or the whole town would have been a heap of ruins tonight."

Three months after the fire, in an effort to rebuild the first block of Main Street, town council called for a new survey of the property lines initially established in 1882. The new town of Moose Jaw would be constructed along more accurate measures, with brick and mortar rather than blankets and wood. A new fire code called for the use of brick or stone in new construction, and the business of brickmaking skyrocketed. The Boan family, still residing in Moose Jaw generations later, capitalised on the new opportunity by opening a limestone quarry with two firing kilns in 1899. Located just east of the city, the Boan enterprise produced bricks that were used in the construction of the City Hotel, the Cecil, Joyner's and Alexandria School, among many other buildings.

Before the new building standards could take effect, another fire broke out, on May 11, at the intersection of River and Main, but was more easily brought under control. The "Great

Below: Firemen in action at the Central Fire Station on Fairford Street West. A Lewis Rice photograph.

BEGINNINGS — 21

Fire" was a wake-up call for Moose Jaw, and inasmuch as the fire was a tragedy, it focussed the city on important steps needed to be taken in order to redevelop and grow, though a full-time fire fighting service wouldn't be achieved until 1905, with a permanent fire hall in 1908. Motorised fire vehicles chugged their way into the city in 1914.

However, the fire helped Moose Jaw move from being a haphazard, wooden shack town to a substantial town with architectural character and greater socio-economic weight.

...Full of Sound and Fury

Although Regina had been founded earlier, within a few months of its creation, Moose Jaw was a social and economic rival to the older, larger centre. With trains arriving on her doorstep day and night, money continually rolled through the city. The small town in the middle of nowhere soon became the centre of commerce between the Bow River in Alberta and the Red River in Manitoba. Regina and Moose Jaw angled and pitched to gain positive recognition from politicians in Ottawa. And although Regina had been proclaimed official capital of the North West Territories in August, 1882, this was a race for capital status of a different kind − a race for prestige. To all those who lobbied on behalf of Moose Jaw there was little to erode the belief that dominance of the region hung in the balance.

With the decision in 1883 to locate the CPR divisional point in Moose Jaw − an earlier roundhouse in the capital city had burned down − Regina began to lose much of its influence as a social centre, and many visitors questioned the wisdom of having selected the barren area as capital. It was an academic question for many travellers west. By the

The *Times* building about 1894. Founded by Walter Scott, this was the city's second newspaper.

mid-1880s, Moose Jaw appeared as much a capital as any other major centre on the prairies, and far more in many respects than did Regina. In 1894, Moose Jaw welcomed the arrival of its second newspaper, the *Moose Jaw Times*, led by Walter Scott, who would go on to be Saskatchewan's first premier. The new paper followed carefully the economic boom of the town, served as a check to the municipal government, and as a fresh source of input for its residents.

The animosity between the two towns soon grew acrimonious. Nicholas Davin, the journalist and member of Parliament from Regina, referred to the competition as "Loose Jaw." A war of economics and influence peddling soon followed the war of words and the ultimate decision to make Regina the capital of the new province of Saskatchewan in 1905 left bitter feelings in the city to its west and elsewhere.

The decision had been made, though, and Moose Jaw had to lick its wounds.

Four Premiers with Moose Jaw Connections

Walter Scott

Walter Scott, who went on to become Saskatchewan's first Premier, was born in London, Ontario, in 1867. At the age of eighteen, he went to live with an uncle in Portage la Prairie, where he was introduced to the publishing business when he became a printer's apprentice. He later worked as a journalist at the *Manitoba Free Press* and *The Regina Journal*. In 1892 he helped found the *Regina Standard* with other disaffected ex-employees of the *Journal*.

In 1894 he went to Moose Jaw to start the *Moose Jaw Times*. With him he brought the seventeen-year-old Thomas Miller to be the foreman of the paper. Miller would eventually buy the paper and would be the editor of the *Times*, *The Evening Times*, and later the *Times-Herald*. Miller would also help found the Western Associated Press (a forerunner of the Canadian Press), of which he was a director until he became the only Lieutenant Governor from Moose Jaw in 1945.

Scott lived in Moose Jaw while he was publisher and editor of the *Times* in 1894-1895. He sold the *Times,* and then bought it again the following year. In 1895 he bought the Regina *Leader*.

In 1900 he was elected to the House Of Commons as a Liberal. He was closely involved with the writing of the Autonomy Act, which would result in the formation of the Province of Saskatchewan. In 1905, after being elected a second time, he resigned from the Commons to become leader of the Saskatchewan Liberal Party. In September of 1905, he was appointed the first Premier of the brand new province by the equally new Lt. Governor A.E. Forget. Shortly after, he won the first provincial election and became the first elected premier as well. He served as premier for eleven years before ill health forced him into retirement.

Upon his death in 1938, Premier William Patterson said of him, "Walter Scott established the government of the province.... He established a foundation based on sanity and right.... The parliament buildings and the University of Saskatchewan are a permanent tribute to his wisdom."

Charles Avery Dunning

Charles Avery Dunning was born in England in 1885. He came to Canada in 1902 at the age of seventeen and worked

as a farm hand near Yorkton. He then settled on a homestead in the Beaverdale district in 1903, and became a member, then a director and later vice-president of the Territorial Grain Grower's Association. In 1911 he was one of the founders, and then became general manager of the new Saskatchewan Co-operative Elevator Company, a post he held until 1916. During those years, the company became the largest single grain handling company in the world. In 1912, the co-op acquired a seat on the Winnipeg Grain Exchange as a result of Dunning's efforts.

He was elected as the Liberal MLA of Kinistino by acclamation in 1916 and was appointed Provincial Treasurer. He also served as Minister of Telephones from 1918 to 1919, Minister of Agriculture from 1919 to 1920, Minister of Municipal Affairs and Provincial Secretary from 1921 to 1922. The MLA for Moose Jaw County from 1917 to 1926, he became Premier on April 5, 1922. As well as Premier, during this time he was also Provincial Treasurer, Minister of Railways, and President of the Executive Council.

Dunning was thirty-seven years old at the time, and was often referred to as "The Empire's Youngest Premier." His administration was particularly concerned with the prosperity of farmers and the development of producer co-operatives. One of his last acts as Premier was to arrange the sale of the Co-operative Elevator Company to the newly-organized Saskatchewan Wheat Pool.

Resigning as Premier in 1926 to move into federal politics, he became federal Minister of Railways and Canals, before becoming Minister of Finance in 1929. He was defeated in the 1930 election, but returned as Minister of Finance during the last years of the Dirty Thirties, 1935 to 1939, trying to restore prosperity. He played an important role in the completion of the Hudson Bay Railway and the selection of Churchill as its terminal. During the last nineteen years of his life, he worked in the financial world of Eastern Canada, until he died in Montreal in 1958.

W. Ross Thatcher

Wilbert Ross Thatcher was born on May 24, 1917, in Neville to Wilbert and Marjorie Thatcher, English immigrants from Ontario. He had three younger siblings, Clarke, Ron, and Joan. The Thatchers moved to Moose Jaw in 1928 and Wilbert began the Moose Jaw Hardware Company Ltd. Ross graduated from Central Collegiate when he was fifteen: he was a bright student that often completed two grades in one year. He attended Queen's University in Kingston, Ontario, on a scholarship and graduated at age eighteen. He worked for Canada Packers for a period, and then at his father's insistence moved back to Moose Jaw to take over the family business in 1939. He married Adrah Leone (Peggie) McNaughton in January, 1938, and they had one son, Colin.

A member in his youth of the Moose Jaw Liberal Association, he served a two-year term on city council from 1942 to 1944, before being elected the CCF Member of Parliament for Moose Jaw in 1945. He left the CCF in 1955, sitting as an independent, and then joined the Liberals in 1956. He was elected MP for Morse from 1960 to 1971.

He led the provincial Liberal Party to victory in the spring of 1964, and remained as Premier until June, 1971. During that time, he was also President of the Executive Council in 1964, Provincial Treasurer from 1964 to 1967, and Minister of Industry and Commerce from 1967 to 1970.

Lorne Calvert

Lorne Calvert was born in Moose Jaw on December 24, 1952. He attended school in Moose Jaw and graduated from Riverview Collegiate. Lorne received his

Bachelor of Arts Degree in Economics from the University of Regina in 1972, and in 1976 completed his bachelor of Divinity Degree in Theology in Saskatoon. In 1975 Lorne married Betty Sluzalo of Perdue. Betty's family still farms in the Perdue area. They have two children, Dave and Stephanie, and one grandchild, Levi. Ordained as a Minister

of the United Church in 1976, Lorne served congregations in Gravelbourg, Bateman, Shamrock, Coderre, Palmer, and Moose Jaw.

Lorne was first elected to the Saskatchewan Legislature as the MLA for Moose Jaw South in 1986. He was re-elected in 1991 and 1995 as the Member for Moose Jaw Wakamow. Appointed to cabinet in 1992, he held several major Cabinet posts, including Minister of Health and Minister of Social Services. He has also served as Minister responsible for Seniors, Minister responsible for SaskEnergy and SaskPower, Minister responsible for the Public Service Commission and Minister responsible for Disabilities issues.

In 1998 Lorne stepped down from cabinet to devote more time to his family.

During 2000, he served as the special advisor to Cabinet on social policy. He became Premier early in 2001.

Becoming a City

Spectacular Growth

At the turn of the century some fifteen hundred people lived in Moose Jaw, but only a decade later the number would mushroom to nearly fourteen thousand. With its population explosion, the city faced critical issues regarding the direction of its growth. New housing divisions were being established at record rates. Public parklands, including the showcase Crescent Park, with its serpentine creek, were incorporated into the city map. All in all, as Moose Jaw rounded the corner of the twentieth century, prospects couldn't have been brighter.

The much coveted new amenity of electricity had made its first appearance ten years earlier, in the form of a temporary generator at the Simpson's lumberyard. The first full service power plant didn't arrive until 1905. A fire on May 24, 1912, destroyed it but it was quickly rebuilt. The city was by then so dependent on electricity for lighting that, to help cope with the lack of power, it became the first place in western Canada to institute "fast time" or daylight saving time.

Recognizing that visiting travellers would continue to drive a significant portion of Moose Jaw's economy, competition in the hotel industry was fierce. James Kern, one of the town's leading businessmen, opened the Brunswick Hotel, which rivalled the Ottawa Hotel for travellers' dollars throughout the

Opposite: Spring Carnival Day on Main Street about 1912. A Lewis Rice photograph.

1880s. Several years later, Kern built the Maple Leaf Hotel directly across from the CPR station on the site later to become the Cornerstone Pub. At the turn of the century, Kern, who had established himself as Moose Jaw's top hotel builder, began construction of the "new" Brunswick hotel that opened in 1903.

The appeal of Moose Jaw spread far beyond municipal boundaries. According to the *Times* of February 14, 1900, 237 people had applied for land permits on one day, for a total of 19,720 acres (7,980 hectares). The paper's edi-tor challenged "any other district in the NW to make a better showing than this."

Even within Moose Jaw, prospects for the growth of the city were so high that, in 1912, the development of a new subdivision known as Britannia Park was proposed.

Designed in fifty-foot housing lots and meant to provide housing for the Linseed Oil Company, the area was to have a grain elevator, flax mill, new roadways, four public parks, trolley tracks and a twenty-four-hectare exhibition ground. Although the plan never came to fruition, it speaks directly to the magnitude of growth Moose Jaw was experiencing, and its hopes for the future. A brochure advertising the new and unabashedly modern development at Britannia Park bragged: "Moose Jaw is proud and rich, and is mightier today and (will be) still mightier tomorrow...for the world lies at the door of Moose Jaw, and the smile of confidence is on her face."

Despite the failures of the Britannia plan, Moose Jaw's growth *was* spectacular. Its population grew by 4,692 in the five years ending in 1906 and the national census that year showed Moose Jaw to be the largest city in the brand-new province of Saskatchewan. Its population of 6,250 bested its arch-rival Regina's by 37.

As Moose Jaw continued to flourish and downtown traffic became congested, traditional dirt roads grew increasingly impractical. The thaws of summer and rains of fall often left the

Workmen paving Manitoba Street with the disastrous creosoted wooden blocks, about 1910.
A Lewis Rice photo.

town mired in mud, and the introduction of the automobile made driving in the mud a virtual impossibility.

In 1910, in response to a growing need to construct a solid Main Street, city council adopted what turned out to be a disastrous idea: building streets from creosoted wooden blocks. They were considered superior to asphalt paving on several counts but the decision to "pave" Main Street in wooden blocks remains one of Moose Jaw's most infamous decisions; it was a choice that served up continued frustration when blocks would float away due to excess rain or spring thaw waters. The blocks worked well for about five years, but after that, the water-soaked blocks became problematic. Luwilla Paine, who moved to the city in 1912, later recalled, "Every time it rained, up they popped."

Tunnels of Sanctuary

Like every other town on the Prairies, Moose Jaw has several Chinese restaurants. These cafés are solidly established, their owners well respected members of the business community. It wasn't always that way.

The development of Moose Jaw's storied tunnels as a tourist attraction has raised new speculation about the use Chinese may have put these underground caverns to a century ago. Stories abound of opium dens, and of large-scale communities of Chinese seeking to avoid taxes and immigration fees. There's little evidence to support either legend, but the stories persist.

There's no question that Moose Jaw's small Chinese population had to endure rank discrimination, though no more here than elsewhere in the West, or throughout Canada, for that matter. The Chinese were relegated to second-class citizenry, marginalized both socially and economically. Still, many of them stubbornly hung on in their new homes.

In the latter half of the 1800s, the economy of China was suffering badly, spurring many Chinese men to leave their homeland in search of better opportunities. The majority of the immigrants settled in the United States, primarily California. For the vast majority of them, the plan was merely to make enough money to return to China with greater prosperity. When the Yukon gold rush and building of the CPR presented new economic opportunities further north, thousands of Chinese workers migrated to the Canadian West despite the rampant racism with which they were met. Some seventeen thousand Chinese "coolies" are believed to have been employed in the building of the CPR, but they were relegated to the lowest social order. Agreements within CPR hiring guidelines assured that all local white men and Francophones emigrating from Quebec would be assured jobs before Chinese. In 1878, the west coast newspaper *British Colonist* asserted that "the Chinese ulcer is cutting into the country and sooner or later must be cut out."

In the spring of 1883, a group of Chinese-hating whites attacked the makeshift British Columbia camp where hundreds of Chinese workers slept peacefully. They burned the camp to the ground and beat the workers with axe handles. Four men died, three of them because white doctors refused to treat the injured Chinese.

Despite such obvious and rampant racism, some in Moose Jaw were more enlightened. The fledgling *Moose Jaw News* printed a scathing editorial on the front page of its May 25th issue under the headline "Canada Disgraced." It concluded: "We blush to think that such a combination of paltroonism and cruelty could have occurred in the Dominion. We hope the Government will take prompt and vigorous measures to...prevent the recurrence of such an outrage."

When the railway was completed in 1885, the growth of anti-Chinese sentiment throughout British Columbia had grown so great that many workers began to drift eastward. Many Chinese sought new opportunities in fledgling prairie towns like Moose Jaw, though typically they were relegated to dead-end jobs and often fell into a cyclical lifestyle that propagated stereotypes about the Chinese, sterotypes which often exaggerated the use of opium and the vices of gambling.

If some Chinese men did make use of the tunnels, they were most likely motivated by the simple desire to avoid public persecution, to remain out of sight, and to dispel fears that the Chinese population would adversely affect

Successful businessman Yip Foo with his wife and baby daughter, Dora, about 1920.

the local economy.

Key Wong, a born-and-raised Moose Javian, recalls his father arrived in Moose Jaw in 1905 as a thirteen-year-old. Yee Chee emigrated from China to find economic success with his own father. Chee eventually ended up running the Commercial Lunch Café on River Street.

Discrimination continued to grow until the clash between the whites and Chinese of Moose Jaw reached a crescendo in 1908. As Moon Mullins recounts the story, passed on from his father, a group of disgruntled railway workers had lost their jobs and sought to pin blame on Chinese workers who took CPR shifts at much lower rates of pay. "The Chinese labourers were working hard, and of course the laws were all against the poor fellas to begin with." One night, a gang of drunks went to the railway station with pick axes "and tore into them and beat the living hell out of them. Dad said it was one of the worst things he'd ever seen in his life, said he couldn't believe it, how cruel men could be." According to Mullins, his father claimed the Chinese went underground afterwards.

The 1908 riot has to been seen in context, though. The CPR was involved in a long and bitter labour dispute and Chinese labourers were hired to replace the striking union members. In the tumultuous labour scene of the early part of the twentieth century, violence against "scabs" was fairly common, so the incident described above was as much about labour unrest as it was about race.

Eric Chow, a third-generation Moose Javian whose family immigrated from China before 1920, agrees that some Chinese, including his grandparents, likely did live in underground spaces, but he explains "that there were two things happening. One is that (the Chinese) were scared they'd get beaten up because of unionised workers, and the other thing was that the early Chinese settlement was really poor," limiting the choice of accommodations. According to Chow, living in tunnels had little to do with smoking opium but everything to do with the Chinese community being barred from Moose Jaw's mainstream society. Still, there's no explanation why Moose Jaw's Chinese might have gone underground when those in other prairie cities did not.

As late as 1912, the provincial statutes of Saskatchewan continued to propagate racism by exhorting, through law, that white women were prohibited from working "in any establishment operated by a Chinaman." The alienation of the Chinese community is one of Moose Jaw's darker historical tales, but one that saw vast improvement as the years progressed.

One man who bucked the trend was Yip Foo, who arrived in Moose Jaw in 1903 and found the climate refreshing.

By 1910, Yip was a successful business-man and, with his partners Arthur Latham and A.E. Hopkins, had built the Russell Block, on the corner of River Street and 1st Avenue NW. Built in the style of the Chicago School, it was one of the most modern buildings in the West and became famous for its beautiful facade, its marvellous spiral staircase, and decorative ceiling. It was a well-used and multi-cultural building, housing Latham's Hardware Store, the Chinese Methodist Mission, a pool hall, a Chinese importer, a barber shop, and the offices of the Royal Northwest Mounted Police. Yip also constructed another building that bears his name.

So impressed was it with Yip, the *Times* held him up in 1913 as "a fair example of what is possible in the case of anyone who gets fair treatment at the hands of the white men in the

The Russell Block.

midst of whom he lives." The article goes on to say that "in proportion to the number of Chinamen in the city there are remarkably few brought up in the Police Court for breaking the law.... In Moose Jaw it is sufficient to say that the Chinaman as a whole are [sic] remarkably good citizens."

The YMCA, always a leader in tolerance, opened its doors to Chinese members very early. In 1915, the Red Ribbon Circus – an annual Dominion Day fundraising event – featured the Foo New Shàn troupe. The program describes them as a "Chinese Gymnastics Troupe," but photos in the YMCA scrapbooks show demonstrations of what is obviously *kung fu*.

The Jewel of the Prairies

Moose Jaw passed a rite of passage on November 20, 1903, as it officially moved to city status. Charles Unwin was elected mayor, and, with a population of twenty-five hundred, the new city was poised to make an indelible impression on the twentieth century. The flames of aspiration held for Moose Jaw's future were bright on

The YMCA Foo New Shan Troupe.

the night of November 20, when the city hosted a huge bonfire along Main Street to celebrate the momentous occasion. The *Times* proudly announced that day that "during the past twenty years the growth has been rapid, the buildings are substantial, and on the whole, the town is said to be the best built on the prairies."

Moose Jaw soon looked ahead to consolidate its new status. In the area of public works, city council experimented with concrete sidewalks and by 1905 many suggested that the city's waterworks and sewage projects were better than those of their rival to the east, Regina. In 1903, Moose Jaw was also to build the exhibition grounds and opened its first library – a reading room that required buying a ticket to borrow books. At the corner of First Avenue and Fairford Street West, a new city hall was built in 1904, complete with an opera house on the third

Top: The second CPR Station in 1912.
Bottom (Left to Right): The General Hospital; Moose Jaw College for Boys; Alexandria School.

floor. It sat in the centre of a large public garden and athletic field.

In 1906, the General Hospital opened, with twenty-six beds. Cognizant of its responsibility as a bearer of civilization and colonial values, the new city took education very seriously and began to expand its school system. Alexandria School opened in 1905, King Edward in 1906, Central Colle-

giate and Empire in 1909, King George in 1911, Prince Arthur in 1912, and Ross in 1913.

Another educational advance was the opening, in 1912, of the Moose Jaw College for Boys. It was a Presbyterian school that would have an enrolment of about 100 boys per year. It sat atop a hill overlooking the river. It built a reputation for scholarly excellence and

was a favoured place to send boys for a good academic education coupled with strong moral training.

The growth of Moose Jaw continued unabated, even though the new city lost a 1906 bid to Saskatoon to house Saskatchewan's first university. In 1908, some 728 new entries had been made through the Dominion Land Office, a record the December 25, 1908, *Times* announced "has never before been approached and which without doubt will remain unbroken in ages to come."

Phenomenal growth was by no means exclusive to Moose Jaw, of course. A 1926 census of the prairie provinces indicates that, in 1901, there were some ninety-one thousand residents. By the end of World War I in 1918, that population had exploded to seven hundred thousand.

Telephones followed quickly on the heels of electricity as the latest technological advance, and Moose Jaw published its first phone directory in 1910. A fire in 1911 destroyed the orig-

inal flour mill, but it was replaced in 1912 by one of Moose Jaw's enduring landmarks for many decades, the Robin Hood Mill.

Mayor James Pascoe opened the Moose Jaw Library in Crescent Park, replacing the reading-room system, in 1913. Turned down by the Carnegie Foundation, which funded many public libraries throughout the prairies (the plans were deemed too elaborate for the city's population), the city had raised the necessary $50,000 itself.

Clockwise from left: The Post Office in 1906; The new City Hall about 1906; The Walter Scott Block about 1910; Houses on Oxford Street during the building boom of 1910-1912. Photos by Lewis Rice.

With that cultural achievement behind them, civic leaders began to consider the need for social and athletic facilities.

A 1913 meeting at the YMCA led to the birth of an aquatic club that, a mere three months later, boasted the opening of a clubhouse built on the banks of the river, with baths and showers, an up-to-date locker room, and modern boathouses. The building, all peaked roofs and gables, was covered with shingles and decorated with electric lights that reflected off the water in almost kaleidoscopic patterns. The entire second floor was occupied by a beautiful and spacious dance floor of highly polished maple that soon became a focal point of the social life of the city.

After twenty years, Moose Jaw had grown from an insignificant tent on the windswept prairie, to a city with significant economic, political, and social influence.

Luwilla Payne remembers well the newly incorporated city, when its limits extended to 9th Avenue West and Oxford Street North. Born in 1893, she arrived in Moose Jaw as a young woman in 1912 and took an immediate liking to the place. She has fond memories of taking meals at the Savoy Café, going to the movies in the evening with friends, and weekend dances at the armoury. "In the early days, you were all like one. You could go to any of your friends any old time, and you were welcome."

Top left: Canoeing on Plaxton's Lake near the Aquatic Club in 1913.   Top right: The Robin Hood Mill ablaze.

Two Horsemen of the Apocalypse

The First World War, "the war to end all wars," has often been cited as the single most important event in the growth of Canada as a sovereign nation. It was "a coming of age" for Canada, and, in both its victories and defeats, Moose Jaw played an integral part.

With war looming in Europe, the 60th Rifle Company, under the command of Lt.-Col. Herbert Snell, a Moose Jaw merchant active in local politics, was created in 1913. When war was finally declared, the 60th was mobilised to be part of the third Canadian contingent. But before the company could be sent overseas, 106 of its men were seconded into the Princess Patricia's Light Infantry and another 250 were taken to join the first contingent overseas.

Snell got his chance finally in 1915 with the formation of the 46th Canadian Infantry Battalion (South Saskatchewan), with him in command.

The 46th, born and based in Moose Jaw with contingents from all of Southern Saskatchewan, although more than half its members were from the Moose Jaw area, was to take part in most of the major battles of the war: Ypres, the Somme, Vimy, and Passchendale. In action, the 46th displayed a heroic, almost reckless, courage and gave itself the nickname "The Suicide Battalion." By the end of the war it had seen 4,917 men killed or wounded out of 5,374. In thirty months in the trenches, the 46th received 337 decora-

The 46th Battalion, "Moose Jaw's Own," at the CPR Station on August 23, 1916, leaving for WWI.

to fight overseas, many women took over the duties traditionally held by men. The war created an unprecedented demand for wheat exports into Europe, a direct benefit to the economy of the city and area. Lastly, from a social perspective, the war gave rise to farming associations and unions, two forces that would continue to grow and shape the lives of the people of Moose Jaw.

As if the war in Europe weren't enough hardship and torment for those on the home front, the epidemic of Spanish influenza in October, 1918, delivered yet another emotional blow to the city. Started in Europe and having spread to North America, the epidemic left thousands dead in the US and Canada in a matter of weeks. In one month, from mid-October to mid-November, 1918, the influenza killed a staggering 253 people in Moose Jaw. The death toll was so high that graveyards couldn't keep apace of the burials needed. Schools were closed, a bylaw was passed prohibiting public gatherings, people wore face masks, and local merchants allowed their employees to stay home or to volunteer with medical efforts.

tions, including the last Canadian Victoria Cross recipient of the war, Sgt. Hugh Cairns.

Snell was never to lead his men into battle, though. Badly injured by a grenade during a training exercise in England, he was forced to serve behind the lines for the rest of the war.

The Canadian Expeditionary Force also included the 68th Battalion, an entire company which originated in Moose Jaw; the 210th, the 128th, the 229th, the 16th Mounted Rifles, and the 27th Light Horse, all of which trained in Moose Jaw and drew significant numbers of recruits from the city and surrounding areas. As casualties

mounted, the survivors of the 128th, the 210th, and the 229th were absorbed into the 46th, which by the end of the war was truly "Moose Jaw's Own."

Other young men, and even some women, joined the navy, the field ambulance, and the fledgling Royal Flying Corps. Many of them died. For those who returned with injuries, Ross School was temporarily converted to a convalescence hospital.

The war meant more than the loss of life in Moose Jaw households. It had a profound effect in every aspect of life. For women, the war was a major step toward equal social recognition. As men lay down their hoes and tools

When Johnny Comes Marching Home Again

The old rivalry between Moose Jaw and Regina resurfaced even as the war-weary soldiers returned from Europe. It expressed itself immediately in an incident that, in retrospect, seems quite petty but, at the time, aroused strong passions.

In June of 1919, with contingents of the Canadian Expeditionary Force straggling home, most of the South Saskatchewan regiments were demobilised in Regina. But when word reached Moose Jaw that the 46th Battalion was scheduled to be decommissioned in the capital, it raised the collective hackles of an entire city.

Mayor James Hawthorne fired off a telegram to Ottawa; veterans, civic officials, and prominent citizens complained, cajoled, and lobbied. The 46th was born in Moose Jaw and drew most of its men from Moose Jaw, they argued. If there were any justice at all, the 46th would return to its place of birth to complete the circle.

When the *Times* reported the good news on June 6 that the 46th would be demobilised in Moose Jaw after all, the city felt vindicated. The mayor proclaimed June 9th a civic holiday to mark the occasion.

The homecoming was a mixture of pomp, joy, and military pride. Hundreds of people were on hand as the train pulled into the station. The men piled off and marched to Manitoba Street between First and Second Avenues, N.E. For forty minutes, family and friends mobbed the men of the battalion, shedding tears of happiness and relief, slapping backs, shaking hands. It was a gentle, joyous chaos, full of pent-up emotion finally unleashed.

With bayonets fixed, and wearing steel helmets, the men of the 46th

Peace Day Parade on July 19, 1920.

began to march to the cadence of three military bands. Up Main Street they marched, followed by automobiles carrying the wounded, and past a reviewing stand at High Street, to the grandstand at the Exhibition Grounds, there to be greeted by all the city's schoolchildren, waving tiny flags in furious fluttering welcome.

Later, there was a banquet in the armoury, served by seventy-five young women. The men of the 46th and their families broke bread together for the first time in several years. Then the 46th Battalion passed into history.

Its memory was vividly evoked just over a year later, though, when a still jubilant Moose Jaw threw a party to end all parties, a three-day "peace celebration" that featured parades, games, sporting and musical events, and a midway. One of the highlights was a "Bolsheviki parade," in which prizes were awarded for the shabbiest clothes and punishments were meted out to those whose dress was too "respectable."

For a city that had enjoyed social growth and economic prosperity for nearly four decades, the First World War and the influenza epidemic changed the dynamics that propelled the city. Death had made an indelible impression on the city, women had shifted their status, and an entire generation of men had been seriously diminished.

Still, on the eve of the twenties, Moose Jaw had begun to recover from the losses of the previous six years. It was a new decade, an age of new hope, of money, of new-found spirit and unbridled enthusiasm. It was the beginning of Moose Jaw's most exciting age: the Roaring Twenties.

A float with miniature houses in the Peace Day Parade.

THE ROARING TWENTIES

The World at Peace

Modern Times

The 1920s began in Moose Jaw with optimism. The darkness of the war years had begun to dissipate and people turned with renewed energy back to the business of carving their province out of the wilderness. Even the climate co-operated, for a change. Despite the crushing burden of the war debt, and the postwar depression, it seemed that better things were on the way.

Saskatchewan was looking to the future. The population had risen to 833,262, but the province was still characterised by windswept, wide-open spaces. In the countryside, the nearest neighbour might be fifteen or twenty kilometres away. Loneliness and isolation were still the closest neighbours for the many people in the rural areas.

The latest of the string of revolutionary technologies of the twentieth century – the automobile – changed all that. But, as with most technological solutions, this created new problems. Roads that were good enough for horse-drawn buggies and wagons could not survive heavier, faster, more destructive automobiles, and Moose Jaw faced the challenge and cost of paving its streets.

During the war, Moose Jaw had been a staging area, a training area for the local regiments before they left to fight. Many of those enthusiastic young men

Opposite: Police Chief Walter Johnson and the police force about 1915.

came back in much worse shape than when they left. Some of these tough former soldiers, now convalescing at the converted Ross School, directed their manual skills to handiwork.

Rose Kain, then a sales clerk at Woolworth's downtown, recalls waiting on wounded men who came to buy wool and other supplies for their embroidery. "They did the most beautiful work, those boys in that hospital."

She remembers one man in particular who "wanted to have his crest of his regiment. He drew it beautifully, and it had maple leaves all around it, and he wanted to know if he could get cushion tops to embroider, stamped like that pattern.

"So I got the address in the office and I wrote for him, and they said they could do nothing but twelve dozen and that was a lot of cushion covers. Anyway, he talked to the other boys up

at the hospital and they decided to pay for it, and there was twelve dozen, they had the maple leaves all around them, and they had their crest and their regiment number and so on. I used to make a lot of trips up to that military hospital. Cause they were making mats on a frame with nails. I used to buy the wool for them."

Many returned men had no problem finding work, their old jobs waiting for them. But for others, neither jobs nor readjustment came so easily. Henry Swaberg remembered:

"In 1920, my dad was back and not doing anything except any job he could get. Like unloading coal for the coal dealers. He'd unload a car of coal – a thirty-ton car for $7.50 – 25 cents a ton. [I'd] help him sometimes."

Wounded soldiers convalescing at Ross Military Hospital.

Many of these jobless men in Moose Jaw got a new break when the federal government opened up an Indian reserve for homesteading. But many others remained without permanent work, misfits in the society they had fought for.

"The Trains Were Always Full"

The war had put a temporary stop to immigration from Europe. Now, a new wave of immigration brought thousands of war-battered Europeans to the prairies. Many of them wound up in Moose Jaw.

Most people in Saskatchewan agreed the province needed more peo-

Ross Military Hospital.

The third CPR Station, built in 1920, taken some time in the late 1920s. The flower gardens visible in the 1919 photograph have disappeared.

ple. A larger population would mean greater potential for economic growth. But there was argument over who these newcomers should be.

Although Moose Jaw itself was predominantly British, the new immigrants were largely from elsewhere in Europe. Actually, that wasn't new. From the 1890s on, the prairies had seen an influx of Jews, Ukrainians, Russians, Germans, and Poles looking for a better life. Now the immigrants seemed even more "foreign." Mennonites, Hutterites, and Doukhabors, with their strange clothes and stranger customs, puzzled and discomfited residents who themselves had so recently been immigrants. South Hill, the working class suburb south of the CPR tracks – where whole neighbourhoods were built in the twenties to accommodate the employees at the new industries in the area – became known as Garlic Hill.

In Moose Jaw, it was widely felt that immigrants should be quickly assimilated into the predominantly British culture and ethos. Dr. J.W. Edwards, head of the Orange Order of British North America, spoke of immigration to the Moose Jaw Canadian Club in July 1923. It was, he said, important to populate the vast underdeveloped lands of the west and to increase the general population of Canada to spread the burden of taxation and national debt. But, he emphasized, it was essential to encourage the "right kind" of immigrant, specifically, those who embrace the "British ideals" upon which the country was founded, and who would "bring [Canada] to the forefront as a British country." The seeds of a new wave of racism were being planted.

Hard Times in the Gold Mountain

Moose Jaw has, at times, shown a profoundly ambivalent attitude toward its ethnic and racial minorities. In the newspapers and documents of the day can be seen varying examples of outright bigotry, a kind of tolerant disrespect, and a surprising warmth and affection toward racial and religious minorities.

The Cree and Sioux peoples had been in Moose Jaw for centuries before the railway arrived and the city existed. In the early days, they had supplied a pool of cheap labour, the women acting as cleaners, cooks, and general domestic workers. By the twenties, the native population had all but disappeared from the Moose Jaw area, shunted off to distant reserves. At one time, the city had a substantial Metis population – many of the early settlers in the area were Metis who had obtained grants to prime land on the Moose Jaw River east of town – but by the twenties, they had shrunk to a small minority.

One ethnic group, the Chinese, were not part of the new immigration wave. The federal government had banned any new migrants from China in 1923. But, while the Chinese population in Canada began to decline, in Moose Jaw it grew. There were only 188 Chinese in the city in 1921, but by the mid 1920s the population had grown to more than three hundred, making Moose Jaw's Chinatown the largest in Saskatchewan.

The days of the tunnels, fanciful or true, were behind them, and Moose Jaw's Chinese became entrepeneurs, specializing in laundries and restaurants.

The first recorded Chinese-owned business in the city was Lee Kee's Chinese Laundry, which opened in 1889. It was the ideal business for a poor immigrant – a man's clothes always got dirty, and there were plenty of single white men on River Street, or working on the railroad. It required almost no capital to start a laundry – just a willingness to work long hours up to your armpits in hot, soapy water. By the twenties, *Henderson's Directory* showed between fifteen and eighteen laundries operating in Moose Jaw – the only one not owned by Chinese was the large

The men, and three young boys, of the Chinese community about 1920.

commercial Moose Jaw Steam Laundry.

Soon the Chinese were also running cafés and small grocery stores, and in 1920 market gardens along the river south of the city. According to one source, the first Chinese-owned grocery was Star Fruit, which opened in 1925, but the *Henderson's* for 1919 lists five Chinese merchants, and throughout the twenties there were many confectionaries listed with Chinese names. By the end of the second decade of the twentieth century, more than 50 per cent of Moose Jaw's restaurants were owned by Chinese and other Asians.

Moose Jaw's small Japanese population was also the largest in the province. Twenty-five of the fifty-seven Japanese living in Saskatchewan in 1916 were in Moose Jaw, many of them working for the CPR. Naka Nakane, the manager of the CPR lunch counter, later opened his own café near the station. Many Japanese names appear in *Henderson's* later as tailors and proprietors of confectioneries and cafés.

Despite laws that barred Asians from government employment, and other forms of discrimination, there were a number of examples of Asian business-

men who achieved high levels of success and respect in Moose Jaw, following in the footsteps of Yip Foo, the turn-of-the-century entrepreneur. In 1927, Chin Foon built the Ace Hotel. Moose Jaw even boasted a Japanese-owned dental laboratory. Naka Nakane was elected to the executive of the Chamber of Com-

> Despite laws that barred Asians from government employment, and other forms of discrimination, there were a number of examples of Asian businessmen who achieved high levels of success in Moose Jaw.

merce in the 1930s.

Although some black people from Oklahoma had settled in Maidstone and Rosetown in 1905-06, later contributing the first black player in the NHL, African-Canadians were rare in Moose Jaw in the 1920s, largely due to the determination of the federal government to keep them out.

The racist attitudes of the time can

be seen in the newspaper coverage of minority groups. In the early days of the century, nonwhites, and non-Anglo-Saxons in general, were flagged in newspaper reports, especially in negative stories. A headline in the April 20, 1920, *Daily News* read: "Chinks Pay Fines for Smoking Opium," while the *Times* put it a little less flamboyantly: "China Boy Arrested on Opium Charge." Ethnicity of any kind was flagged in the newspapers: Poles, Ukrainians, French, Negroes, Indians – anyone but a white British man was duly noted.

But that attitude wasn't universal in Moose Jaw. The Rev. W.G. Wilson, speaking at St. John's Church in 1920, chided his parishioners for wrapping themselves in a cloak of superiority. "Because some persons are different in colour, have their eyes at a different slant, or otherwise differ in their facial appearance, it gives no grounds that they should be looked on as of a more menial race," he told them. "All persons are equal in the eyes of the Maker."

This was not a voice crying in the wilderness. The people of Moose Jaw could show remarkable hospitality, respect, and even affection to people of colour. In fact, despite a reputation for showing a very British reserve, they could be quite effusive in their affection, as is clear from the following incident.

In early 1920, the board of directors of Zion Church has a problem. The church's minister is planning a well-deserved vacation and will be gone for six weeks. One board member tells his colleagues about a minister he met while travelling through the small town of Hot Springs, Arkansas. It being a Sunday, he stopped into a church, where he heard a young, charismatic preacher of great power.

The board is convinced to write to this young preacher and invite him to come north for the summer, even though the Rev. Dr. Joseph Hill is a Negro.

Rev. Hill turns out to be an early and outspoken advocate of civil rights and black pride. In Moose Jaw, he preaches about the lack of respect his people received, of the indignity of centuries of slavery and of the need to provide higher education for the poor blacks of the South, of their need to provide their own doctors, their own

lawyers. He speaks with respect of the British Empire, which was the first to ban slavery, and of the hospitality accorded him in Canada, telling the Times that "never have I been made

The Reverend Joseph Hill.

to feel so much of a man."

The visiting minister's popularity is enormous, his sermons so well attended that extra seats are installed in the alcove at the entrance of the

church to accommodate the crowds, and still there are standing-room-only crowds. In his five weeks in Moose Jaw, he is in great demand as a speaker, appearing before a number of service groups, and is one of the most popular attractions at that summer's Chattauqua show.

After a speech to the Rotary Club, the Times calls Hill "one of the greatest attractions ever invited to visit our city. He is the topic of favourable discussion in the home, places of business, on the street, in fact everywhere two or three people are gathered together."

When Hill returns home at the end of August, his congregation gives him a farewell party, expressing their gratitude with a donation of $760 for his charity work.

This affection toward a man of colour was not unique. Later the same year, poor health forced Yip Sam to retire after ten years as the superintendent of the Chinese Mission (the Zion Chinese Mission). Hundreds of well-wishers from all races attended his going away party, a story carried on the front page of the Times.

A Passionate Process

Moose Jaw takes civic politics seriously. At the same time it never hurts a politician to be colourful, even a little eccentric. Local politicians were sometimes stupid, sometimes venal, sometimes lacking in courage, and sometimes even crooked. Sometimes they were dull. But, for much of the city's early history, politics often provided drama even local theatrical groups couldn't match.

One of the more colourful local politicians was Sam A. Hamilton, sometime alderman, sometime Conservative MP and – from time to time – mayor. He was not afraid to make himself noticed and was often in the news. Never one to step softly, Hamilton resigned as mayor August 1, 1918, in the middle of his first term over a jurisdictional dispute with City Commissioner George D. Mackie.

The mayor's resignation was not without consequences. He left office without signing the papers for a bond issue. Without his signature, the bonds could not be sold. The city was on the hook for $10,000, which was never recovered.

Despite the fiasco of the debentures, and the hostility of many councilmen, Hamilton ran for and won a second term a mayor. Soon he became embroiled in an issue council often argued about – gambling.

Over the past year, punchboards had begun to appear in local poolrooms and cafés. Punchboards were low-tech precursors to the scratch and win lottery. Council had begun to take notice. There were those who thought they were intrinsically evil and ought to be banned. Some on council were beginning to feel that the way to control vice was to control the venues where vice thrived. The way to control the venues was through their licenses. On the night of Feb. 25, 1920, the discussion at council was heated – and ended with an eruption of violence when Hamilton took a swing at Ald. R.J. Jackson, a vehement gambling foe.

Something Jackson said brought Hamilton to his feet, his face red with anger. According to newspaper accounts, he reared back and "violently [struck] Jackson in the face." Jackson staggered back in surprise and the mayor, overbalanced by the power of his own punch, fell to his hands and knees on the floor. The two men staggered up, both enraged. Before they could do more damage to each other, the police chief, Walter Johnson, inserted his considerable bulk between the two men to prevent further "fistic encounters."

The next day, Jackson charged Hamilton with common assault. The mayor pleaded guilty and was fined $5.

Local politics often seemed to be consumed by River Street and activities that centred on it: gambling, alcohol, prostitution, and the police. Investigations of the police in 1913 and 1915 were followed by the Bence Commission of 1922; the embarrassment of a police theft ring in 1924, with the loss of more than half the uniformed force; the firing of the chief in 1927; and endless attempts to gain control of the police commission. Council seemed to be obsessed by the police.

Public morality was often on the minds of local politicians. Curtains in restaurants were a frequent worry. In 1922, a local restaurateur complained to council about the "sick and disgusting" behaviour that went on behind the curtains in his restaurant. Gambling was almost as bad. Jackson continued to crusade against dice and cards. In 1921,

Opposite: Main Street looking south from Ominica Street about 1920.

he surprised council by pushing through a motion calling for an investigation of gambling in chartered social clubs. In the election later that year, his campaign was centred on the issue. The same year, W.F. Dunn campaigned for mayor on a platform railing against the non-enforcement of the law, an obvious attack on the police administration.

Another issue that dogged local politicians was water. Although the city was built on three streams, there was never enough water. Shortages were common, and got more so with the popularization of indoor plumbing. In 1920, the city was optimistic that the large new reservoir at Britannia Park would solve the problem, but by the mid-twenties the shortages returned. The water supply was an issue that would return to haunt councils for the next seventy years.

Moose Jaw was not afraid of setting precedent. In the 1919 election, Mary Allen, a housewife, was the first woman elected to council and the board of the Collegiate Institute. In another progressive experiment, the city flirted with proportional representation. A referendum on Nov. 12, 1920, authorised its use but the experiment ended with another referendum in 1925. It was generally believed to be a better and fairer system, but voters found it too confusing.

The Modern City

"Times Were Really Good"

The economic decade began with neither a bang nor a whimper. Unemployment was intermittent. Farmers went begging for labourers at harvest time and special trains were chartered to bring thousands of men from the East. Twenty-two excursions brought twenty-two thousand harvesters to Saskatchewan in 1920. By late fall, those jobs had disappeared and migrant harvesters in the Moose Jaw area, often at loose ends, were frequent customers of River Street and the local bootleggers before most of them headed home.

For years, the city government ran various relief projects, especially in the winter, when construction and farm work was unavailable. In the first three weeks of the relief program in 1921, over $5,000 was distributed. For one such project, the city bought tons of rocks for the jobless men to crush into gravel, which was sold. Much of it was used, for example, in the construction of the Harwood Hotel in 1927. In 1925, just as the postwar recession came to an end, City Council asked the province to pay one third of the cost of relief for people living in the city. The province ignored the request, setting the stage for intergovernmental wrangling throughout the years of the Great Depression that followed.

Moose Jaw's economy was fundamentally sound. It had the lowest gross school debt, and was in third place for tax levies per capita among cities in the

Main Street looking north from River Street. The Metropolitan Store, where Rose Kain worked, is on the corner.

three prairie provinces. In those early years, the city's income was derived largely from a local income tax, though authority over municipal taxation rested with provincial governments. The province struck the city a severe blow in 1920 when it doubled the basic personal exemption, cutting municipal income tax revenues by half. Shortly thereafter, the province abolished municipal income taxes entirely, leaving cities with property taxes as their only source of tax revenue.

Moose Jaw's economy grew from the beginning of the decade, as did the city itself. Although never reaching the giddy heights of the period just before the war, the number of building permits rose in both number and value throughout the 1920s, and many major construction projects gave a boost to the local economy. The Bellamy Block, the CN Depot, St. Joseph's Catholic Church and the Public Comfort Station on Fairford Street West started a decade-long building boom in 1919. The CP station was built in 1920, St. Louis College in 1921, the Convent of Our Lady of Sion in 1923 and the House of Israel in 1926. The Saskatchewan Wheat Pool seed clean-

ing plant, the C&W Grayson Building (later Eaton's Department Store and now Eaton's Place), and the provincial Normal School (which became the Teachers' College, and later the home of SIAST), were all built in the latter half of the decade.

The railways, as always, were prime movers in the economic fortunes of

> Moose Jaw's economy was fundamentally sound. It had the lowest gross school debt, and was in third place for tax levies per capita among cities in the three prairie provinces.

the city. In addition to their new stations, both the CN and CPR began work on laying new track.

Business increased and many businesses expanded. Slater and York Men's Wear's new building on Main Street was illustrative of the optimism of the period – it was constructed on a foundation strong enough to support two

more stories should the need arise.

Marshall-Wells, one of the largest hardware wholesalers in Canada, built a new warehouse on Manitoba Street. In 1928, Eaton's department store opened on Main Street to great fanfare. The store opened for business on November 6, 1928, and, as the *Times* reported that day, "People from as far north as Elbow were visitors (and) the fine weather and good roads brought many from West and South.... Main Street for several blocks north and south of the store was thickly parked with cars."

McBride's Ltd., which owned ten retail grocery stores in the city in 1919, built a small shopping centre at the corner of Hall and Main Street in August of 1920. With a grocery, a pharmacy, and a meat market, this $15,000 mini-mall, the first of its kind in the city, was decades ahead of its time.

New and innovative industries were courted. Land was surveyed in 1920 for a site for a multi-million-dollar plant for making paper from straw. Derby Motor Cars of Saskatoon established an automobile manufacturing plant, although it closed before producing any cars. In 1927, it was announced that Moose Jaw was to be the headquarters of the Prudential Oil Company Ltd, with eighty-five hundred hectares at Readlyn Valley, just south of the city. Attempts to locate a supply of natural gas beneath the city continued through the decade. Some was found, but a reliable source remained elusive.

Much of the growth was due to the vigorous and innovative Board of Trade (later to become the Moose Jaw Chamber of Commerce), the first of its kind in Western Canada. It began in 1888, and from the start fought for the health and expansion of business in the city. To support the retail trade, the board arranged special "Shopper" trains to bring people into Moose Jaw in the fall after harvest, for the annual fair, for Chattauqua and for Christmas. The CPR brought people from as far away as Broadview, Outlook, Swift Current, Elbow, and Davidson.

Moose Jaw was the retail centre for an area that included the smaller city of Swift Current, 30 towns, 110 villages, and 130 hamlets. In peak periods such as Christmas, these trains brought as many as four hundred and fifty people

a day into the city to spend the day – and spend money. Some of them would wind up at Robinson-McBean's five-floor department store (the home of Lasting Impressions – later the largest crafts mall in the province) where Rose Kain recalls a special added attraction: "A real nice rest room. They had nice seats – padded seats. People'd sit down, and there was carpet and paper, people could sit and write letters. I had a brother-in-law used to come in, he used to bring their kids with 'em. There was three girls at that time, and they would bring in a neighbour with them, and she would look after 'em in that rest room, while they went shopping."

By the mid-twenties, the postwar depression having run its course, employment in the city reached its highest level since 1920. Optimism and enthusiasm continued to grow and, with them, the size of new projects. Jobs were plentiful, and relatively easy to come by. "Times were really good until the thirties hit," recalls Luwilla Paine. "There was lots of work for people.... If you weren't satisfied with a job you were on, you could go right on and get another one."

The flour mill in 1922. The Robin Hood on the mill was painted by Harry Bell.

Gambling on the Land

To be a farmer is to be a gambler. You throw down the seed and wait. If the rain comes, but stops in time, if the wind stays calm until the seeds germinate, if the grasshoppers and the cutworms don't come, if the rust, and the blight, and the midge stay away, then you've got a crop. That is, as long as

The Rigden farm at Buffalo Lake about 1914.

you're not hailed out, if the autumn rain and early snow don't keep you from harvesting, if you can find men to get the crop in, then you've got a crop. Now you just have to pray that the railways will get your crop to the lakehead, where you pray the longshoremen don't go on strike and leave your wheat to rot in the hold or on the docks. That is, if somewhere in the world there is a demand for your wheat, and the price they pay is more than it cost you to get the seed in the ground. You don't need River Street and crooked card games; life is a gamble – you're a farmer.

The CPR may have made Moose Jaw, but agriculture sustained it. As long as farmers in the surrounding countryside prospered, Moose Jaw prospered.

In the vast expanses of farmland surrounding the city, wheat was king, and the twenties were good for wheat. The decade began with the biggest crop since before the war, and prices were consistently high, jumping spectacularly in the second half.

Wheat wasn't the only crop. Farmers around Moose Jaw also grew oats, rye, and barley in abundance. And some innovative farmers went much further afield, like Charles E. Rigden of nearby Buffalo Lake, who grew gooseberries, cherries, pears, and even managed to produce oranges.

In the twenties, the city also saw the rise of secondary agricultural businesses. Moose Jaw was completely self-sufficient, with four creameries to buy the output of the many dairy farms in the area. The Robin Hood Flour mill, refurbished in 1920, supplied the whole country with flour and oatmeal, producing four thousand barrels of flour and over seventeen hundred barrels of oats daily. Its towering elevator, a city landmark still in use, although not by Robin Hood, held 1.7 million bushels of grain. Even larger in capacity was the Dominion Government storage elevator, a thoroughly modern facility that held 3.5 million bushels and which could treat damp or off-grade grain. Capacity was increased to five million in 1930, just in time for the agricultural downturn. Moose Jaw was also the headquarters of the Saskatchewan Registered Seed Growers Limited, which distributed large quantities of registered, standardized seed of distinct varieties. Its half-million-dollar sixteen-storey reinforced concrete building was one of the last big construction projects before the Depression.

In 1925, the Moose Jaw Grain Exchange was revived, with a hundred seats selling for $250 each and, briefly, it was predicted that Moose Jaw would soon rival Winnipeg as a major centre of the grain trade.

The city was also a livestock centre. The Southern Saskatchewan Stockyards, with its eight hectares of pens and direct connection to both railways, was the largest in Western Canada after Calgary and Winnipeg. It held seven thousand head of cattle, three thousand pigs, and five thousand sheep. Swift Canadian had a large packing plant, processing 270 cattle and 750 hogs a day, and the Harris Company, which later became Canada Packers, had an abattoir and packing plant.

The March of Progress

All during the Roaring Twenties, Moose Jaw continued to flex its muscles.

By the end of the Great War, it had a modern streetcar system, with tracks running east along Athabasca as far as

A 1920s Moose Jaw Electric Company streetcar.

The Fourth Avenue Viaduct under construction on October 11, 1929.

ply power to many of the smaller, surrounding communities.

Two new bridges to South Hill were built, one at Manitoba St. East and Second Avenue and another – the Thunderbird Viaduct (also known as the Fourth Avenue Bridge) – at Manitoba and Fourth N.W. The concrete viaduct, built in 1929 and decorated with cameo-like portraits of famous Indian leaders, and lights atop graceful and elegant stanchions, replaced the functional if ugly creosote bridge that had spanned the river and the CPR tracks for decades.

Ninth Avenue. A few years later, the system had expanded, after much loud and exasperated lobbying by the residents of South Hill, south of the river.

The publicly owned power plant continued to increase production, contracting to supply energy to the Moose Jaw Electric Railway Company and Robin Hood in 1920. Larger coal-fired generators were purchased in 1922, when the street railway agreed to buy electricity from the city, and again in 1927, when capacity was increased to five thousand kilowatts. It was a profitable venture, which not only enabled the city to light the streets and provide almost the entire population with electricity, but also turned a profit of over a half million dollars a year. By the end of the decade, it had contracted to sup-

Although the city had its origins with outside companies, and outside companies such as the CPR and Robin Hood Mills were the largest employers, most of the economic growth originated from within. Moose Jaw's pioneer spirit was exemplified by entrepreneurs like Richard Harwood, a local hosteller since 1911, when he bought the Alexandra Hotel on River Street. His ambition since his arrival from the East in 1902 was to build the most modern and up-to-date hotel in the city, a hotel that would impress even the most cosmopolitan visitor from the most sophisticated places.

The supporting columns under the Viaduct.

The Willard

Gary Hyland

On the cover of *Home Street*, one of my early poetry chapbooks and one of first publications of Coteau Books, is a Robert Currie sketch of the Willard Hotel, quite fitting since the house where I grew up was on the same block as the Willard and the hotel dominated my neighborhood.

Approaching South Hill over the Fourth Avenue Bridge any time from the 1920s to the mid 80s, you would see four structures rising above the one-storey homes in the background – the tall white Seed Pool, to its right Swift Canadian's gigantic smoke stack; and to the left of the Seed Pool, Empire School. In the foreground was the Willard Hotel, a three-storey building, the only hotel and public beverage room on South Hill. How the original owners managed to get the area zoned for a commercial hotel and bar is a mystery. There it was plonked incongruously in the middle of the 400 block of Home Street, otherwise occupied by private residences.

The Willard was built to accommodate the rough and ready crews who worked at or delivered to the stockyards, the coal and lumber yards, the two packing plants and the flour mill, all within a three block radius. In the early days there was also a blacksmith shop, stable and hide-buying operation half a block away. Many of the South Hill men who worked at the CPR or B.A. Oil refinery would stop in on their way home from work. Profits came largely from the beverage room, which was not known for its refined decor. Occasionally, a room was rented to a farmer too drunk to walk to his truck or, on a monthly basis, to someone on a low budget in need of temporary lodgings.

When I came to it in the late forties and early fifties, the Willard, like nearby Thunder Creek, the gopher-ridden fields under the bridge, and the lumber yards, was one of our neighbourhood play zones. It was owned by former Woodrow merchant Harry Silverman, who lived with his family in the house next door. Most of the time, Harry was successful at keeping us boys out of his halls and off his fire escape, but we still derived some income and entertainment from the place.

The income came from hustling at the front and back entrances of the bar. "Can I have a nickel?" was our usual blunt request and even blunter were the usual

gruff responses. One summer, we failed miserably trying to sell Kool-Aid from the back of my wagon at the front door. The men had sterner refreshment in mind, forcing us to pour over half a jug of grape drink onto Mrs. Silverman's flowers. As we grew older and could stay out later we found panhandling at the back door near closing time (11 p.m. in those days) much more profitable

Entertainment came from watching the antics of inebriated patrons as they left the Willard. Only sadistic pre-TV youngsters could enjoy watching a drunk trying to unlock his truck with his house key or crawling under his car to grope for a dropped cigar. Encountering the fresh air seemed to activate the bladders of many of the patrons, who watered well the alley fences and telephone poles. Always fun were the clownish ones, tilting grimly as they tried to keep the world horizontal. I remember helping one old-timer out of a snowbank where he had collapsed and watching him stagger into the alley where he fell face first into another.

The Willard occasionally housed some colourful characters. Buddy Brown stayed there with his mother almost a whole school year. Thin, diminutive and precocious, Buddy told great lies and kept garter snakes and snapping turtles in the window wells at the side of the hotel. He also claimed to hear the moanings of a ghost on the top floor, the spirit of the first owner who had jumped from the roof after losing the hotel in a poker game. We spent a long five minutes one cool autumn evening stretched on the fire escape, our heads inside the third-floor exit door watching and listening, but all our vigil produced was a wonderful striped pattern where our stomachs had pressed the metal slats. Buddy had a potent imagination. The snakes froze to death, all except the one we put into Mr. Silverman's car. It got stomped senseless by his wife.

From time to time, all the patrons would burst out of the bar to watch a fight. Sorry bouts these were with not many good exchanges and dubious outcomes. A few were downright vicious and brought the police. I recall one that featured a couple of heavyweights from the packing plant. I had to stand on Mr. Silverman's front step to see, over the heads of the raucous crowd, the blood-spattered combatants going at it for at least five minutes until a cruiser arrived. One of the fighters, bleeding profusely from the face was taken to the hospital. Later, as we combed the area for coins, one of my friends found a pulpy piece of flesh, the tip of the loser's nose bitten off and spat out by his opponent.

Such were the ways of the Willard. Some time in the 1970s new owners renamed it The Bridgehouse. I believe it was in the early 80s when it burned to the ground. I could look it up, but I'd rather just remember it.

For years, he planned, saved and prepared. Finally, in 1927, he bought the plot of land on Fairford Street East once occupied by Barr temperance colonists who had stopped there in 1883 on their way to Saskatoon. Then he began to build his dream, spending $64,000 – a fortune in 1927 – and doing much of the construction himself.

The fine six-storey hotel opened late in the spring of 1928. It was the first hotel in the city with a bath in every room. It boasted that it offered the best possible personal service that any guest could want – with one notable exception. Harwood was an almost fanatical teetotaler and he not only refused to sell alcohol, but was known to search suspicious packages guests brought with them. Anyone caught with intoxicants was asked to leave.

Moose Jaw was already well known for its tolerant attitude toward strong drink, but Harwood's no-booze ban didn't seem to adversely affect his trade, and his hotel became famous, not only throughout the province but nationally.

Around the same time that Harwood was building his dream hotel, another one, even bigger and grander,

was being planned a block north on Main Street and Cordova. The Grant Hall was the work of James Walker, an American. With the backing of a large hotel chain, which put up $50,000, Walker raised over $200,000 from 486 local shareholders, the most successful stock offering in the city's history. The hotel opened on May 19, 1928. The lobby was a large rotunda, with black marble walls, and surrounded at the top by a decorative frieze. An immense fireplace graced one end. A marble staircase led up to the mezzanine and the only musicians' gallery in the province. All in all, it was considered to be one of the most modern and beautiful hotels on the prairies. Most important, despite the idea's foreign origin, the hotel was predominantly a local enterprise.

A Nice Place to Visit

Moose Jaw had always been a destination. Some people, of course, had come for the spurious pleasures of River Street, but others had been drawn by perhaps less wild but nonetheless equally natural attractions.

Moose Jaw was built on the confluence of three waterways: the Moose Jaw River, which drains the land to the southeast; Thunder Creek, which comes from the west; and Spring Creek, which comes from the northwest. Spring Creek, however, was not nearly as significant as the other two. In the hot, dry days of late summer, it slowed to a trickle, and all but disap-

Richard Harwood's dream hotel in 1931.

Automobile tours were becoming a favourite holiday getaway. It was cheaper driving and camping than taking trains and staying in hotels. In 1932, for example, the camp had 3,843 visitors in 1,134 cars.

The idea for the Wild Animal Park began innocently enough in 1926 when local businessman Frank McRitchie's mother happened to mention that in all her seventy years, as a girl in Ontario and later in Saskatchewan, she had never seen a buffalo. Well then, he replied, let's go to Banff and see one. No, she said sadly, she was too old and unwell for such a trip. "O.K. We'll bring them here."

McRitchie had been enthusiastically recounting a trip to the Rio Grande Valley in Texas to his sister Mary. What an asset beautiful scenery could be to a country, he told her. What about Moose

peared in dry years. The river, of course, with its natural wild beauty drew many visitors, as did the newly established Wild Animal Park. Many people came from the surrounding area for the dance halls, theatres and concerts.

By the 1930s, the automobile had supplanted the train as the main form of transportation, and Moose Jaw benefited by its location on the Trans-Canada Highway, that seemingly endless, dusty trail, stretching most of the way across the country. In a decade, it had grown from an ambitious idea to a long, if mostly unpaved, reality.

In 1922, the Tourist Camp was opened in River Park. The Rotary and Kiwanis clubs built a community building there and the next year six hundred people in two hundred and fifty cars camped in the park. Over the following years, there were a number of improvements and additions at the camp and it remained popular and successful even in the depths of the Depression.

River Park Cabin, also known as Ashton's Canoe Rentals, about 1930

Dignitaries at the 1929 opening of the Wild Animal Park. L-R: James Gardiner, J.R. Green, Mayor Dunn, Senator James H. Ross, John M. Uhrich, and W. Baker.

Jaw? she scolded. Was it not surrounded by natural beauty? A lovely winding creek? Lush trees? Why could a group of people not find some land and get government permission to have a few buffalo and deer?

McRitchie was inspired and, within a few months, had entered into a partnership with farmer and early environmentalist John R. Green, who owned large tracts of land south of the city, for development of a wild animal park, although the project didn't come to fruition until 1928. "We were like the dog that chased the train and when the train stopped, the dog did not know what to do about it," McRitchie later wrote in a memoir.

With pleas to the public and a variety of fund-raising schemes, McRitchie and his supporters, including lawyer and politician J. Gordon Ross, as well as the local MP, E.N. Hopkins, managed to raise $6,000 to build a 2.5-metre fence around the park. By March 1929, they had six buffalo, three elk, three mule deer, and two Rocky Mountain sheep. The superintendent of Banff National Park pronounced the new Wild Animal Park one of the finest of its kind.

The park was an instant success, with bears, coyotes, and badgers added to the mix. It was officially opened on May 24, 1929. For the day, it was renamed "Sitting Bull Park." The ceremonies were held on a natural amphitheater on the east side of the river. Cree and Sioux, who camped in wigwams on the flat, performed a mock robbery of the "Jean Louis Legaré General Store," all the while firing shot

The founder of the Park, Frank McRitchie Sr., and friends about 1929.

were at large for many days and road-grading equipment was needed to clear away the dunes around the fences.

At first they had no cages at all. The large animals roamed the two hundred hectares. Birds lived on the river. McRitchie and the Green family were adamant that the animals should remain completely unmolested, to the extent that they would not allow banding of migrating birds. But the influx of wounded racoons and porcupines brought to the park by local children required cages, and the park changed subtly.

The park began as a refuge for native species. In 1931 it received a pair of peafowl from Boston, but it was a long time before they started to get exotic and foreign animals. Eventually it expanded its repertoire until it

gun blanks into the air. They were then "apprehended and subdued" by a group of Mounties.

In the early years of the Depression and accompanying drought, feeding the animals became a serious problem. Despite the almost total crop failure in 1931, many local farmers donated wheat sheaves, oats, corn stalks and hay to keep the animals alive. In 1935 and 1936, the same thing happened and hay had to be brought from as far as Manitoba. The province also provided financial assistance in the lean years.

Top and bottom: Enjoying the Park in September, 1956

The blowing dust also created a problem. At times the drifts grew so high that the fences were covered, allowing several elk to escape. They

Top: Looking at the wolves in September, 1956. By today's standards, the enclosure is terribly inadequate.

Bottom: "Through the trees on the Moose Jaw River." The photographer, Lewis Rice, was an ardent environmentalist and conservationist, who crusaded to save the Moose Jaw River from the damage that was already afflicting it around 1910.

became a more conventional zoo. This was ironic given the early insistence that it was most definitely not a zoo.

The park remained popular throughout the 1940s and 1950s, but began to decline in the 1970s as interest in small zoos dwindled. By 1987, the future of the Wild Animal Park, now losing over a quarter of a million dollars a year, became doubtful. The provincial government finally decided to move toward privatization.

After a couple of failed private ventures, including an amusement park and an attempted return to the original concept of a sanctuary for wild animals (which included a project to reintroduce the swift fox to central Saskatchewan), the park closed its gates permanently in 1995.

A Sense of Identity

Taming the Wild Landscape

Seen from above, the Moose Jaw of today shows a lush and rich canopy of green. Even the traffic islands on Main Street grow twenty-foot weeping birch trees.

But in 1920, the endless, treeless, mind-numbing, preternaturally flat expanse of prairie was more than a mere memory. Less than a generation before, the prairie – flat, featureless, and bald beyond imagination to eyes that learned to see in Britain or Eastern Ontario – licked at Main Street. Photos from the turn the century show no trees, except a few around the riverbanks. Even Crescent Park, later to be a sylvan jewel, was treeless away from the creek.

"Mother said her eyes used to ache for trees," recalls Luwilla Payne.

Planting trees became almost an obsession.

In 1924, with the postwar recession receding and life returning to normal, the city distributed thirty-five hundred trees in May, more than in any previous year, with a mind to "making the city a beauty spot." Two thousand were given for use on private land; four hundred were planted on civic boulevards; and seven hundred were taken to Rosedale Cemetery, on the tabletop flat prairie on the western outskirts of the city, where, according to the *Times-Herald* of May 7, 1924, "in a few years they will spread a leafy shade over that now desolate place."

Opposite: The Shepley family, pioneers at Boharm, picnicking in style at Crescent Park in 1895.

A gathering at Crescent Park about 1912.

The Parks Board had been appointed in 1911 and its first project was to plant three carloads of trees along the streets of most of the city. So important were trees felt to be, their planting took precedence over capital improvements such as drains, gutters and sidewalks. Arbour Day was celebrated every year. It was an official civic holiday, with businesses and schools closed. People turned out in large numbers to plant trees, often with great ceremony.

It took more than trees, though, to tame the wilderness that lurked just beyond the boundaries of civilization. Trees made the prairie habitable, but flowers made it civilized.

Crescent Park sits in the middle of the city, one short block from the business district. Today, it is eleven hectares of green grass, trees and flowers. In the earliest days of the city, though, it was a large patch of prairie grass unequally bisected by a ravine through which trickled Spring Creek. Soldiers from Nova Scotia bivouacked there on the way to engage Louis Riel's forces in 1885. Cattle grazed there. At one point, people complained about the stench

from the garbage and human waste that befouled the ravine.

By the turn of the century, however, people began to see the value of a green space in the middle of the growing city. The lawns of "the Crescent" became a favourite spot for picnickers. As the city expanded and surrounded it, the park remained as it had been – two and one half blocks wide by three blocks long. George Champion, superintendent of parks in Winnipeg, designed Crescent Park in 1911.

The large flat, still treeless, expanse of grass to the east of the ravine was ideal for sports. By 1920, it was home to baseball, cricket and football fields. Originally owned by the CPR, it was leased to the city for 999 years. In 1921 the Cenotaph was built to commemorate those who died in WWI.

The area west of the ravine was a little more civilized. The library, to the north near Athabasca Street, was the centrepiece of the park, with a complex pattern of paths and formal flower gardens surrounding it. Eventually, the entire park was transformed into a beauty spot of great repute.

While Crescent Park is the heart of the city, Moose Jaw's waterways are the

Crescent Park

Ethel Kirk Grayson

Down the long, steely stretch of water, curving between the poplars and the weeping-caraganas that in spring wear gold coronets in their hair, down the quiet water and under ornamental bridges drifts the queenly swan, proud as Juno, cruel as Cinderella's step-mother, and with breast white as glacial snow; while blowing in the wind, smiling in the rain, a Tyrian conflagration - flicker the thousand, thousand blossoms of sweet rocket.

And so I return to the coulée, who in her barefoot childhood was known to me, if I may so personify her, while she went paddling in the creek, her dear familiar, and the draggled end of her green petticoat caught among the brookmints and buttercups, and her pocket spilled wild strawberries. But she grew up, slovenly, accumulating tin cans and torn papers, and I was content to nod at her in passing. Yes I knew her as a slattern, at her worst; then she became newly rich almost over night, and baroque bridges spanned the creek that had shrunk to a discouraged trickle, and its waters were replenished; and to lend her neighbourhood grandeur nesting swans were enthroned on reedy islets. The coulée, even in her lean years, had preserved something of charm. In the time of industrial depression it proved her means of salvation. To out-of-work labourers was assigned a task worthy of their hire; the transforming and beautifying of the rude gulch. Now with no apparent effort the swans move slowly, through glimmering mists of wisteria-tinted sweet rocket.

Today the coulée is bounded by a park-like area, a summery composition of trees and flower borders; a bandstand and a children's playground trumpet the holiday mood; a Memorial Cross honours in perpetuity the names of the Fallen. Leisurely strollers are observed, and often the voices exchanging jests are recognizable as Dutch, Esthonian, Polish, German voices – to such strange usage has our language come – of "displaced" persons.

Yet the coulée in her feminine character persists; upon the watery surface of her mirror, the creek, are imposed the wavering reflections of changing history. Call it my whimsy that she views therein the days of lightfoot youth, when she was but a wilding, and unambitious; there too must be imaged the phases of materialism, when men went mad over real estate values, and the coulée was scoffed at as "no account." Then on her mirror rest the shadow of drought and depression, and of an enforced introspection that gradually turn opinion toward a belief in the coulée's potentialities. Her natural comeliness had been defaced, but comeliness might be restored. And the mirror records war, and aeroplanes in flight, and dispossessed persons pausing for a survey of the swans - "where light and shadow cross."

And occasionally I catch a glimpse of the coulée as I knew her first. When the last leaf has whirled slowly to its death, and the swans, through fear of an imminent frost, have been removed; when the bluish shreds of fog lurk among the skeletal bushes, and long-legged birds halt in their migration and mince about drearily in the drained creek-bed – then my fancy evokes the earlier madcap, a wreath of withered rose-berries in her matted hair. Unmindful of her intellectual associate, the library, she roves at will; yet she is a timorous phantom, and prone to take cover in the wind-stripped glades of sweet rocket.

Above R-L: Ethel Kirk Grayson with friends Frances Pascoe and Dorothy Miller at Crescent Park.

Crescent Park with Zion Church in the background in the 1920s.

veins and arteries pumping the city's lifeblood, providing more than six hundred and fifty hectares of natural parkland along their banks and beaches.

The river and two creeks, so important to the city's development, were also a major source of recreation, and an important meeting place. The Aquatic Society produced both world-class athletes and important social events from its birth in 1913. The clubhouse, which sat sixty metres east of what is now the First Avenue bridge connecting South Hill to the rest of Moose Jaw, "was the Mecca" in the summer, recalls Jack Freidin. Many beaches along the riverbank attracted large crowds throughout the summer

too. The beach at the General Hospital saw seven hundred to a thousand bathers at a time in the heat of the summer. The Plaxton family's motor launch tours of the river were famous for decades. People fished, rented canoes, and rowboats, and picnicked on the banks. Connor's Park, a mile or so south of the city, had both a large dance pavilion and a dock where revellers could rent canoes. Many a summer's night was spent dancing under the stars, with occasional romantic interludes on the river itself.

The river was not always benign, though, and every year, many people, young and old, drowned.

A regatta at the Aquatic Club in August of 1924.

All Singing, All Dancing.

Moose Jaw has always had a split personality – part rounder and part evangelist – but it was a place with a distinct personality. It was a community. Everyone knew everyone and there were few secrets and fewer surprises.

In those days, Moose Javians liked to get together. There was no television to get in the way, radio and the movies were still novelties. People got together for fun and frolic, but for serious purposes as well – church, political meetings, and Chattauqua competed with parties, picnics, and parades to draw people out and draw them together.

Rose Kain, who was active in the St. Boniface Church, recalls the fun she had at dances and socials. There were "quite a lot of women around the same age as I was. I spent a lot of time there." As a young single woman, she also went to the movies with friends a lot. "There used to be a serial on every Friday night you see. And of course they'd take it off just at a very exciting

time and they'd make you go the next Friday. And you'd sit with much the same crowd on Friday night. They'd be in their favourite seat, and [you'd be in] your favourite seat."

The Princess Theatre opened in 1911. It was followed by the Monarch, the Sherman, and the Allan (which became the Capitol Theatre in 1919). There were, at times, up to fifteen theatres in the city, as well as the Opera House on the third floor of the old City Hall.

The Capitol Theatre, which still exists, albeit divided into three mini theatres, was one of the most elegant and up-to-date. It became only the sixth theatre in the West to show "talkies" – ceremonies began at midnight June 15, 1929, with a speech by Mayor James Pascoe, followed by a showing of *Close Harmony,* "an all-talk-

Dancers who entertained between shows at the Capitol Theatre in 1928.

More Capitol Theatre dancers in 1928.

ing, all-singing, all-dancing" musical starring Buddy Rogers and Nancy Carroll. The Capitol was also the first theatre in Canada to show legendary Hollywood director Cecil B. DeMille's first talking picture, the now all-but-forgotten epic social commentary *Dynamite*. Throughout the 1920s, many films had their Western premiere in Moose Jaw theatres. People took pride in these "firsts," boasting of Moose Jaw's location on the cutting edge of technology and culture. Moose Jaw was a city of culture.

Of course, in those days, movies were only a small part of the fare offered by local theatres. Live drama, vaudeville and concerts appeared on their stages, often followed by the latest film. Moose Jaw was a stop on major theatrical and literary circuits. Major stars of the day walked the boards at the theatres of the city. Vaudeville acts like Sir Harry Lauder and the Dumbbells (a kind of Canadian Monty Python) passed through the city, along with, as Kain recalls, "dancing girls, some of them with not very much on

their stages, often followed by the latest film. Moose Jaw was a stop on major theatrical and literary circuits. Major stars of the day walked the boards at the theatres of the city. Vaudeville acts like Sir Harry Lauder and the Dumbbells (a kind of Canadian Monty Python) passed through the city, along with, as Kain recalls, "dancing girls, some of them with not very much on

and so on. That," she adds with a wink, "used to draw quite a crowd."

Like young people everywhere, young Moose Javians loved to dance. From Main Street's Masonic Temple to River Street's notorious Academy Room, where gangsters, drugs and booze were frequently found and which was known on the street as "Gonorrhoea Alley," there were plenty of places to dance, and bands to dance to.

But in 1921, a very special place was born. Musicians loved the place for its nearly perfect acoustics. Dancers loved it for the sprung dance floor, where you could dance for hours without tiring. The eccentric pseudo Tudor décor provided some cosy dark corners where couples could be alone despite the hoards of revellers. Temple Gardens soon attained almost leg-

Temple Gardens soon after it opened.

Wilson MacDonald and the cast of "In Sunny France" in February, 1924.

THE ROARING TWENTIES — 71

endary status and became the main place for teenagers to go for more than fifty years.

Moose Jaw was interested in higher culture as well. Poets and other orators on cross country tours often stopped in the city. Pauline Johnson had been a hit on Sept. 23, 1897. Charles G.D. Roberts came to read in 1925, and in 1927 the city's poetry lovers were thrilled to hear three of the countries leading literary lights: Bliss Carmen, E.J Pratt, and Alfred Noyes. (In modern times, the city is home to its two official poets laureate, Gary Hyland and Bob Currie.)

The "pop star" poet of the twenties who had the biggest impact on Moose Jaw, though, was Wilson Mac-Donald. A Canadian who toured extensively, he was a musician as well. A slim, dapper man, he was always turned out in immaculate, well-tailored suits, his walking stick, grey Homburg, and monocle accentuating his aristocratic looks. Although time has not been kind to MacDonald's reputation, he was highly regarded in the past, though no one was as impressed as he was with himself, claiming that his "Ode to a Whip-poor-will" was the equal to Keats'

"Ode to a Nightingale" and Shelley's "Ode to a Skylark."

He performed for a number of audiences in October 1923, including the Canadian Club and the Local Council of Women. Less than a year later, he was back with the opera "In Sunny France," which he wrote, composed, and directed. MacDonald stayed in town for several weeks rehearsing the mostly local cast and crew. He wrote in a letter that he had been "treated royally," that he had "not one unpleasant word said to me," and that the mer-

The studio of radio station 10AB in 1925.

chants of Moose Jaw were "glad to have the chance to assist Canadian art."

Art and commerce merged in radio in the twenties. The first commercial radio station in the province was CKCK in Regina, which first broadcast in 1922. It was, however, a bit of a late-comer. A year earlier, a group of enthu-siasts had formed the Moose Jaw Ama-teur Wireless Club. Their first experi-mental broadcasts occurred in 1921. With the call letters "10AB," it was the first amateur broadcasting station in Canada.

On Nov. 1, 1922, two weeks after CKCK first went on the air, 10AB made its first broadcast on a 10-watt trans-mitter from the fire hall on Fairford Street West. A few months later, the sta-tion was moved to the YMCA building some three blocks to the east and power was increased to 50 watts.

In late 1923, financial problems almost killed the station, and it went off the air for a short time. A new organiza-tion, the Moose Jaw Radio Association, took over. On Dec. 15, 1923, in its new home on the fourth floor of the Bellamy Furniture store on Main Street, it made a triumphant return to the airwaves. It stayed in that studio, operating as an amateur station for eleven years. It was the only amateur station that could be heard in all parts of the United States.

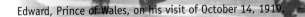

Edward, Prince of Wales, on his visit of October 14, 1919.

Commercial radio came to the city in 1928 when Winnipeg stock brokers James Richardson and Sons started station CJRM. The radio station broadcast from the top floor of the $100,000 stone building on Main Street, one of the few Art Deco buildings in the city, where the brokerage firm had its offices.

With its heavy British population, Moose Jaw had a great love for the monarchy. When a royal or even vice regal visitor came to town, the whole city exploded with respect and affection.

Royal visitors dropped by quite regularly. The Prince of Wales, who owned a ranch in Alberta, was a regular visitor, stopping in the city in 1919, 1924, and 1927.

Prince George, the future king of England, and future father of Queen Elizabeth, paid a quiet visit in 1926 and managed to spend two hours walking incognito in the city, without being found out. The twenty-four-year-old prince, travelling as a private, if somewhat privileged, citizen, was crossing Canada on his way home after a tour of duty with the navy in China. When his train stopped in Moose Jaw, the prince,

escorted by two bodyguards but largely unnoticed, got out to stretch his legs and buy a record at a Main Street music store.

...and everyone Played the Game

Much of the recreational life of the city was based on sports. Many businesses sponsored their own teams, manned by their own employees in most organized sports. On a summer's night, every one of the city's innumerable ballfields was occupied until dark.

Crescent Park was not the only public space containing sports fields; the exhibition grounds had, at various times, a football field and cricket pitch. Even the park at City Hall had an athletic field.

Organized baseball had been an important part of Moose Jaw life since the beginning. The city won the territorial championship in 1895.

The city had not only amateur, but also professional baseball. The Moose Jaw Millers were a first-class team in the Western Canada League. The Millers held spring training in Oregon and scouted in California for new prospects. Millers often ended up in the major leagues. In 1920, for exam-

The Territorial Baseball Champions of 1895 included future Premier Walter Scott, second from the right in the middle row.

The Moose Jaw Ball Club of 1921.

ple, Denny Williams was sold to the world-champion Cincinnati Reds.

The Millers played most of the twenties in the new stadium built on land donated by Senator J.H. Ross between Ross and Oxford streets two blocks east of Main. The land was the location of the "Ross Well" – the source of water on one of the original plots of land claimed by Senator Ross – which gave the new park its name, Ross Wells Park.

As baseball dominated summer, hockey was the game of winter. In 1920, the city built a new, thoroughly modern indoor rink for the princely sum of $24,900. A Moose Jaw team had played in the Allan Cup finals in 1913. In the twenties, Moose Jaw had two senior hockey teams – The Robin Hoods and the Maple Leafs. Before Prohibition, there was also the Maroons, a professional team sponsored by a local brewer.

Almost every boy in the city played shinny on outdoor rinks, on the river and creeks when they froze, even on the streets and the back alleys. Hockey wasn't nearly as organized in those days as it is now, but there was a high school league with teams from Central Collegiate, Ross Collegiate, and Moose Jaw College. The Moose Jaw KORCS (named after the local regiment The King's Own Rifles) played in a two-team league with the Regina Pats (named after the Princess Patricia Regiment).

Combative sports were also popular in Moose Jaw from at least the turn of the century. Professional boxing and wrestling matches were a staple of the sporting clubs of River Street, and always attracted big crowds. World-class fights were not unusual in larger venues and often attracted a lot of attention. One of the more colourful was a twelve-round match in May 1924 between two hometown middleweight boxers, Kid Moose and Jack Reddick, both of whom were making names for themselves internationally. The "Kid," just back from a successful tour of England, was a schoolboy boxing sensation. At nineteen, he stood a little under 5'11" and weighed only 160 pounds.

The twenty-year-old Reddick's family ran the Windsor Hotel. He could not fight under his real name – John Runner, Jr, because his mother did not approve of his choice of careers. He had started a boxing club in the Hammond Building, then moved to the Arena Rink. Promoted by Jack Whelan and Jack Wesley, he had fought world middleweight champion Henry Gib, light heavyweight champion Paul Berlenbah and Kid Norfolk, the light heavyweight "champion of the South." He was generally considered a world contender, who, said the *Times-Herald,* "was a natural in the ring. He could hit like a trip-hammer and possessed plenty of boxing know-how." He'd won the light-heavyweight championship by beating Sailor Jones in Toronto earlier in 1924.

The fight at the Arena Rink, which was touted as the biggest fight in Western Canada, was also remarkable for some of the antics that preceded it. Reddick was well known for his big white malamute dog, Jack, which travelled everywhere with him. So Kid Moose's handlers got him a dog too - and milked the story for all the publicity value they could, first dropping hints the dog was a fierce hound that would require a special chain and six men to hold it. The dog turned out to be a husky puppy, but served its purpose well. Six thousand fans attended the fight to see Reddick defeat the Kid on points.

Kid Moose soon disappeared from the ring. Reddick, who most thought was destined for a world championship belt, injured his back in training a few years later and retired from the fight game, his promise unfulfilled.

The Moore-Quinn fight at the Arena Rink on September 21, 1923.

SINKING FAST—NO REGRETS

Every vote will be needed to complete the downfall of King Booze in Saskatchewan, on Monday, December 11.

The Decade That Roared

A Failed Experiment

After many battles between those who enjoy a glass of spirits and the temperance movement, the "dry" side finally prevailed in 1919, ushering official Prohibition into Canada.

The Canada Temperance Act allowed the provinces to decide for themselves, based on the results of provincial referenda, whether to apply the federal legislation. Saskatchewan was the first province to act, and a referendum was held Oct. 25, 1920, with the "drys" scoring an overwhelming victory. Prohibition lasted until 1924, but throughout its existence it proved to be a law-enforcement headache.

In Moose Jaw, where the dry forces won the day, the issue split the community along many different lines, including ethnic and religious. River Street might have been a centre for the provision and proliferation of vice, but Moose Jaw as a whole was law-abiding and proper: a bourgeois town. Ironically, while Saskatchewan voted decisively for prohibition, the province would soon be responsible for sixty per cent of all the illicit still prosecutions by the RCMP in the country, and Moose Jaw would play a major role in that illegal trade.

Of course, the real problem was not whether alcohol was legal or not, but enforcement of the laws. Despite the fact that Moose Jaw voted overwhelmingly for Prohibition, many people just did not pay much attention to the antibooze

Opposite: This Temperance cartoon ran in the *Grain Growers Guide* on November 29, 1916.

law. The stigma attached to a conviction under the Saskatchewan Temperance Act was minimal. To be a drunk was disgraceful, to be convicted of selling a bottle of beer was negligible. Simple subterfuges were used to hide the booze being sold.

Tap Kwan, whose parents owned the Commercial Lunch on River Street, recalls that "River Street at that time was crazy. People came into town to gamble. My dad told me they served liquor in a bowl, but not openly. People would come in and have a bowl of soup. They'd know what they want. They wanted a bowl of whiskey."

Even the city's movers and shakers turned a blind eye to Prohibition.

In testimony to the Bence Commission, appointed by the provincial government to look into allegations of police corruption in Moose Jaw in 1924, Deputy Police Chief Tony Townsend said he had delivered confiscated booze to Mayor W.F. Dunn's house. The mayor and his wife denied getting any liquor from the police but readily admitted to having some on hand; it had come, they swore, "from other sources."

While the domestic consumption of alcohol was barred by Prohibition, it was legal to warehouse it and to ship and sell it outside the province. Consequently, there was money to be made from exporting booze, and Moose Jaw cashed in. The Bronfman family, which became rich during Prohibition under the leadership of brothers Sam and Harry, based most of its operations out of Yorkton and Regina but maintained a warehouse in Moose Jaw. It was run by brother-in-law David Gallaman, who committed a small indiscretion – he sold booze to a couple of police informants. That careless act almost sent Harry to jail.

Harry was already under fire – he had been accused by a customs official of attempted bribery (a charge he later beat), and a Bronfman employee had been murdered, allegedly by American

Looking west from Main Street onto River Street West in the 1920s.

bootleggers, in Bienfait, a town close to the American border.

Before Gallaman's trial, the two informants – who turned out to be River Street habitués who occasionally turned informant in order, ironically, to earn money to buy booze – disappeared. Stories circulated, helped along by Bronfman business rivals, that the two had been spirited away on a long transcontinental train trip. They were, the yarn went, supplied with rivers of hooch and disappeared from the train somewhere in the US midwest. Without the star witnesses, the case against Gallaman collapsed.

The Crown alleged that Harry was behind their disappearance, and he was charged with obstruction of justice. The basis for the prosecution's case was the testimony of bootlegger and some-time police informant John Denton. During the trial, Denton's testimony proved to be somewhat flexible and was often revealed to be outright fabrication. Ultimately, the jury didn't believe a word he said, and Harry was acquitted.

Moose Jaw was in an ideal position for the transit of booze, both legal and not. It was the busiest rail centre in the prairies. Trains from all directions passed through the two depots. The Soo Line trains came straight from Chicago and Minneapolis. Highway 1 brought east-west automobile traffic;

> Moose Jaw was in
> an ideal position
> for the transit of booze,
> both legal and not.
> It was the busiest
> rail centre in
> the prairies.

Highway 2 led straight to the US border. Even after the end of Prohibition in Canada, the export of liquor remained a big business, as the US remained dry until 1933.

Harry Swarberg, who at the time was a young man, recalls seeing men loading cars with boxes of alcohol from a stash in a barn on the north side of the Fourth Avenue Bridge. "About 5 o'clock in the evening these big cars would come out there, and they would load 'em with it. And they would head south and over the border. They didn't use trucks. They had these long Daimlers, which were sixteen- or seventeen-cylinder cars."

Of course, River Street was at the centre of this industry. The boys of River Street had the experience, the know-how and the proximity to the railway and Highway 2.

Moon Mullins' dad was a **rum-runner**, and the young Moon was drafted into service, driving loads of booze in Model T Fords, when he was twelve or thirteen. "My Dad 'n' them figured they wouldn't stop a kid," he remembers. Mullins started with short hauls, but in 1927, as a seventeen-year-old, he made three trips to the US, "hauling down liquor to Minot, North Dakota, from here – the Brunswick Hotel. It was shipped in from the East."

The trips south were dangerous, Mullins remembers, with rival gangs sometimes gunning for the haulers. "Across the line down there, these guys played for keeps. They'd shoot you off the road, rather than try to stop you."

Considering Moose Jaw's notoriety, in later days, as a hotbed of boozing and bootlegging, the city was, in fact, surprisingly free of the worst excesses of Prohibition-flouting, however.

Provincial liquor commissioner Allen G. Hawkes zealously pressed his pursuit of bootleggers but had little success in Moose Jaw.

One day in the winter of 1924, for example, Hawkes, looking "like a wild man," according to the *Times-Herald*, led a late-evening police raid on the Princess Café. But after an exhaustive search of the restaurant, not a drop of liquor was found.

On another hunt, Hawkes raided the Veteran's Pool Room, coming up with just one bottle of beer. Undaunted, he and an investigator moved on to the Cecil Hotel, where, after an exhaustive search, they seized a trunk containing fifty-three bottles of beer, seven barrels of beer hidden in a specially built basement stash and a bottle of wine a waiter was unable to ditch in time.

Hawkes' zeal sometimes rebounded against him. On another expedition to Moose Jaw during Prohibition's dying days, he and his men found seventy-two empty beer bottles and three kegs of beer during a raid on the Royal George Hotel. They also found a heavy trunk, which they proceeded to break open with a crowbar. There was no liquor in it and the trunk's owner had Hawkes

Allen G. Hawkes.

charged under the Criminal Code with "wilfully committing damage to the trunk." He was convicted and fined $20 plus costs.

Ironically, just as Hawkes was in court, the first legal booze was being unloaded a few blocks away on High Street West in preparation for the opening of the first Government Liquor Store a few weeks later.

The Reverend W.P. Reekie was another anti-booze zealot who had little

The Princess Café in the 1920s.
(Or it could be McIntyre's Café.)

success in Moose Jaw. The secretary of the Regina-based Saskatchewan Social Service Council, an ecumenical organisation devoted to the solution of social problems, Reekie was convinced that the cause of much social blight was the demon rum.

Reekie's job description did not include acting as a law enforcement officer, but he had little faith in the police. So when he got wind of a carload of beer sitting in the railyard at Moose Jaw in September 1923, he decided to check it out himself. Arriving in the city in late afternoon, he found the railcar near the Robin Hood Mills, its contents labelled "Aerated Waters." After reporting his findings to the Liquor Commission and police, he and three friends set up a vigil in case someone tried to unload the cargo.

What followed was a bit of a Keystone Kops caper. At 1 a.m., a lone policeman showed up, but was uncertain, since the car was on CPR property, whether he had the right to confiscate the contents. He telephoned headquarters for advice. At 3 a.m., a sergeant appeared on the scene and explained he didn't have the manpower to stake out the boxcar, but would try to have a man check it every hour. Reekie tried to persuade CPR police to move the boxcar to a spot where it would be easier to watch, but they were too busy. Exasperated, he underook to watch the car himself.

A short time later, sure enough, a gang of men arrived and began to unload barrels into a truck. Reekie rushed to the telephone and was told help was on its way. But by the time a policeman arrived, on foot, the truck was long gone. Reekie's subsequent letter to Mayor Dunn accused the police of, at the very least, incompetence.

The mayor was forced to convene a Police Commission inquiry, which did not sit until 1924. The commission consisted of Judge F.A.G. Ousely, Magistrate H.S. Lemon, and the mayor, who, by then, was W.W. Davidson. Reekie told his story in great detail, and with great fervour. He was at a disadvantage at the inquiry, however. He faced cross-examination not only from the counsel for the police but from the three commissioners themselves. At one point, exasperated and feeling that he, not the police department, had become the subject of the investigation, Reekie cried out, "How many counsels are there for the police?"

Of course, the police version contradicted most of Mr. Reekie's terstimony, and, after three days of testimony, the inquiry ruled in favour of the cops. The commissioners didn't find "any evidence to substantiate any of the charges made against the police department or any member thereof."

A footnote: the spectre of the war against alcohol continued to haunt the prairies into the 1930s and it seemed as if the controversy would never go away. After Prohibition's official end in 1925, liquor was easily obtainable in government stores and profits from its sale become one of the government's main sources of revenue. When word spread, in early 1934, that the province was going to allow sale of beer by the glass, delegates of the Women's Christian Temperance Union from Moose Jaw and Regina met with the provincial cabinet to protest. Facing the imminent election that would wipe out his party, Tory Premier James Anderson realised that he was facing a no-win situation, since he could afford to antagonise neither the "wets" nor the "drys." He avoided having to decide by calling for a plebiscite on beer by the glass simultaneous with the election.

It was the last stand for Moose Jaw's temperance movement. Twelve hundred people packed Zion Church in March and unanimously adopted a resolution to campaign to defeat beer by the glass, but it was to no avail. In the election, beer lovers won by a big margin and, even in Moose Jaw, the "wets" won a narrow victory. The city's first beer parlours opened on May 1, 1935.

Turn Left and You'd Think You're in New Orleans

River Street was a legendary centre of sin and merriment. Later, when its time had passed and a nostalgic glow had softened the hard edges of memory, children would still be afraid even to walk its sidewalks for fear of contamination and the wrath of their mothers, such was its reputation.

In fact, River Street sat in the middle of the business district, and in business hours it was almost respectable. For River Street was more than a nest of brothels and gambling houses. In 1924, for example, seven of the nine hotels in Moose Jaw were on River Street, as were two of the six jewellers in the city.

"River Street was business," Rose Kain recalls. "There was a most wonderful hardware store on River Street. They had good stuff and good low prices, so people did go on to River Street to that business." The best Chinese restaurants in town were on River Street too, along with a Greek restaurant and an ice cream parlour called the Princess, Kain says. Then there was the Savoy, to which, according to Jack Friedin, "people would

come from Regina for their steaks."

But at night, River Street was transformed. It was a world away from the respectable society of Moose Jaw. One block north of the CPR station and turn left, says an old-time reporter quoted by James Gray in his book *Red Lights on the Prairie,* and you'd think you were in New Orleans. After dark, it was the domain of the pimps and the madams and the bootleggers and the gamblers, and, of course, the whores. There were numerous brothels in private houses, and it was said that every hotel, even the most respectable ones, had a floor where you could find rooms that came complete with female companionship. Gambling dens were common and impromptu casinos in the basements of many establishments were the source of many of the stories of an underworld underground.

River Street was the place where the fast life and the straight and narrow collided.

But River Street was actually highly disciplined, its skin trade as discreet as that trade can be. There were very few streetwalkers – other streets closer to the railway had an even worse reputation. "Manitoba Street East was really a bad street," Kain recalls. "There were a lot of prostitutes down there."

Violence was relatively uncommon, confined mostly to disputes over card games within the gambling halls and drunken brawls. It would occasionally spill over on to the streets, though. An argument at a River Street poolroom once erupted into a pool cue- and blackjack-swinging melee that had police responding in force.

But those who worked in the stores near River Street sometimes had their eyes rudely opened.

Kain was a young girl from Souris, Manitoba, come to Moose Jaw with her mother and father and six younger brothers and sisters in search of better opportunities and higher paying jobs. In Souris, she made $7 a week as a sales clerk. In Moose Jaw, the boomtown, in the same job, she could make the grand sum of $10.

Coming to the city was a shock for a small town girl.

"I didn't know there was so much crookedness until I came to Moose Jaw," she says with a laugh. She found a job at Woolworth's, on the corner of Main Street and River. "We used to get some pretty tough customers in there."

Some of the girls were from elsewhere, chased out of other towns, abandoned by lovers, husbands, sold by their fathers, left with no choices and no place to go. Others were local poor girls, trying to make a living. Kain, who often waited on them at Woolworths's says most of them "were very nice.... They were well dressed on River Street. [But] they weren't of good character, you know. They were there for the business."

Moon Mullins, who sold newspapers on River Street as a boy, recalls some of the street's prostitutes taking an interest in the paperboys. "'Soiled doves'...we called them that. They were good to us kids. They'd protect us like a bunch of mothers."

Kain did have one bad encounter with a prostitute, whom she caught shoplifting. "She was quite tall, very attractive, and she had a Hudson seal coat right down to her ankles, and a big fur hat," she recalls. "She was a good-looking

Hotels on the second block of River Street West in the 1920s.

woman" – so good looking that Kain kept her eyes glued to her when she came into Woolworth's one day, and she saw the woman pocket some candies. "I was so darned mad because a woman that was in a Hudson seal coat, in this

Above: A Hudson Seal coat from the 1920 Robinson McBean catalogue.

beautiful hat, was stealing candies."

The police were called and Kain told them what she'd witnessed. "They searched her and she really had her pockets full" – not just of candy from Woolworth's but items from Joyner's, Robinson-McBean's, and Binnings', and other stores along Main Street. The woman tried to grab Kain, snarling, "I'll get you, I'll get you," but one of the policeman told her, "You cool it. You're in enough trouble now!"

Kain remembers she was frightened by the threat and for months afterwards would only leave the store in the evening with a co-worker. "I used to be scared to death that she would be waiting for me with some of her friends."

Everytime the woman came into the store, she'd give Kain a "vicious look," and eventually Kain left Woolworth's and moved to the lingerie department of Robinson-McBean's department store a little farther up Main Street.

There, she often waited on prostitutes shopping for the lacy lingerie the store specialized in. She never had trouble with any of them again, but, years later, she recalls with a shudder that she'd always wash her hands after handling the money they paid with.

Gangsters and Gunmen: Al Capone and the Dubious Chicago Connection

The Roaring Twenties was something between the honest anarchy of the frontier town and the thinly veneered civility of modern corporate society. In October, 1927, United Church minister E.F. Church said from the pulpit that Moose Jaw had a reputation as a "city of freedom." This was not meant as a compliment. The apathy of good people, he said, resulted in the "harbouring of criminals who cannot find refuge in any other place...prostitutes, to menace the life and hope of men and women...so-called hotels used as bawdy houses...restaurants where liquor is sold and drunk, a screen for the bootlegger...[and] places which are protected by bribery where various forms of gambling are carried on."

River Street was the centre of a peculiar universe. Every day, men and women got off the train from Chicago, from Minneapolis, from Toronto, from Vancouver. After long hard days riding the rails, or in the luxury of a Pullman sleeper, or even on the day coach from Regina, they came seeking the diversions of River Street. Indeed, Moose Jaw was sometimes known as "Regina's

The Saskatchewan Provincial Police detachment in Moose Jaw in 1929 includes (L-R) Constables Bond, Pyne, Kistrack, and Cassidy, and "Mac" the dog.

red light district." Anything you wanted, you could get – booze, drugs, dames, an all-night game – they were all there for the asking.

And come they did. Gamblers and grifters, pimps and prostitutes, gunmen and thugs – the unknown and the famous alike. Two-Gun Cohen is known to have passed through on his way to fame as bodyguard of Sun Yat Sen and confidant of Mao Tse Tung.

But the biggest infamous name associated with Moose Jaw is Al Capone, the notorious king of Chicago who made a fortune during Prohibition in illicit liquor.

From the twenties on, rumours have persisted that when things got too hot in Chicago, Big Al would hop on a train and take off for the Jaw. In fact, there's no evidence that Capone ever even heard of Moose Jaw, let alone

spent any time there, but the rumours have stuck.

Fred Stearns, an engineer for the Great Northern Railroad on its freight run between Chicago and Moose Jaw, used to swear he hauled private cars filled with gangsters to the city, and he was sure Capone himself was sometimes a passenger, though he never saw him. Stearns' tales have passed down to his grandson Dale, a Moose Jaw businessman, who continues to tell them today.

Other people were said to have had contact with the Chicago mob chief.

Moon Mullins claims his friend Bill Beamish, now dead, used to boast of meeting Capone. "He was a barber, and he had told me that he had met Al Capone right here in Moose Jaw. He had cut his hair twice, he said."

And so the stories persist. There's even another tale that Big Al had to get his wisdom teeth pulled in Moose Jaw, but corroboration is hard to find.

Even if Moose Jaw didn't have Scarface, it had its share of petty thugs and desperadoes.

During the twenties, the Wild West still existed in part. Bandit gangs preyed on small towns and cities throughout the West, both in Canada and the US. Johnny Reed, the mastermind of a gang that terrorized Saskatchewan/Montana border lands, once made Moose Jaw his base of operations. Armed robberies were common. The post office was robbed of $35,000 in a daring daylight holdup on December 1, 1924 – a year later, four men were arrested and sent to prison for long terms.

In the fall of 1924, the city was buzzing with the exploits of John Harrison, an American drawn to Moose Jaw by the lure of the fast life and easy pickings. A small, pale and thin-faced man of twenty-six, he was nevertheless stocky, tough, and brash as the gold tooth that glinted when he talked. He liked to call himself the Pittsburgh Kid.

On October 28, Harrison and an accomplice known only as the Frenchman stole a car from the parking lot outside the Arena rink, only to wind up in a smashup. The accomplice beat it on foot, leaving an unconscious Harrison to the police. After two weeks in hospital, he was transferred to jail, where he escaped by impersonating a hobo who had begged a night of warmth at the jail and shared a cell with him. In the morning, while the

hobo slept, Harrison convinced the jailer that he was the overnight guest and to release him. By the time police realized their error, he was long gone.

The Pittsburgh Kid's escape was one of the slickest tricks the city had ever seen. But the kid was too cocky for his own good. He stuck around town and, four days later, a CPR policeman making his usual rounds of the train yards recognised Harrison as one of two men shooting at a tin can with a Smith and Wesson .44 calibre revolver.

The CPR cop, W.C. Birch, outsmarted the tricky Harrison. Donning a pair of torn, greasy overalls and rubbing a little dirt on his face and hands, he transformed himself into a grubby hobo. Walking up unnoticed on the target-shooters, he was easily able to get the drop on them. Harrison was sent back to jail and was ultimately sentenced to four years in prison.

A Man of Some Repute

Chief of Police Walter Johnson stepped out onto the porch of his small white house on the northwest corner of Fairford Street West and First Avenue North. He gazed out upon his domain

and smiled. For the chief, life was good.

It was 1920. He had been chief of police for fifteen years. In that time, his force had grown from one to a staff of twenty-one (including civilian clerical staff and jail guards) plus his deputy, Tony Townsend. The River Street crowd was under control: they didn't roll their customers too often, and they kept their affairs confined to the two blocks of "The Street," where respectable citizens could ignore them. Moose Jaw was relatively free from serious crime, and, apart from the occasional intrusions of nosy pesky politicians and annoying reformers, he could run the force as he pleased. His bank account was substantial, and his large modern farm to the north of the city was thriving. He was fifty-five and still had his health. Life was good indeed.

Moose Jaw was well policed in the 1920s. Besides Johnson's municipal force, the city was also served by local detachments of the RNWMP and the Saskatchewan Provincial Police. In addition, the railways had their own police, who had powers of arrest and carried handguns, and were thus more than mere night watchmen.

Relations between the various forces were not always the most amicable. Their jurisdictions were separate but overlapping. The provincial police and the Mounties would not enforce city bylaws and the Mounties preferred to leave provincial statutes alone, but all three forces upheld the Criminal Code. Often, one force would defer to another when called on to enforce unpopular laws, such as Prohibition. The provincial police were often left to themselves in the fight against illegal booze, which was, after all, what they were created to combat.

Despite this large police presence, pimps, bootleggers, and gamblers seemed to have a more or less free hand, as long as they kept their activities discrete. And, perhaps because of their numbers, the police, especially those of the city force, occasionally fell victim to temptation. Long before the most famous incident, when most of the uniformed force found themselves behind bars, the Moose Jaw police managed to embarrass themselves from time to time.

The force was notoriously lax in its bookkeeping. Fines collected in Police Court were often just tossed into a desk drawer. One day in 1921, the chief received a message from the attorney general demanding $1,400 in fines and forfeited bail that had not yet been turned over to the province. Not knowing what had happened to the money, Johnson blithely wrote a personal cheque to cover the missing amount. The money was later found stuffed behind a desk drawer. It's hard to say which is more remarkable: the fact that money was misplaced, or that Johnson could so insouciantly toss off a cheque for what was, for the time, a large amount of money.

Although he ran a tight ship, Johnson was not universally popular. Local politicians were often unhappy with him. Unfortunately for them, though the city provided the police budget — around $40,000 in the early 1920s — council had no control over the chief or his men. The police commission at the time was appointed by the provincial government and consisted of the District Court judge, the city magistrate, and, ex-officio, the mayor.

The problem was, according to Alderman W.G. Ross (nephew of Senator J.H. Ross), that having judges who officiated in criminal trials control the police was a clear conflict of interest.

This conflict came to a head in the

Police Chief Walter Johnson.

notorious case of Mah Pon, an RCMP undercover agent assigned to infiltrate Chinese drug and gambling operations in the city. Mah's testimony was responsible for a number of conviction but ultimately he wound up on the wrong end of the law himself, arrested by city police and charged with possession of opium. Mah was the son of a wealthy businessman from Saskatoon. Troubled by the devastation that drugs caused in the Chinese community, he had volunteered as a police undercover agent. Mah insisted the drugs had been planted by the police. He also challenged

Magistrate Lemon, demanding he excuse himself from the case because he was a member of the police commission. The judge brushed aside his concerns and Mah was convicted and sent to jail.

His appeal created a quandary for legal authorities, since District Court Judge Ouseley was also on the police commission. Instead, his case was assigned to a Weyburn judge who agreed the drugs had been planted, probably by the police who had arrested him.

The resulting furor was enough to make the provincial government appoint Saskatoon lawyer J.R. Bence to head a special commission to investigate the Moose Jaw force.

Bence looked at a number of issues, including alleged tampering with records, lack of co-operation with the Mounties, and strife within the police force itself. The commission sat for eleven days, heard fifty-four witnesses, and examined sixty-seven exhibits. Despite expectations, Bence exonerated Johnson and Deputy Chief Townsend, pronouncing them to be honest, professional, and not inefficient. The report further

excoriated many of the aldermen who had been critics of the police.

The report split the council down the middle, and a motion of nonconfidence in Johnson and his deputy lost by a single vote.

But Johnson's reign as police chief was to receive an even greater threat.

Early on a July morning in 1923, Annie Moncur entered her millinary shop at 28 High Street West. Something was not right. She scanned the interior of the shop, mentally taking inventory. Then she had it. The hat her staff had finished the day before was missing. Moncour didn't bother reporting the theft to the police, not then anyway. But, two months later, while strolling along Main Street, she noticed a woman in a passing automobile wearing a hat identical to the one stolen from her shop. This time, she went to Chief Johnson, setting in motion a chain of events that would rock the force to its core.

To John Douglas, the only detective on the force, fell the unpleasant job of spying on his fellow policemen because, after a preliminary investigation, that's where the case of the mysterious hat theft seemed to point.

Staking out downtown stores, Douglas observed a series of burglaries by policemen, often involving the use of a flashlight flashing Morse Code all-clear signals.

For more than six months, an epidemic of thefts had plagued city businesses. Some, like those on South Hill, were ordinary, petty thefts, with a few dollars, some cigarettes, or a few goods missing. But many downtown businesses, ranging from the retail giant Robinson-McBean to Kent and Brown Grocery to the Dominion welding works, had been robbed of large amounts of goods. Expensive clothing, automobile batteries, and even Christmas turkeys had turned up missing. The police had so far been unable to solve the biggest and longest running crime spree in the city's history.

Early in the morning of February 16, 1924, the police commission – Mayor Davidson, Judge Ouseley, and Magistrate Lemon – convened an extraordinary meeting with Johnson.

The chief left the meeting armed with a search warrant. Accompanied by Detective Douglas and Deputy Chief Townsend, he raided the house of Constable J.W. Reynolds, where they discovered a large cache of stolen goods. By the following Monday, the entire uniformed force, except the three duty sergeants, had been suspended, and seven of the nine uniformed officers on the force had been charged. Truckloads of stolen goods had been recovered.

Reynolds, according to the Crown, was the ringleader of the group. At his trial, he maintained his innocence, claiming he had come by all the goods found in his home legitimately. The jury wasn't convinced and on the second day of his trial he was convicted and sentenced to four years of hard labour.

The "blue wall" crumbled. Most of the accused cops fell over themselves to testify against each other. Some of them were convicted and got smaller sentences. Some were acquitted, but all were fired and none rehired.

The only constable who survived the scandal of 1924 with his job and reputation intact was Andy Boland, the force's mounted policeman, who to some was the most memorable and beloved policeman on the force. From the prewar years on, he had patrolled the city on his horse, and was often seen at the head of the many parades down Main Street. The portly Boland continued to ride his horse through the city on patrol and parade until the force bought a motorcycle in 1933

> Chief Johnson, despite the fact that almost his entire uniformed force turned out to be crooked, came out of the affair as a hero.

and his horse was retired. Boland himself followed three years later.

Constable Alexander Bell, who was not suspected of theft himself, was dismissed from the force because he knew of the thefts and didn't report them. He was rehired the following year, though, and was promoted, first to sergeant in 1927, then inspector in 1928, and finally became chief of police in 1950.

Chief Johnson, despite the fact that almost his entire uniformed force turned out to be crooked, came out of the affair as a hero. He was lauded for ending the crime spree, and for replacing the recalcitrant constables so quickly. He had landed on his feet once again.

Rumours about the police, and about the chief, continued to spread, though. It was common knowledge that the police were on the take, and that the chief was getting his share. In a few years, even the esteem he gained from the affair of 1924 couldn't shelter him from the glare of public execration.

On July 21, 1927, the Police Commission — now made up of Mayor Davidson, Magistrate G.N. Broatch, and John Crawford, the manager of Macdonald Consolidated Ltd. — convened an extraordinary session. Johnson was not invited. He was the only item on the agenda.

For more than twenty years, the chief had done a good job of keeping River Street under control, but that was no longer good enough. As an editorial in the *Times* was to ask: "What is to be the ideal of the city of Moose Jaw? Is it to be the obsolete ideal of segregation (so-called) and police control (so-called) of the social vice and liquor-law violations? Or, is it to be law enforcement and legal suppression of vice and crime?"

The council asked for the chief's resignation. When he refused to respond, he was fired. It was the end of an era. Johnson did all right, though, and would eventually return to public life – as mayor!

Strange Bedfellows

There was more – much more – to Moose Jaw than the goings on of River Street. In fact, Moose Jaw was a generally law-abiding, church-going community. In a city of some twenty thousand, there were four Anglican churches, three Presbyterian, and four Methodist as well as assorted Catholic, Baptist, Orthodox, Lutheran, Salvation Army, and Seventh Day Adventist churches. It even had a synagogue. It did not lack for moral and spiritual leaders.

And, ironically, Moose Jaw in the

twenties was a centre of the sweeping, if short-lived, popularity of the Ku Klux Klan in Saskatchewan.

Late in 1926 three men got off the train in Regina. Lewis A. Scott, his son Harold, and a man of many aliases, Hugh Emmons – aka Pat Emory, aka Pat Emerson – were KKK organizers from the US. Within a year, they had established branches throughout Saskatchewan, with appeals to patriotism, a British identity, and conservative evangelical Protestantism.

In late September, 1927, the three

men disappeared with an estimated $100,000 in Klan funds. The Scotts and the money were never seen again. Emmons was found hard at work in Alberta, forming new chapters of the KKK. He was tried for embezzlement in May 1928, but was acquitted when the judge accepted his argument that, since he had never promised that he would not keep the Klan's money for himself, keeping it did not constitute fraud. This despite the fact that at a rally on June 7, 1927, he said that the initiation fees had "passed into the

An illustration from *Women of the KKK* fashion catalogue of the 1920s.

coffers of the Klan to be used for the purposes of the organisation." There were some who saw this as a miscarriage of justice and hinted at a conspiracy.

In Moose Jaw, Emmons did most of the work. He told everyone who would listen that he was moving to Moose Jaw permanently and bringing his wife and children. Allied with evangelical ministers, he quickly mirrored their shock at the "painted ladies who plied their obnoxious trade and other visible offences against God." Dark forces were at work in Moose Jaw, he said, forces that would stop at nothing to preserve their vile and sinful business. They had threatened his life, he said. Nevertheless, he said, he was prepared to die for the cause. If the worst should happen, he wanted his skin to be tanned and made into a Klan drum so his mortal remains could continue to fight the good fight, even after his spirit had passed on.

Not to be outdone, the Reverend Mr. T.J. Hind of the First Baptist Church prayed aloud on the podium that his life be taken instead so that Emmons could continue his great work.

The first Klan rally in Saskatchewan was held in Moose Jaw on June 7, 1927. Over four hundred members arrived from all over the province on a special CNR train — a far cry from the forty thousand Emmons claimed to have recruited. The crowd — estimated at about six thousand — that came expecting to hear rabble-rousing rhetoric was due for serious disappointment. The speeches dwelt mostly on patriotism, peace, brotherly love, Christian morality, evangelism,

> Ironically, Moose Jaw in the twenties was a centre of the sweeping, if short-lived, popularity of the Ku Klux Klan in Saskatchewan.

and denunciations of civic corruption. The closest thing to the expected Klan rant was Emmons' statement, as quoted in the *Times*, that: "We are not French. We want one flag, one school, one race, and one language."

The second and last big Klan rally in Moose Jaw was held on October 26, 1927, just ten days after a warrant had been issued for Emmons' arrest. About a thousand people attended, although it is unclear how many were actually members. Dr. J.H. Hawkins, an American Klan leader brought in for the day, claimed a total membership of two thousand in the city. He was more explicitly racist, saying "[We] believe that Almighty God created the white race as superior to any other race."

Although most Protestant clergymen who were not themselves members of the Klan remained emphatically silent about the group's activities, there were some, all of them from the United Church, who vigorously opposed the Klan. In Moose Jaw, Rev. E.F. Church denounced the Klan from the pulpit and pronounced himself "happy to be able to say that scarcely any of the Protestant minis-

ters of the city took any part in the work of this shallow organisation."

Rev. Angus A. Graham, dean of the Moose Jaw Boys College, lived up to Church's expectations. Bill McWilliams, who was sixteen and a student at the college at the time,

recalls being part of a group of students watching a Klan rally. "There was about forty, fifty guys in hoods and gowns [burning} three crosses on the top of the hill behind the college. We were leaning in the west window looking out. The old dean come

along and says, 'If one of you guys step out that door to see what's going on, don't come back in.'"

The Klan quickly lost momentum. It existed in the city for another three years, its presence marked by notices in the Announcements sections of the newspapers. There were no more rallies, but in 1929 the Klan sponsored a big Labour Day picnic in River Park, which four thousand people attended. Although there were racist speeches and a cross burning, the emphasis of the day was on sports events. The most notable thing about the picnic was the advertisement in the *Times* that included the decidedly un-Klan-like: "This is an invitation to you – no matter what your religion, your color, or creed."

Emmons later admitted that his primary motivation was the fees that new recruits paid him. The Klan promoted membership by exploiting cleavages within the community, and Emmons confessed that the main tactic was to feed people's "antis." He said, "Whatever we found that they could be taught to hate and fear, we fed them. We were out to get the dollars and we got them." It is worth noting that in southern Saskatchewan

Below: Advertising for the Capitol Theatre's showing of *Red Dance,* starring Dolores Del Rio, in 1928.

THE ROARING TWENTIES — 93

in general and Moose Jaw in particular, the "anti" that the Klan sold was predominantly vice and sin. It would appear that race and religion were not sufficiently strong enough prejudices to exploit successfully.

Reminiscing decades later about his recruitment into the Klan in 1927, a Foam Lake man told of his hesitation to join a racist organisation. He was assured that the organisation "was not anti-Negro (as in the US), anti-Jewish, or objectionable in any way; just a patriotic group who stood for 'Canada for Canadians' and general good citizenship."

Soon after, the Klan faded away, leaving nothing but a slightly embarrassing memory.

By this time, the twenties had all but run out of roar.

THE DIRTY THIRTIES

Nature Untamed

What Goes Up...

October 24, 1929 – Black Thursday.

The Great Depression hit the Prairies harder than other parts of Canada, and Saskatchewan hardest of the prairie provinces. In Moose Jaw, businesses folded, the ranks of the unemployed mushroomed, poverty spread like a cancer. In the surrounding countryside, crops failed under the relentless onslaught of an accompanying drought and farmers went bankrupt.

But people persevered.

With less money in circulation, solutions had to be found to prevent a total shut-down of local economies. Goods were commonly exchanged for other goods or services. People formed co-operatives to consolidate and exchange labour. In the winter of 1930-31, the money economy at times seemed to have almost disappeared, and barter had almost completely replaced money at Harry Connor's tire shop.

The stock market crash and the steadily deteriorating agricultural crisis sent ripples – more like tidal waves – of devastation through Moose Jaw. The unemployment rate soared, reaching unprecedented levels.

As the decade proceeded, a subtle shift began to emerge. Large corporations, owned by faceless shareholders and run by managers from corporate headquar-

Opposite: A Saskatchewan duststorm in the 1930s.

ters in faraway cities, began to infiltrate the city. Eaton's had come to Moose Jaw in 1928, and during the thirties outside interests took over many local firms. "The bigger stores put the little ones out of business," remembers Luwilla Payne, who came of age in the city during the Depression.

Although it was a difficult time, the sense of community remained strong. People of various economic strata did not feel alienated from each other and there was a sense that "everyone is in the same boat." Except, that is, for the economic elites, the Bay Street bankers and politicians back east largely blamed for the misery.

"It was a great time to grow up, I think," says clothier Ted Joyner, whose father's department store survived the Depression despite severely reduced business. "The gap between those who might be perceived as poor and those who might not be poor – I don't remember such a gap. Everybody seemed to be the same. It didn't seem to me that it was odd that my chum had no shoes in the school. I had shoes – my dad had a shoe store." To Joyner, the camaraderie created by shared tough times was "a natural way to grow up. It was fun. We used to do a lot of hiking and snaring gophers and all that sort of thing which kids don't really do today. We didn't run around in a car, because who had a car?"

The decade also saw a demographic change. The apparently inexorable increase in immigration from

> The air would fill with rich black topsoil ground to fine powder, filling the eyes and nose, and blocking the sun – midnight at noon.

non-British lands changed the province and the city. In 1931, Moose Jaw was 87.7 per cent of British origin; in the next census in 1934, that had decreased to 80.1 per cent.

Much of Europe was in turmoil. The after-effects of the Great War continued to reverberate through the continent and economic and religious refugees continued to search for a better life in the wide-open spaces. Many people saw the hard life on the prairies as vastly preferable to the religious persecution of Soviet Russia, or the blasted fields of central Europe.

"Someone's Farm Going By"

By the end of August 1929, it was apparent that the harvest was going to be a poor one. Yields of wheat and barley were well below average. Rainfall had decreased every year since 1925 until, in 1928, the prairies had the lowest rainfall of any year in the twentieth century. Experts had been warning for decades that farming methods that had worked well in Europe were not suited for dry land farming. Their warnings had gone unheeded and the exposed soil was desiccated by the howling winds.

The air would fill with rich black topsoil ground to fine powder, filling the eyes and nose, and blocking the sun – midnight at noon. Rose Gusaas, who lived about a third of a block from the CPR station in Mortlach, a once-thriving small town just west of Moose Jaw, remembers that sometimes the dust was so bad that she could hear the trains but not see them. People would sit looking out their windows at the black clouds hissing past the door. "There's somebody's farm going by," Rhoda Freidin remembers people saying.

"You'd have to have a light on at noon, it would be so dark in the house," recalls Peggy Johnson. "Sometimes it blew all day. It just blew and blew, and when it stopped blowing, it was a miracle it seemed like. All the ditches filled with dirt...and there'd be dust stuck on the windowsills. It was a dreary, dreary, dreary time. It really was, because it didn't seem to be any letup."

The dust accumulated everywhere. It seeped through the cracks around windows and doors, forming tiny dunes on the floor, and covering the interiors of houses with a fine grey film. It settled in large drifts on roads and railway tracks. After a particularly big blow, in April of 1934, accumulations six to eight metres high could be found on the tracks between Moose Jaw and Assiniboia. The CPR used snowploughs to clear the tracks.

Nature could be a joker at times. Moose Jaw's annual cleanup campaign, which every spring brought hundreds of people out to clean up the detritus of winter, was interrupted in 1939 by a dust storm.

Nature could also be a killer.

Mayor James Pascoe makes Moose Jaw's first trans-Atlantic telephone call in 1929. Superintendent of Telephones W.C. Moore is beside him.

Mayor James Pascoe died of a heart attack in 1931 when his car got stuck in soft windblown sand while he and his wife were checking on a report that homes in Snowdy Springs, an outlying area of the city, were without water. The mayor, who was sixty-eight, collapsed while attempting to shovel his way out.

You couldn't win for losing. If no rain fell, there were no crops. But if rain did fall, and there were crops, grasshoppers came in their millions to eat them. Hoppers had always been a prairie plague, but during the drought years they worsened, and, if the sky wasn't dark with dust, it was dark with the voracious insects.

"I seen the grasshoppers so thick in the sky that you couldn't see the sun," recalls Fred Ansell, who farmed in the Moose Jaw area. Crickets were bad too, Ansell says. "You went out there in the morning, you were stookin', put your leather coat down, you came back and there were the buttons there. They'd eat the leather right out."

In Moose Jaw itself, the grasshoppers weren't the menace they were to farmers, but a pretty big nuisance nonetheless. Lawns were picked bare and gardens devastated. The annual garden show was cancelled, but that was nothing compared to the disappointment of people counting on a vegetable garden harvest for food.

"You'd be walking down the sidewalk and they'd be falling off the trees," remembers Jack Friedin, a retired businessman who grew up in Moose Jaw. "You wouldn't have any trees – no leaves – they ate 'em bare. You'd walk down the street you'd be squishing them on the sidewalk. They always had in the paper, 'Don't forget when you drive, you [put] on the brakes, you're not braking on the pavement,' you've got these grasshoppers, and it's like oil, and you'd slide."

The only remedy to the hoppers was a poison bait that would turn today's environmentalists apoplectic. The poison was a "granular green junk...and it was very frightening," Joyner recalls. In 1934, one of the worst grasshopper years, about a dozen tonnes of the stuff was distributed in the Moose Jaw area by the provincial government. Twenty people worked, in day and night shifts, mixing the poison in two machines. They wore gloves and rubber boots and covered their hands with Vaseline in a pitifully inadequate attempt to ameliorate the danger.

Struggling Through

Despite the grasshoppers and the drought and the dust, things were not uniformly bleak. Farmers who could hold on were sometimes rewarded for their patience. In 1934, the drought eased a bit in the Moose Jaw area and a wheat crop was produced.

The drought eased a little more in 1936. For the first time in years, people heard the sweet songs of croaking frogs. Moose Jaw was the centre of the best crop in Saskatchewan. Farmers in the area were producing up to seventy-five bushels per hectare of #1 or #2 Northern Wheat. Strong demand from Europe and Japan drove up prices, as did a heat wave.

An unexpected side effect of the Depression was an increase in the demand for horses. After a few decades of being sidelined by machinery, they began to make a comeback. Price and demand rose in the spring of 1936 and Saskatchewan breeders sold ten carloads of horses in two days to the United States.

The Saskatchewan Feeder Show and Auction Sale, the largest outside Toronto, continued at its long-time venue at the Southern Saskatchewan Stockyards on South Hill throughout the Depression. The drought made it difficult to finish beef properly, and supply was drastically reduced in the worst years. Increased demand in other provinces kept the industry alive. In 1933, prices were low at the feeder show, but once again, those who could hold on were rewarded for their perseverance. In 1934, prices began to increase.

Things were looking up.

The Urban Economy

During the Depression, federal and provincial governments cut back on their spending. In Moose Jaw, that meant the loss of government services and jobs. In October 1931, the province transferred the Moose Jaw branch of the Department of Natural Resources to Regina. Three days later, Ottawa closed the income tax office in the city, transferring the records to Regina. Once again, Moose Jaw lost out to the growing centralisation of government services in the capital.

In 1934, the CNR, which had long been a losing money venture, threatened to close the Moose Jaw station. After anguished cries of protest from the public, the newspaper, and from local politicians, CNR officials changed their minds and the city retained its status as the major railroad hub in the province, and indeed in the prairies.

As the Depression deepened, Moose Jaw College suffered a devastating drop

Packing Plants Before Unions

Recalling the 30's brings on a bit of a chill to think that anything like it could happen again. Well, not likely. Our guys and gals have had a lot of experience and have really stuck together. However, just when you think you are winning is the time to push ahead.

The hog floor. Summer-long hog dust choked the guys, and the Government inspectors ate their share too. There was no ventilation: the roof was solid. Guys fainted on the torches for singeing hogs. In the winter the hog sticker had to climb up and down from his perch in temperature varying from 80 to 30 below. The Fort San T.B. people finally got him for a couple of years.

The tank-house. One day in August, 1938, the guys took the temperature on the second floor. Unbelievably it was 140 above. The tank-house windows had been bricked in about 1938 and there was no fan in the place. The ceiling rained slimy condensation through the steam and stench. In the basement where the tankage was ground, it was regular procedure to throw up one's meal and continue working or lose the job. We won't even discuss the dressing room. Suffice it to note that the latrine was five feet from the lunch table.

The sausage kitchen. There was no fan or proper ventilation over the smokers. The smoker himself was frequently invisible in the steam, heat, and smoke. There was no overtime in those days, so a guy could end up working a seven day, 90-hour week for $20.00. The older female staff recall working excessive hours illegally, but what could you do? Complain and you were out the door.

The pickle cellar. A particular Hell-hole. It was worth your job to have a pickle sore attended to on company time. Blood poisoning was supposed to hold its horses until the then irregular quitting time between six and ten p.m. There was no nurse after six, so no real help, and besides, the bandages were locked up unless, by luck, the watchman happened by on his round. When you went on compensation, it was all your fault, and on the carpet you went, receiving a curt warning that another incident and you would be out on your ear. Did fifteen years service count for anything? Not on your life: you were getting old and slowing down anyway. It was as good an excuse as any for the old "heave-ho." Heavy pull-truck loads were something else. Most guys thought that 1,800 pounds was a heavy load, but 2,000 to 2,600 was standard in the 30's. To top it off,

The young Hubert S. "Hub" Elkin.

weekly wages varied from $8.00 to $14.00.

Carrying and loading beef quarters. Switiching jobs from the pickle cellar to beef loading into refrigerator cars on a cold winter day was a particular joy. You often heard unprintable comments about pickle-wet underclothing, overalls, and shoes refusing to bend. A similar effect occured in July on transferrring back and forth from pickling to zero and below freezers.

The casing floor. This was another place where, without ventilation, the stench could knock you down. In those days there was no such thing as a rest break, so one might grab a bite or get adequate relief. In fact it was

not that unusual for a supervisor to make a point of observing the "relief" operation to ensure maximum efficiency.

Hours of work. Start work one day at 7 a.m., next at noon, next 9 a.m., or be told "Don't come back 'til next week." You had to stay on-call because of the lineup of other guys looking for work. Quitting hours were any old time. If hogs came in they had to be killed. No keeping them over 'til next day: they might eat some feed or lose some weight. Fancy meat and casing floor workers came in at 7 a.m. and the boss would say, "There's no work yet. Go to the dressing room until I call you." (On your own time, of course.) No call, so you had to return home and share your lunchpail with your kids.

Statutory Holidays? You have to be kidding. If there was work you had to go. At straight time of course. Even Xmas and New Year's could mean at least half a day. The closing of the year was also the big lay-off time, which could mean a three- to six-month vacation "on relief." Speaking of vacations: there were none until somebody

got generous with one week for five years service. About the same time there was a sudden wage jump from 25 to 30 cents per hour. A big organizing drive by the UPWA in the US was no doubt the explanation for the unusual display of generosity.

Wages. Wage rates were always a big secret. Most of the foremen had not even seen the list. So they would go to the "speed-up" department to get the rate when urged by nervy pork-cutting guys and return with what was said to be the rate. However, the foreman would observe, "You've been on the job only three years and you are not quite up to snuff. So, we can't see our way to pay you the full rate until you brush up a bit." And that was that.

Seniority. A great system in the 30's. Based on speed and beer. The trouble with speed was there was always another guy or gal who could go faster. Buying beer also had its problems. The competition could be very expensive, leaving a big problem. Feeding the boss or feeding the family.

Problem solving. Of course, every place has its troubles and there needs to be some

means of solving, or at least having the appearance of being able to solve, problems arising. So we had a "Company Union." It worked like this. There were ten company guys and ten workers on a committee who could judge whether Johnny should be fired for not going fast enough. There were ten for and ten against, so Johnny got fired because of the rule "In case of a tie, the company wins."

Books could be filled with stories of what went on and no doubt still goes on in old or new ways in the slaughtering and other industries. Hopefully, comparing what you know of conditions today, this brief account will convince doubters that union organization has already brought about many real improvements in our industry. Also, while obviously there are still many problems to be solved, the remedy lies in continued worker solidarity in our own plant and organization of the unorganized everywhere.

Fraternally, H.S. (Hub) Elkin, 1942.
President, Packing Plant Employees
Federal Union, No. 75.

in student enrolment. Economic conditions meant that many families could no longer afford to send their boys to a private school and in 1931 the college closed. The teachers were laid off and the principal and students were relocated to Regina College.

Moose Jaw was not always the chief manufacturing centre of the province. Before the Crash, both Regina and Saskatoon produced more goods. In 1929, for example, the value of manufactured goods in Regina was $34 million, in Saskatoon $15.9 million, and Moose Jaw $14.6 million. Output collapsed with the stock market in 1929 and bottomed out in 1932. From then, growth in Moose Jaw and Saskatoon was steady, while output in Regina continued to shrink. By 1935, Moose Jaw was the top manufacturer in the province, producing almost as much as in 1929.

The Sterling Refinery, a Moose Jaw-based firm which started in 1915, did well through the Depression. Even in 1932, it produced twenty-five thousand gallons a day, and employed twenty workers. In 1934, the refinery was sold to the British American Oil Company, seriously weakening the already tenuous local control of the economy. It was a development which would have serious results later in the century.

The company increased the size of the refinery, buying six blocks of property from the city, and spending $250,000 on expansion. The city provided a sweetheart deal, agreeing to tax improvements made in the first year at a reduced rate for twenty years. In a turn that would eventually be revealed to reek with irony, the city gave the refinery the right to use water from the river and return it after use "...provided that the returned water shall not in any way contaminate the river."

Things did improve somewhat through the thirties, and the Depression saw the birth of many new businesses. The Army and Navy store opened in the summer of 1933, in the old McBean Building on Main Street, and a year later opened a second floor.

In 1934, one of the worst years of the Depression, James Thompson reopened his soft drink bottling plant, which had been closed eleven years before. Kresge's opened a "five and dime" store later in 1934 and that same year Prairie Airways Ltd. was formed from the Moose Jaw Flying Club. The club was not allowed to use its planes for commercial purposes, so five members of the club, including the redoubtable Walter Thorn (who had been involved in nearly every big project in the city from 10AB radio to the Natatorium and was active in the community hotel group which built the Grant Hall Hotel), went into business for themselves. Prairie Airways became successful as a feeder line for major airlines, and a commuter service to Saskatchewan cities.

By 1935 many merchants were doing quite well. Jack Scot Jr. had started Scotty's Scooters and Taxi Service in his father's carpentry shop a month before the Crash. His small fleet of motorcycles and small delivery trucks kept busy despite the tough economic times. By 1935, he owned a fleet of new Chevrolet taxis, four delivery vans, and a filling station.

The Tees and Persse Building, once a wholesale warehouse and later a hostel for unemployed veterans, became the new home of Prairie Bag Company in 1937. The company, whose principal customer was Robin Hood Mills, turned out twelve to fifteen thousand bags per day in the second week of production, and that number soon doubled. The company employed thirty people.

A light could be seen at the end of the Depression's long dark tunnel.

Nobody Knows You
When You're Down and Out

How Do You Spell Relief?

As the unemployment rate soared, working people, who had lived close to the edge at the best of times and had next to nothing in reserve, were hit particularly hard. The demand for "relief," as welfare payments for the poor and unemployed were then known, increased significantly by the end of 1930 as another crop-year ended in disaster. By 1933, 18 per cent of Moose Jaw's population required some kind of relief, the highest rate of any city in Alberta and Saskatchewan. Throughout the Depression, up to 25 per cent of the population of the city was on relief at any given time.

The postwar recession of 1919–1922 had been, in retrospect, almost a blessing. Local groups – from churches to the Trades and Labour Council – which had organized to provide relief during that difficult period were still active and, although hardly adequate to the task, were at least able to make an effort. From that earlier recession on, the different levels of government had fought to avoid taking responsibility for the victims of economic downturns. All agreed that someone needed to help, but all wanted it to be someone else.

As early as 1928, local politician Sam Hamilton had said that relief should be the responsibility of the city rather than churches and private charities. This was the next step in the evolution of the handling of the poor.

Opposite: There was work for some, including the Reg Fysh road-building crew, about 1930.

Mob Panic Real Cause of Break on Stock Markets

F. R. Phelan Issues Statement On Break In Stock Market And Gives Reasons

Montreal, Oct. 31.— F. R. Phelan, President of Financial Service, Limited, Canada's largest financial statistical organization, issued the following statement on the break in the stock market:

Two questions on the lips of everyone most out of the market on Thursday were What caused the precipitous crash" and When will it stop? The answer to both questions is not difficult to find if one uses a little thought.

The fundamental cause of the break is the fact that stocks had been forced up in many instances out of all proportion to values. This upward movement, expanding to an ever increasing way over the past few years kept on until the buying wave commenced to slow up through sheer exhaustion and lack of ability of the public to buy any more. The last phase of the buying, running over ...

GRAIN INSPECTED AT MOOSE JAW

(October 30, 1929)

Total number cars inspected 102
Number of cars of wheat ... 85
Number of cars coarse grain 17

WINNIPEG LIVESTOCK

Winnipeg, Oct. 31. — Receipts: cattle 1,100; calves 100; hogs 200; sheep 400.

Good killing cows $6.50; bulk up to $6; heavyweight butcher heifers $8; killing steers, good $8.50, plain steers $6; bulls $4; shdin ledium $6; bulls $4 to $5.50; stockers and feeders $7.50.

Hogs, bacons $9; butchers $8.95. Good killing lambs $8 to $9.50.

Wall Street

New York, Oct. 31.—(By Stanley W. Prenosil, Associated Press finan...

Weakened Marginal Accounts Wiped Out by Wall Street's Wide Open Break at Opening

Huge Blocks of Shares Poured Into the Market by Big Operators Who Could No Longer Stand the Pace; Rumors Of Brokerage Failures Legion

Toronto, October 29.—(By the Canadian Press.—The "market which could not come down," broke into a frenzied panic at this morning's opening in Wall Street following a steady accelerating slump of weeks which had gathered alarming momentum in the last few days. Nothing less than the outbreak of another war could have set the continent by the ears and word came that the European exchanges had broken, making the debacle a worldwide affair. Men hurried along the streets in the cities of Canada and the United States, faces pale and lips quivering; little knots formed in offices, with working discipline gone as often garbled versions of the break, which could hardly be exaggerated, flew around. The afternoon newspapers were besieged by telephone calls and many of the voices at the other end, some feminine, were hysterical.

Word went around in Toronto that Nickel had dropped to 24, but this greatest Canadian mining issue did not go below 29 in the morning. The New York break in the first half hour was precipitate. As eager traders watched the tape, expecting an uncertain recovery, they saw, instead, huge blocks of sacrifice shares poured into the market, one after another releas...

Wheat Takes Drop But Recovers for Loss of About 3c

Winnipeg, Oct. 29.—(By the Can...

Moose Jaw *Evening Times* headlines at the end of October, 1929.

From church to private charity to city government...to what?

Following the Crash, Conservative Prime Minister R.B. Bennett at first refused to get involved, saying "people do not want charity," but eventually relented, with cities paying one third and the two senior governments the rest. Through the Depression, Ottawa continually reduced its share, putting extra pressure on local governments. The problem was so serious in Moose Jaw that the city threatened to get out of the relief business entirely, a threat it continued to make regularly for the next few years.

Moose Jaw's city hall did not get along with the Conservative governments in both Ottawa and Regina. In 1934, this animosity came to a head when J.A. Merkley, the provincial minister of railways, labour, and industry, publicly claimed that something was seriously wrong with the administration of relief in Moose Jaw. He would not make any specific charges, but hinted they would come later. He dispatched three "inspectors" to investigate. The investigation, which made headlines for months, found nothing wrong with relief in the city – hardly surprising, since the city's program in Moose Jaw was widely seen as both efficient and well run, and was used as a model for other cities in the province.

As governments feuded, private charities continued to help out, often making the difference.

Not surprisingly, the winter holidays brought out people's generosity. The Rotary Club and the Salvation Army treated eighty-five men to a lavish Christmas dinner and party in December 1930, and the Elks Club threw a Christmas party for a thousand children at the Orpheum Theatre. In October 1931, the Boy Scouts collected more than three thousand toys for the Legion Boy Scouts Toy Shop, which repaired, refurbished, rejuvenated and redistributed the toys to needy children.

The YMCA and the YWCA were in the vanguard when it came to helping the dispossessed. The YMCA came to the aid of many of those hardest hit, opening up blocks of time in the gym and the pool for the unemployed. Children from underprivileged families were also given classes and gym time.

Opposite: A Children's Toy Matinee, close to Christmas in 1934. Admission was free with the donation of a toy for an underprivileged child.

Unfortunately, the Y had always been on shaky financial ground and the extra costs and lowered income hit it particularly hard. The problem became serious in 1932 when, already $5,000 in the hole, the YMCA found itself in need of a new heating plant. Positions had been cut, salaries lowered, and other expenses had been pared to the bone. If a solution could not be found, it looked as if the building would have to close. Only frantic fundraising saved the Y from its own generosity.

As the need for relief increased, it became increasingly evident that there was too much redundancy and overlap of services. Churches, service clubs and charity groups were often doing the same thing and resources were being wasted. At the same time, it was clear that private charities could not keep up with the demands made upon them. The Depression was beginning to hurt everyone; even people with jobs were having trouble as wages were cut, and in some extreme cases people who still had jobs were actually living on less that those who received relief. Citizens demanded that the city take sole responsibility for the poor, but the city had its own financial troubles.

Civic politics throughout the 1930s were dominated by one issue: relief. Council had to provide financial aid to the poor, and the costs were enormous. In 1930, relief was costing $2,000 a month. By 1933, this had risen to almost $12,729. The first six years of the Depression cost the city over a million dollars.

The problem was exacerbated by the decline in tax revenues. The Depression hit everybody, and the lack of payment of property taxes became a serious problem. As early as 1932, Moose Jaw won the dubious distinction of being second only to one other western city in the amount of unpaid taxes. In the years 1931 and 1932, some 40 per cent of

In the early thirties, despite many charitable acts, the Y managed to pay off and then burn its mortgage.

taxes were unpaid.

With revenue down and so much money going to relief, there was less left for wages. Something had to give.

By 1935, the financial burden of relief had brought the city to the verge of bankruptcy. With a new Liberal government in Ottawa, federal and provincial contributions rose, with cities' share dropping to 20 per cent. By this time, though, even that was too heavy a burden.

The story of relief in Moose Jaw was also characterized by an underlying fear that people would abuse the system and that the unworthy would profit from the plight of the needy. People needed to be reassured that only the truly needy were receiving relief. The *Times* ran daily stories profiling deserving families. A 1930 article tells a story about a married man, the father of six children, that is positively Dickensian.

The man, the paper reported, "has had less than six weeks work in the two years, though he has picked up other small jobs wherever possible. His health has been bad, and at the present time, he is in hospital. Investigators from the Central Relief Committee found that his family had a little flour, a few potatoes, but not another thing in the house to eat...."

The city was unwilling to give cash to relief recipients, instead providing vouchers that could be redeemed at local stores and taxpayers were assured that their hard-earned money was not being wasted. Elaborate, increasingly unwieldy systems were set up to distribute not only groceries and clothes and coal, but also to supply dental and health care and other services.

Peggy Johnson, who was a teenager during the Depression, recalls her family getting coupons "for sugar and syrups and sweets." Everyone got the same coupons, according to their family size and income, she remembers. "If you didn't use your amount of sugar coupons, if you were a family that didn't use much sugar, why you were allowed to, you know, pass it around and share. Maybe what somebody didn't have somebody else would. A lot of sharing went on."

Farmers, despite their problems, still had access to livestock, poultry, fresh milk and eggs, and produce from their gardens. In Moose Jaw, City Hall offered plots of city-owned land to the unemployed to grow vegetables, which provided many families on relief with much-needed fruits and vegetables.

Relief trains were regular, if infrequent. Trainloads of salt fish from the East Coast, and of fresh fruit and vegetables from British Columbia and Ontario, would pull in a few times a year. People would line up at the train station patiently waiting for their share.

"Everybody looked forward to the apples particularly because, hopefully they had enough," Johnson remembers. She says she never went hungry, but knew many others who did.

At least the winters were relatively mild, so there was less need for warmer clothes and, especially, coal.

"Coal was hard to come by, and

The YMCA and the Central Oil Service in the first block of Fairford Street east of Main about 1930.

you were only allowed so much, and you had to do your best to make it do," Johnson says. "You went to bed early and got up late sort of thing. Lots of families, like with us, all we had was a cook stove. Generally, you tried to bank it so there was a little bit of coal there in the morning, and lots of times it was out."

Coal became a particularly touchy subject in Moose Jaw. In 1935, council noticed that all the tenders submitted from coal suppliers were identical, and were higher than private citizens paid, for poor quality coal. Council suspected collusion and rejected the bids, calling for tenders again, but the same thing happened.

The city had too many families on relief. The cost was becoming prohibitive, and new, more radical solutions had to be found. In 1931, Ottawa began offering families on relief uncleared Crown land in the north and a loan of $500 to buy building materials, livestock, food, and clothing. That year, sixty-eight Moose Jaw families took advantage of the offer. The next year, the federal government reduced the loan to $300 and suggested that the province and cities each contribute $100, a deal the city and province hesitantly agreed to. In 1932, when the program was renewed for another year, 108 families applied.

The deal stalled when council balked at Moose Jaw's $100 share, but reversed its decision a few days later with the proviso that only seventy-five families from the city be accepted.

It was a hard life, indeed: hard enough that many of the putative settlers could not take it, gave up and tried to go back south. Both the province and the city refused to grant relief to anyone who failed at the homesteading scheme and tried to return. If the economy could not be fixed, at least some of its victims could be warehoused and kept off the unemployment lines.

And there were some, it was said, who just squatted on the land and waited for the relief supplies to come. In a letter to City Council, the provincial department of municipal affairs called attention to this kind of abuse and as evidence cited one unnamed farmer who had broken less than a hectare in four years. No one suggested why anyone living in a relatively comfortable city would want to move almost a thousand miles north into unbroken bush and live in primitive conditions just to receive what they were already getting.

In fact, most people didn't want to leave the city, even if they were in dire economic straits. Moose Jaw had one of the best relief systems in the province, and it was still a good place to live.

"I would say that…Moose Jaw in those years was a pretty great place to be," Ted Joyner says. "The food lines were probably longer in Regina than they were here."

At the beginning of the Depression, relief was looked on as a kind of loan. It had to be paid back, either in money or labour. This was the genesis of such relief work as the famous rock pile, in which men were put to work with sledgehammers turning big rocks into little rocks. Despite the fact that the resulting gravel was put to good use by the city on streets and roads, it was not the best or most productive use of the men's labour.

By the mid-thirties, it became obvious that relief debts were going to be a crushing long-term burden and, in 1935, with the Liberals back in power, farm relief debts from 1931 were forgiven by Ottawa. Through the remainder of the decade, relief debt continued to be forgiven, up to a total of $40 million.

The city initiated a number of relief work projects through the years. For example, it paid to heat the nearly finished Technical High School so construction could continue through the winter and thus keep seventy-five men off relief.

One of the most ingenious plans involved exploiting a so-far-untapped natural resource: hot water.

In 1928, G.M. Ross, a local financial broker, had unveiled a scheme to build a world-class health spa around the health-giving features of hot mineral water. The water had been accidentally tapped into a few years earlier on the south bank of the river on the grounds of the power plant, just south of the General Hospital, during an abortive search for natural gas. It would rival the hot springs at Banff and the salt waters at Manitou which drew the rich and famous from all over the world to their soothing and healing waters. Ross formed a company, and set about to get financing for the scheme.

Ross negotiated a deal with the city whereby the new company would get the rights to the water for twenty-five years at a yearly rental of $1. In return, the company would refurbish the well, and pipe the water to the surface. But the plan petered out and was finally killed when the stock market crash of 1929 put an end to most of the

"I would say that... Moose Jaw in those years was a pretty great place to be.... The food lines were probably longer in Regina than they were here."

luxury trade and severely cramped the travelling style of even the elites of the world.

Three years later, the Depression was firmly entrenched and almost a quarter of the city's population was on relief. Skilled tradesmen, unable to practice their trades, scrambled for any work they could find. Reviving the Ross plan for a geothermal pool as a make-work project seemed like a natural.

In 1930, the city had sold the power plant to the National Light and Power Co. Part of the deal was establishment of $150,000 Industrialization Fund, an incorporated company jointly administered by the city and the utility and intended to be used to create or attract new industries to the city.

The idea was to have the city build the pool and then lease it to the fund, which would run it. The senior governments agreed to pay 70 per cent, and the city would finance its share from already extant relief funds.

Crescent Park was picked as the location for the pool, which was modelled on one built in Hamilton for the British Empire Games. The CPR, which had veto rights over use of the park property under the terms of the 999-year lease agreement with the city, agreed to the location only if the pool was not allowed to make a profit.

The contract was awarded to Bird, Woodall, & Simpson for a price of $63,700, but only after the plans were changed and the size of the pool

The Natatorium soon after opening.

reduced, because all the original bids were too high. This proved to be a decision that would rebound on the pool sixty years later, when it would be closed partly because it was too small for high-level competition.

The pool, named the "Natatorium" (Latin for swimming pool), was built with amazing speed, with nearly a hundred men working on it, and opened for business on Thanksgiving Day, October 10, 1932. Three thousand people showed up just to take a look, and another one thousand to take a dip in the warm mineral water.

Moose Jaw's first great relief project was a rousing success and the city put relief workers to more good use in Crescent Park. The ravine was trans-formed: trees were planted, the creek was deepened, lined with stone, and turned into the Serpentine that still exists. The east side of the ravine — which had been bare prairie and sports fields — was landscaped and planted with trees and flowers.

By this time, it had become obvious that having skilled tradesmen crushing rocks into gravel was a waste. The Moose Jaw Work Committee was formed to encourage people to hire skilled workers. Even at low wages, it was better for the men to be working than not. In 1934, the city provided labour — men on relief — for home repairs, if the homeowner supplied the materials. This caused some discontent, because the relief workers felt they were subsidizing people who, by definition, were not as badly affected

A transformed Crescent Park.

by the Depression.

The city also began to employ men on larger capital projects. The senior governments were reluctant to provide money for major projects, but the city continued to lobby. The Natatorium was the most ambitious and well-known project, but many other improvements to the city's infrastructure were made during the thirties. Two hundred men worked on improvements to the water system at Snowdy Springs and Caron.

As early as 1930, the city government talked of paving the downtown streets, replacing both the wooden-block and dirt surfaces, but could not find the money. The question arose again in 1933, and, finally, in the spring of 1935, council voted to pave Main Street up to the exhibition grounds. The contract was awarded to a Winnipeg company, which upset some people who thought that a local firm should get the work, even if their bid was not the lowest. Despite the out-of-province contractor, it was a made-in-Moose Jaw project. The surface material, bitulithic Warrenite, was made from crushed rock purchased from the city and oil from BA refinery, using power from the local utility. The project provided jobs for many of the unemployed men of the city.

In 1935, paving was started on Highway 1 near the city as part of a public works project financed by the senior governments. The project was continued the next year, including the construction of a bridge over the river at Manitoba Street East. At that time, the highway entered the city at Eighth

The opening ceremonies at the Natatorium on October 10, 1932. The warning, partly hidden by the flag but familiar to generations of children, reads, "Sliding, rough play or pushing others is dangerous and strictly prohibited."

Avenue at Manitoba Street, then continued west to Fourth Avenue, north to Caribou Street, then west out of the city. Caribou Street West was paved and the highway was continued as far west as Caron. Paving projects provided relief work in the city for the rest of the Depression.

Although, it was obvious that a lot of people needed a lot of help, and that without that help, the province would become a vast depopulated wasteland, there were those who were not happy with the way relief was administered. This was especially true of those farmers who had prospered in the years leading up to the Depression, who had, through frugality, careful planning, and good management, not only thrived, but managed to put something away for the future.

"My grandparents were really quite unhappy about relief," recalls Larry Gusaas, a Moose Jaw artist and musician who grew up in Mortlach. "They had saved about $20,000 by the end of the twenties for their retirement. When the time came, they planned to pull up stakes and head back down to the Norwegian colony in North Dakota. Then the Depression hit, and they had to dig into their savings, and by the end of it they had used almost all of them, for living, new taxes, and so on. People who didn't have those resources got relief. So they felt that they actually subsidized the relief takers, actually were punished for being prudent."

Even with all this machinery, it seems horses were still necessary in building roads.

The Union Makes Us Strong

In the early days of the Depression, the city enjoyed a "we're-all-in-this-together" sense of camaraderie. For example, when in 1931 the employees of the Moose Jaw Electric Railway Company were faced with wholesale layoffs, senior employees volunteered to split their work with their juniors, so everyone would be able to work half time.

Similarly, when, in 1932, City Council decided to cut the wages of city workers 12 per cent, the employees reluctantly agreed. After all, it was better to work for less than not to work at all.

As the Depression got worse, though, government spending cuts got deeper. In 1934, arguably the worst year, the school board cut salaries by 35 to 50 per cent, eliminated kindergarten, and charged resident high school students $9 per month. The city was so desperate, that it tried saving on electrical costs by turning off the streetlights in the small hours of the morning. Angry letters from travellers forced to walk from the CPR station to hotels in pitch blackness quickly shamed the city into changing its mind, but the damage to Moose Jaw's prestige had been done.

Cuts in municipal spending inevitably led to friction between city workers and those on relief.

Every day, men would show up at the offices of the Civic Relief Committee on High Street West. Work crews

Below: A funeral at "The Hall" on February 15, 1931.

"The Hall"

Don Kossick

As a child, I am standing on the floor of "The Hall" on Lillooet Street, as people swirl around me dancing waltzes, polkas, and Kolomankas. I still remember the warmth, friendliness, and the sense of belonging that the Hall provided. It was a safe, secure place in a city where being Ukrainian was certainly being different.

Ukrainian Canadians lived in the other Moose Jaw. The South Hill of Moose Jaw, sometimes referred to as Garlic Heights. South Hill in those days underscored the separateness within Moose Jaw of class and culture.

Moose Jaw had a strong working class tradition, and Ukrainians were part of it. Coming from the "old country," and working hard to create a new life that would offer an education for their children and grandchildren. They worked in the meat plants, on the railway, in the flour mills.

They strove to protect the dignity of who they were. The Hall served that purpose as the cultural, social, and political centre for the left Ukrainian population in Moose Jaw. We were taught Ukrainian dancing and music there. And we sat through interminable banquets as speakers talked about the Workers Benevolent Fund

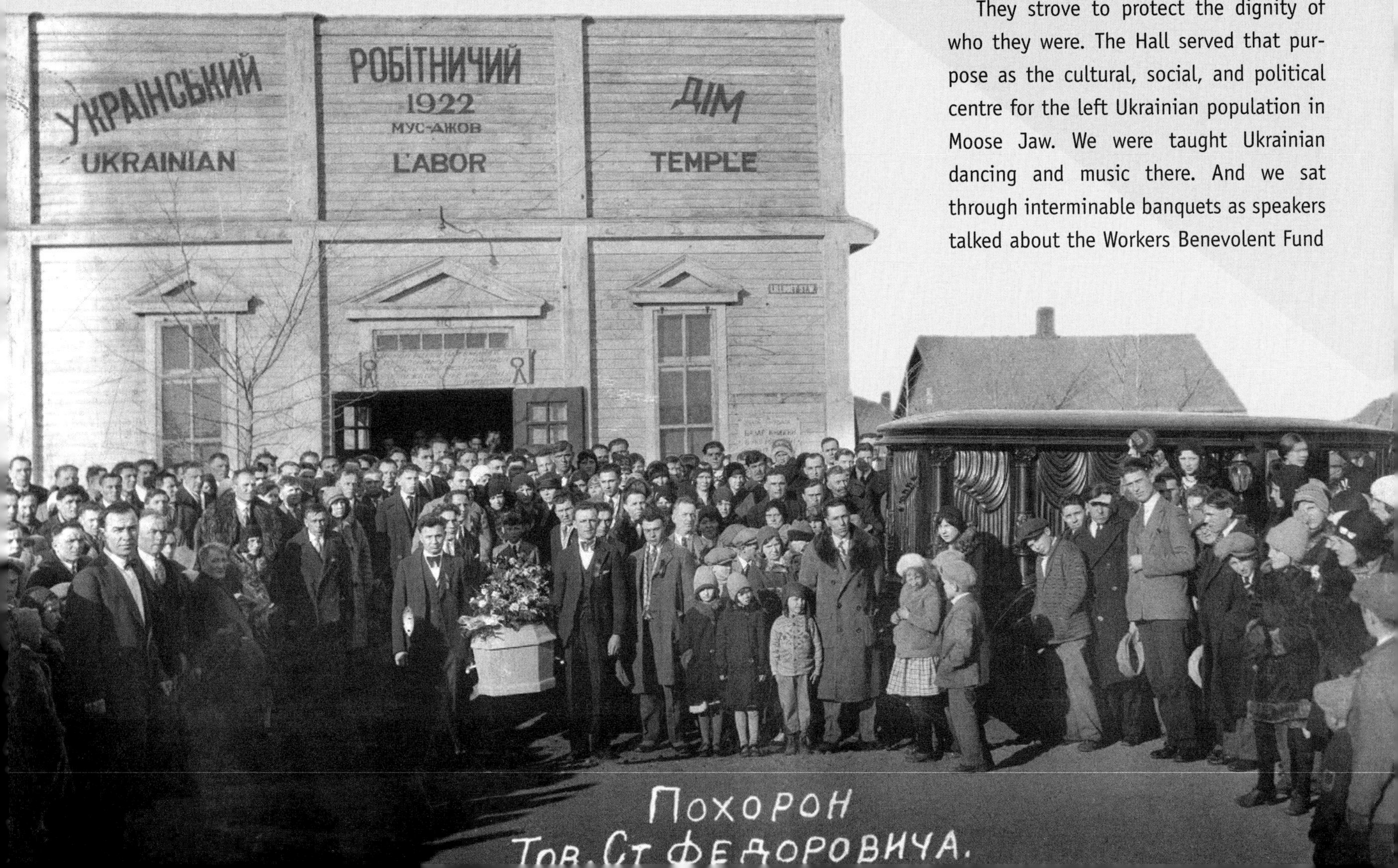

УКРАЇНСЬКИЙ
РОБІТНИЧИЙ
1922
МУС-АЖОВ
ДІМ
UKRAINIAN
L'ABOR
TEMPLE
Похорон
Тов. Ст Федоровича.

and other social issues and we simply wanted to eat the great food.

As children, we were greeted with friendliness by the old people who showered us with sweets. They all had stories that we came to understand more deeply as we grew up. The hardship of coming to Canada and leaving families behind forever. Of enduring the Great Influenza Epidemic of 1918. How they as young people built the Hall in the 1920s so it would be a place of social sustanence as they strug-

gled to survive in Canada. How the unemployed were forced to build Crescent Park in the thirties, and the recrimination when they demanded more rations. How the Hall was an important organizing point during the On to Ottawa Trek. How young unemployed men linked to the Hall fought in the Spanish Civil War against Facism. How many youth raised in the cultural life of the Hall were in the Second World War.

I especially remember our Babas who made perogies for every cause. For more than fifty years their work kept the Hall running and the social and cultural network intact. They shared the gossip, and they always wanted to know how we were. And our Babas planted incredible gardens on South Hill – the raspberries, the dill, the abundance for all.

It was sad through the years to witness the shutdown of the industries – Swifts meat packing plant, Robin Hood Flour. Because we knew that this meant economic and social hardships and that people had to leave the fabric of the community they had built. The Hall endured, but eventually closed down because the young had become old.

They did leave us with their legacy. A real appreciation of how people collec-

tively can organize a cultural, social, and political life over many decades. And that you can have ideas and causes of social justice that may not be accepted by the dominant power structures, but with a strong base in the community you can hold on.

The Ukrainian Labour Temple on South Hill is gone, but the legacy of those who built and sustained the community is still present in our lives.

The police force in front of the library in 1930.

would be assembled and gangs of men would be set to work cleaning the streets, or clearing the storm drain grates, or doing minor repairs on the sidewalks. City employees were not happy with this. They feared the relief workers would soon replace them and they would find themselves fired and on relief themselves, doing the same work for a lot less money. They did not want to carry the weight of the Depression on their shoulders, brawny though they might have been.

Many of the unemployed were also not happy with the system. It was humiliating, they said, to be forced to go out and do less-than-menial labour for the pittance that relief provided. It was bad enough that they did not get money directly, instead getting grocery chits, but to be forced to work on what looked like a chain gang from a southern American prison was a lack of respect that they could not stomach.

Ironically, while many people worried about the unworthy poor getting something they did not deserve, there was plenty of abuse from the other direction. Those for whom the relief recipients did jobs had power over them. And many were not above abusing that power.

Percy Hill, a local farmer, union and environmental activist, recalls his father, a drayman, being cheated by Walter Thatcher, father of the future premier of the province, Ross Thatcher. "He would go down to city hall and pick up a voucher, and then he'd go and haul something away and the person he'd do the job for would pay him half, and sign the slip, and he'd take it back to city hall and they'd pay him the other half.

"So once he went down to Thatcher's hardware store, and he hauled away the ashes [from the coal furnace] and he went back and the old man wouldn't give him any money. He'd just sign the slip and say, 'If I don't sign this you won't get anything, so this is my half.' My dad was so easy-going, he just let it go."

As discontent with relief grew, people started to organize. The first demonstration took place in December of 1930.

On Sunday, Nov. 30, a large

crowd gathered at the Ukrainian Labour Temple to hammer out a list of demands for City Hall. At the top of the list: a cash payment of $25 per week for every married unemployed man, $16 for every unemployed single man, and an additional $2 for every dependant child.

The following evening, hundreds of people gathered in front of the CPR station to hear speakers – called communist agitators by some – rail against the capitalist system that had brought them so low, yet made others rich. Denied a permit to march, the protesters nevertheless "strolled" up Main Street, filling the wide sidewalk. As they approached City Hall, a skirmish line of grim-faced policemen took up position, backed by a line of Mounties. Another contingent of police was in reserve inside City Hall.

Only three delegates were allowed to meet with council, which refused their demands but offered jobs for two hundred men on the following Wednesday. Despite this concession, discontent continued to grow. A showdown appeared imminent and, despite a quickly passed ordinance forbidding mass demonstrations, another demonstration and march were held. This time, violence erupted when the police moved in, swinging batons. The marchers fought back and, when it was over, nine "red agitators" had been arrested and charged with unlawful assembly. Chief John Fyvie warned people, "No further assembles [sic]...will be tolerated, and the citizens...attend at their own peril and risk."

The Central Relief Committee distanced itself from the demonstrators, which it labelled "red agitators" from outside the city.

Further demonstrations led to the formation, in 1934, of the Union of Unemployed Workers, which demanded an end to "forced labour" and an increase of 10 cents per hour for those who chose to work.

Discontent among the unemployed nationwide climaxed in 1935 with the "On to Ottawa" trek, which passed through Moose Jaw just days before its abrupt and bloody halt in Regina.

Starting with a handful of dissatisfied men in Vancouver, the trek built strength and, by the time it reached Moose Jaw on June 12, there were over thirteen hundred men riding the rails. They were organized like an army, in divisions, platoons and squads. Discipline was tough.

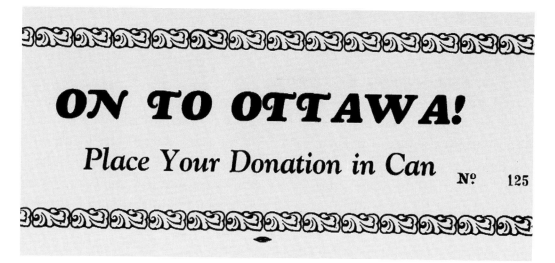

ON TO OTTAWA!

Place Your Donation in Can Nº 125

A banner to be put on cans for collecting donations for the Trek.

Violence was prohibited, steal and you were out, drink a beer and you were out. Even smoking in public was discouraged. The whole point was to gain the sympathy of the public.

"We're just young Canadians like yourself," one trekker told the *Times*. "We only want a good chance to work at a reasonable wage. We're not rioters, and we're not Reds; but we feel that things have gone far enough."

Hours before the scheduled arrival of the stock train from Swift Current, hundreds of spectators gathered on the bridges over the west side of the CPR yards. The crowds were disappointed, though, when the train pulled in close to the Robin Hood Mills to let the men off with a clear path to the streets.

The train stopped. The men stayed put and waited. Finally the order was given and the highly disciplined army disembarked. Each car disgorged a platoon of twenty-five men. The men fell into line, squad by squad, platoon by platoon, company by company. Escorted by Chief Fyvie and Inspector Alex Bell of the city police, the army marched through the streets of the city to the Exhibition Grounds at the north end of Main Street.

An advance party which had arrived the day before had done its job well. Temporary washing facilities

"We're just young Canadians like yourself. We only want a good chance to work at a reasonable wage. We're not rioters, and we're not Reds; but we feel that things have gone far enough."

awaited the men, grimy from the dust and soot of traintop travel. Meal tickets were distributed. The lucky ones were billeted in the curling rink, while most unrolled their bedrolls on the ground, anticipating a cold and wet night's sleep. Pickets were set up around the camp and sentries patrolled in the rain while the rest of the men slept.

The next day, many marchers, unfazed by heavy rain, spent the day out on the streets, raising money for the continuation of the march and talking with Moose Javians. In the afternoon, they held a rally at Ross Park, in the east end of the city, which was attended by enthusiastic members of local labour organisations and members of the general public.

The marchers favourably impressed most people, who showed their support both verbally and financially. The *Times* covered the story sympathetically, and Mayor Harris Johnstone publicly complimented the men on their discipline and restraint. He was sympathetic to their plight, and understood that they were victims of international forces beyond their control, he said, making the point that both the railway and the federal government had given tacit approval for the march.

The trekkers stayed in Moose Jaw for two weeks, resting and gathering strength and public support. At a rally on June 29, at Central Collegiate, a

Trekkers waiting to board the train after the Regina Riot on July 1 or 2, 1935.

resolution moved by H.A. Speers, a Moose Jaw teacher, calling on the Governor General to dismiss the government, was passed.

The next day, the trekkers moved on to Regina, where Prime Minister Bennett had drawn a line in the sand.

On July 1, as many of the trekkers and Reginans gathered downtown for a rally, hundreds of Mounties, city police, and railway police armed with batons and sawn-off baseball bats attempted to arrest march leaders, setting off the Regina Riot that left one policeman dead and dozens of strikers, bystanders, and police injured.

The following year, things came to a head in Moose Jaw with a strike by the Union of the Unemployed in March. The union demanded an end to "forced labour" and an additional 10 cents an hour in cash. They warned that the unemployed were running out of patience and that the city was becoming a powder keg.

The irreconcilable differences between city council and the strikers was summed up in this exchange between Alderman R.J. Jackson and John McKinnon of the union:

Jackson: "Why do you call it forced labour?"

McKinnon: "Because we either have to work or our wives and families starve."

Jackson: "If you don't work, you go off relief; if a working man does-n't go to work, he is off the payroll. It's the same thing. Everybody is forced to work for a living. That goes for everybody."

The unemployed, weighed down by seven years of bad economic times, did not mind working, but strongly objected to being told they had to do work they considered meaningless.

The strike had tragicomic over-tones, since the only labour the strik-ers could withdraw was the labour they didn't want to do in the first place. Without a strike fund, their action could hurt no one but them-selves and their families, although they tried to disrupt the work gangs from time to time. The strike lasted three weeks, when the twenty-seven men capitulated and accepted work tickets.

The same year, even the transients organized. Around a hundred men were stranded in the city when the police and the railways cracked down on men riding the rails. They organ-ized and demanded the city supply relief work at 40 cents per hour or 50 cents in direct relief. They were pow-erless, of course, but the constant

T.C. "Tommy" Douglas in the 1930s.

bickering made their plight real in the eyes of the public.

Discontent continued, and people became more and more politicized. In 1937, even lowly housekeeping staff were sufficiently agitated to go on strike against the General Hospital for more than a week.

The CCF, and the United Church

The thirties, with its economic turbulence, saw the rise of political movements which had previously been on the margins, both the left and right. This was a worldwide phenomenon, and Saskatchewan and Moose Jaw were no exceptions.

On October 14, 1935, Bennett's Tories were swept out of office when MacKenzie King's Liberals won the federal election by the biggest majority in history. The leftist Commonwealth Co-operative Federation (CCF) established a bridgehead, electing eight members, including a young Baptist minister from Weyburn, Sask., who would go on to have an indelible imprint on the province – Tommy Douglas.

The CCF had already established itself in Saskatchewan, where, the previous year, it won five seats in the provincial election that also saw the Liberals sweep to power, enough to become the official opposition. The first CCF club started in Moose Jaw a month after the election. Four years later, the CCF doubled its representation in the legislature to ten – and in 1944 it would sweep to power in one of the most remarkable elections in Canadian history, pulling Moose Jaw along in the socialist euphoria.

The longer the Depression lasted, the more attractive radical ideas became – from the right as well as the left. In the 1935 federal election, the right-wing Social Credit Party – which won power in Alberta, took about 16 per cent of the votes in Moose Jaw. Tim Buck, the leader of the Communist Party of Canada, attracted over a thousand people when he spoke at the auditorium of the Technical High School that same year.

Not all of the progressive movements were political. In Moose Jaw, one Christian congregation came close to having a woman minister, which would have been a first for the province, perhaps the nation.

The United Church, which had come into being through the amalgamation of the Methodist, Presbyterian, and Congregationalist churches in the early part of the 1920s, was becoming a leader in social thought and action.

It was in Moose Jaw that the new church broke new ground and ordained its first Canadian woman minister, only the second in North America.

Even though the United Church didn't initially allow the ordination of women, Lydia Gruchy, a farmgirl who grew up to be an honours graduate of Saskatoon's St. Andrew's College, was hired as assistant minister of Moose Jaw's St. Andrews Church in 1935. She became the first woman to be ordained by the United Church the following year, although she was transferred to other duties in Toronto before getting a chance to serve a Saskatchewan congregation. Later, she had congregations in several Saskatchewan communities, but never again in Moose Jaw.

Dust Bowl Culture

Recreation in the Bad Times

As the hard times of the 1930s continued and money became scarce, life went on and people used their ingenuity for fun and recreation.

This was before television, of course, and, as Ted Joyner recalls, "some people never had a radio, and nobody had their own car when they were in high school. You might be lucky and borrow your dad's car on the odd Friday night – for a graduation prom – something important." Instead, Joyner remembers, "our fun in those days was 95 per cent outside," with the rest "in the home with your sister and brother and your mom and your dad."

People played ball in the summer, curled on natural ice rinks in the winter, and watched all manner of sports, both professional and amateur, all year round.

In the winter, Moose Jaw was dotted with homemade outdoor ice rinks. Joyner remembers "there was one right across the street from where I lived on the corner of Henleaze and Saskatchewan, and right after school it was packed with kids playing hockey. Those were the days when you didn't count how many were on each side. You took everybody who had a hockey stick (who) wanted to play, divided in two, and that was how many were on each team. There weren't any boards. No bench time. Everybody played, and everybody had fun."

But there was also organized hockey league play. From the two-team league

The runners-up in the Stanley Cup Finals in 1933. Ken Doraty is in the back row, second from the left.

in the 1920s, it had expanded to a much more competitive, all-but-professional exercise.

From the 1930s, when organized league play got started in earnest, the Canucks would produce many NHL stars and future members of the Hockey Hall of Fame, like Doug Bentley and his brothers Reg and Roy, and Ken Doraty, who, while playing for the Toronto Maple Leafs, scored what is considered one of the greatest goals in NHL history, breaking a scoreless tie, in the fifth and final game of the 1933 semi-final series with the Boston Bruins, with a goal at 4:46 of the sixth overtime period. Upon his retirement, Doraty returned to the city and ran the Connaught Billiards for decades. The poolroom, decorated with memorabilia from his NHL days, was one of the primary places to hang out for generations of very cool people. Elmer Lach, the former Canuck who went to the Montreal Canadiens in the 1940s, retired in 1954 as the NHL all-time scoring champion. Goalie Emile 'The Cat" Francis went from the Canucks to an illustrious NHL career as both a player and executive. Fifteen Canucks from that generation went on to the pros.

Moose Jaw was also a serious baseball town. A Moose Jaw team that included Walter Scott, who would eventually become the first premier of the province, had won the territorial championship in 1895. The Moose Jaw Baseball Association was organized in 1903. Seven years later, the Moose Jaw Ball Club Ltd. was started. It was the beginning of a long tradition of semi-professional baseball in the city. Moose Jaw won the provincial championship in 1913, and the Moose Jaw Cats were the provincial champions for 1931.

The other important sport was football. Moose Jaw has for a long time been in love with the game. Moose Jaw loves to cheer for the beloved but often hapless Saskatchewan Roughriders, and junior and high school football is an important part of the city's life. Football fields dot the city, and even in bad times there seems to be money for their construction. John Livingston, whose father, Robert, played and coached junior football, recalls with pleasure the Hamilton Tiger Cats sweater he owned for many years, passed on to him by his dad who got it when players with his Moose Jaw Maroons traded sweaters at the end of the 1929 national junior football championship game.

The elder Livingston coached the Maroons through the thirties and into the early forties, when they folded. "They probably just didn't have enough guys staying around after high school to compete with Regina and Saskatoon," John Livingston says.

All of these sports came into their own during the Depression, but, like everything else, they were hit hard by the bad economic times.

The Lawn Bowling Club fell $73.75 in arrears for its water bill in 1933, putting a temporary stop to play.

The bowlers weren't alone.

The Arena rink fell behind in its taxes and other bills and stood on the edge of bankruptcy. The Moose Jaw Falcons, contenders for the provincial hockey championship, cancelled a February, 1933, game when their Regina opponents could not afford to make the trip. The arena management, desperate for money, insisted on payment of $50 for the cancelled game. The Falcons could not afford to pay for a game they did not play and refused. A few days later, when the Falcon players arrived at the rink to pick up their equipment, they found the doors locked, and the management standing there demanding payment before they would produce the key.

Nothing could escape the ubiquitous effects of the Depression.

Well, almost nothing. The river continued to be an important source of recreation through the Dirty Thirties, as it has been all through Moose Jaw's history. The valley was secluded, and the river continued to run even through the worse of the drought, providing a refuge of green in a dry and dusty world.

River Park had fire pits scattered through the trees around the perimeter. The large central campus contained many ball diamonds interspersed amongst the bush and trees. At a time when most people had little money, and diversions were few, you could always get a gang together and play a game of baseball. Equipment was optional. As long as you had a ball and a bat, you could play ball.

In those days, as Joyner says, entertainment was "self-made."

"You could go down to the park, which is now Wakamow, and on a Friday or Saturday night, if your gang of kids wanted to have a roast at one of the fire pits, you had to send someone down at four o'clock in the afternoon just to save it. That park was that well used. On a Saturday or Sunday you couldn't find a sandlot to play ball. They were all full."

The river was lined with parks and other recreation areas that were not public parks but were offered to the public by corporations and private individuals. Kingsway Park, south of the city, was owned by the Moose Jaw Electric Street Railway Company. A large part of the park was left untouched - wild, tangled, and impenetrable - but parts of it were more civilized, with a dancing pavilion, a refreshment booth, a boat house, and a bathing beach. On the riverside were tree-shaded picnic areas. It also had large clearings used as softball fields and football pitches.

The General Hospital beach was another popular spot. The volunteer Hospital Beach Organisation maintained the beach, organized programs and obtained equipment. On hot summer days, up to a thousand people could be found in the water at a time. The city built a diving tower, supplied a log for kicking practice and a floating pier, and the Kiwanis donated a water slide and a small raft.

The beach was the centre for educational and recreational activities. Sixty-nine beginners learned to swim in the summer of 1932, and 175 took a first aid and life-saving course offered by the Royal Life-saving Society. In August of that year, a Regatta with swimming races, diving competitions, and boat races marked the transformation of the Hospital Beach, as the *Times* said, "from a swimming hole to a full-fledged bathing beach."

This was especially significant in the midst of the Depression, when money was short and holiday trips were out of reach for many in the city. It was also a boost for the city's tourist industry, which was already an important factor in the economy.

In 1937, when the prolonged drought dropped the level of the river to record lows, the city created the New

The "New Beach" at River Park in the late 1930s.

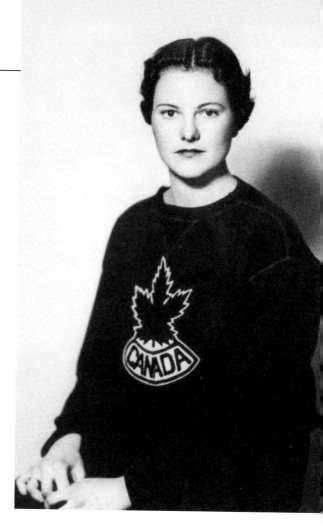

Beach in River Park. The river bottom was dredged and a sand-and-gravel beach was constructed east of the iron bridge. City crews, augmented by relief workers, built diving boards, rafts, and water slides on the river, and picnic tables, drinking water, and sewage facilities on the shore.

The river was rife with beaches and the river was still at the centre of much of the social life of the city. The Aquatic Club had become a landmark in its two decades of existence.

"They had their nice clubhouse and a dance floor upstairs," Joyner recalls with a wistful sigh. "We used to go dancing there when we were high school age.

"And canoes you could rent. I remember they were only 10 cents an hour. If there were two of you and your girlfriend had a dime you could go out for two hours."

The instructors at the Aquatic Club produced many competitive athletes. The teams from the club did well in competitions at the provincial, national, and international levels. Their biggest star was the dark horse Olympian, Phyllis Dewar.

After five years of dust, wind and grasshoppers, unemployment and relief, by 1934 the people of Moose Jaw were badly in need of a hero. They found one in the Moose Jaw Mermaid.

Dewar was eighteen years old, tall and muscular, with dark hair and dark flashing eyes. She was about to dive into history.

She attained world fame in the 1934 British Empire Games in London. In the 100-yard freestyle, she trimmed almost four seconds off the record. The next day, she broke the record for the 440. She was a mainstay of the 4 x 100 and 4 x 440 relays. Four events, four gold medals – the city had its hero.

Dewar was not favoured to win at the games. Born in Moose Jaw, she had learned to swim in the river below the old 4th Avenue bridge. At the age of thirteen, she won her first competition at the Aquatic Club Regatta, then went to Banff with the Aquatic Club team and won the Junior Girls 25- and 50-yard races. The next year she went back to Banff and won the 50-yard championship. The same year she won the 100-yard and half-mile races.

In 1931, she won the newly instituted Wrigley Mile Championship, then did it again in 1932 and 1933. That year, she possessed every freestyle swimming title in the province.

The following year, Dewar competed for the first time at the national level in Vancouver. Although she won the 100-yard freestyle competition, the event was disappointing, as swimmers from the East didn't compete, rendering the championship all but meaningless. But that wasn't the worst.

Dewar's blood boiled when she overheard a swimmer from Vancouver tell race officials: "She'll never be a swimmer. She hasn't got the guts."

Back in Moose Jaw, she trained as never before. Every morning to the Natatorium, every afternoon to the Aquatic Club, she swam a mile, then another half mile with the kicking board. Two weeks before the national championships, she asked Don MacKay, the chief steward and coach of the Aquatic Club, to time her training swims at the Nat. He was amazed. She was nine seconds faster than the national record for the 440.

At the Nationals, she shaved those nine seconds off the record for real, silencing any sceptics, but still coming in second to Irene Pirie, a Toronto swimmer with an international reputation.

In the interim before the British Empire Games, Dewar went to Vancouver and, for the first time in her career, trained with professional trainers and coaches.

In London, no one expected her to win. All of Canada, except Moose Jaw, had hopes for the more experienced Pirie. In the 440, South African Jennie Maakal was the favourite. On the final

lap, Pirie was in second place, but began to falter. With a burst of speed, Dewar passed the two rivals and sprinted to the greatest upset of the games.

Returning home to Moose Jaw on September 4, Dewar stepped off a train into the midst of a Moose Jaw crowd gone wild.

"We had a grand time," she told the *Times*. "It was a great trip, and I'm glad Canada won her share of honours. But, personally, what gave me the greatest thrill was the wonderful reception when I got home.... It really scared me, but I sure appreciated everything."

In Toronto the following year, Dewar was in her glory, winning the Canadian Women's One-Mile Swim and Barker Gold Trophy. She set the record for the 100-yard freestyle, the 440, and also set records for 1,000 yards, for 1,500, and the mile itself. But Dewar's Olympic dreams would come crashing down in 1936 when, weighted down with the flu, she failed to win any medals.

She never rose to those heights again, but was loved and remembered by all Canadians in her day. Pools in her hometown Moose Jaw, and Toronto, where she lived out her life, are named after her.

Dust Bowl Culture

Despite all the hardships people had to endure during the Depression, they did endure, and in some ways even thrived. Moose Jaw, with its semi-rural working class, agricultural, industrial nature, nevertheless had a taste for the arts, and hard times alone wouldn't stop that.

The city did not have a permanent art gallery, but many of the city's institutions provided venues for travelling exhibitions. In 1934, an exhibit of war paintings by F.H. Varley, one of the Group of Seven, appeared at the Normal School. The same year, people flocked to the library to see an exhibit of drawings from the English humour magazine *Punch*.

Live theatre was a major attraction. Many local amateur theatre groups played continually through the decade, and touring companies continued to play at local theatres. Sir John Martin Harvey, the leading English actor of his time, brought his London company to the Capitol Theatre in the winter of 1932.

Attendance at the movies dropped steadily through the decade. Theatres tried all sorts of stunts and promotions to entice people. Dish give-aways and publicity stunts were commonplace, and service clubs sponsored special shows for underprivileged children. Movies were a great escape from the hardships of the times, but money was harder to come by, and people hesitated to spend even a nickel.

The library, on the other hand, experienced an explosion of use. It was free, after all. Attendance records were broken weekly. In February 1932, the daily average attendance was 762, with 19,043 books checked out in the month, an increase of over two thousand over the previous February. On one Saturday, fifteen hundred people went to the library and checked out a book. This was one of every fifteen residents of the city. This popularity continued throughout the decade.

It was a mixed blessing for the library. The Carnegie Foundation's early prediction that the city could not support such a large library had been proved wrong early on. It soon became

The Library viewed from Crescent Park in 1938.

She Planted Trees
Edna Jaques

She didn't do much
    that a person could see,
This little old lady
    who lived down the street,
But she planted a tree
    at the side of the house,
And a row of red tulips
    so prim and so neat.
She set out some rose bushes
    close to the walk,
Some pansies and asters
    and cuttings of stock.

She tended her flowers
    with patience untold,
She watered them faithfully, day after day,
She coaxed them along like a mother, I vow,
They answered her care in their own lovely way.
The roses leaned over the gate, full and sweet,
The stocks sent their perfume in waves down the street.

She didn't do much that a person could see,
But the whole street was better because of her toil,
A little old woman as thin as a wasp,
But she cherished this life in the sun and the soil,
And made of her garden a place set apart
Reflecting the peace in her own quiet heart.

From *Dreams in Your Heart,* published by Thomas Allen, 1937

Above: Edna Jaques dressed for flight at Calgary on July 6, 1919.

obvious that the city's estimate of the demand of the library was not nearly optimistic enough. Space became short, and office space was turned into stack space. When the Depression boosted use, the lack of stack room became critical, but nothing could be done to increase capacity until the debentures had been paid off. In 1934, the debt was finally retired and it became absolutely necessary to expand, though that wouldn't happen until 1989.

Moose Jaw writers seemed to bloom in the Thirties. The first two books of poetry by Edna Jaques of the Moose Jaw area, *Drifting Soil* and *Wide Horizons,* published by the *Times-Herald* (the *Times* merged with the smaller *Herald* in July 1935), were so popular that Toronto publisher Thomas Allen brought out her next book, *My Kitchen Window.* With access to a national audience, her fame and popularity grew, and the following year she did a six-week western tour hitting forty towns and villages and reading to more than ten thousand people. She remained one of Canada's most popular poets for another three decades.

The late thirties saw the publication of a number of works by Moose Jaw writers. Joseph Schull, who would go on to prominence as a historian and biographer, writer of books for children, and poet, published the first of two book-length poems in 1938. Angus Graham published *Napoleon Tremblay,* a picaresque novel about French-Canadian lumberjacks, in 1939. Ethel Kirk Grayson published her second novel, *Apples of the Moon,* in 1935 – the only book written in Moose Jaw during the Depression actually set in the prairies. She ultimately published three novels and three books of poetry from 1928 to 1982, plus numerous memoirs. Another former Moose Jaw resident who published in the thirties was Violet Wheeler, a former writer for the *Times,* whose mysteries were published in California under the pseudonym Claire Lee Purdy.

A small spot of glamour brightened the dark mood of the times when it was discovered that sultry film siren Rita Leroy had once lived at the YWCA in Moose Jaw while working as a house maid, under her real name, Ina Stewart. In England, former Moose Javian Bernard Braden became a radio personality on the BBC, and was featured in several films in the thirties and forties.

The Depression gave a big boost to radio. Once you bought the radio set and the yearly licence, radio was a free source of entertainment, and even culture. Radio's popularity was especially sharp in Moose Jaw, which had more radios per capita than any other place in Western Canada.

The rapid growth of radio in North America helped 10AB to grow from its proud but modest beginning as an amateur enterprise in 1922. The station had been central in many relief fundraising efforts, raising large amounts of money for the needy. Now, in 1932, the station itself needed help. The Depression had hurt amateur radio. Membership had decreased and so had its budget. Technology was advancing rapidly and the station's equipment was woefully out of date.

In recognition of the station's importance to the city, the Rotary, Lions, and Kiwanis clubs came to the rescue. They began a campaign to get fifteen hundred new members. As they started the successful campaign, the campaign committee pointed out that operators, announcers, and program directors at the station "have never received one cent in remuneration for the long hours they have spent in arranging and carrying out broadcasts. Citizens of Moose Jaw have a debt to pay to 10AB."

By then, radio had become a fact of life. The federal government was in the process of consolidating the Canadian Radio Broadcasting Commission (known as the CRC, it was the precursor of the CBC), and radio was becoming both more professional and big business. The CRC began to broadcast American shows but also set up a western division with programs from Vancouver, Calgary, Moose Jaw, Regina, Saskatoon, and Winnipeg.

After the afiliation with the CRC, Moose Jaw's programming was more professional, and catholic, but had begun to lose its local flavour, especially the dramatic programs. As the CRC grew, it also became more centralized, with more of the production being done in Toronto. It was but another step in the centralization that would eventually drain Moose Jaw of not only economic power, but talent, energy, and most important, self-confidence.

In 1933, this process almost killed the station.

Following its successful fund-raising campaign the previous year, the amateur group applied for a license for a 500-watt commercial station so it could be self-supporting. The commission gave approval – but only for a 25-watt station, not a large increase from the previous 10 watts. After vigorous protest, the station – its call letters changed from the amateur designation 10AB to the commercial CHAB, which it still uses – finally won approval for a 100-watt operation. Frustrated, organizers decided to accept this and try for more power later.

The CRC withdrew all its programming from CHAB because the new station was not powerful enough. Instead, the national network concentrated all its Moose Jaw programming through CJRM.

This set off a whirl of protest in the city, with public meetings, letter-writing campaigns and petitions, but the CRC was unmoved.

Undaunted, the new CHAB returned to the airwaves, after a five-week haitus, on Dec. 17, with a full line-up of local, amateur programming. The CRC almost immediately changed its mind, apparently as a result of the protests, and the station was airing network programs by Christmas.

The following year, "Nautical Nonsense," a musical variety show directed by Howard Large and Herbert Peachel, moved from CJRM, where it originated, to the CHAB studios on the top floor of the Grant Hall Hotel, and was put on the full network after only a few weeks on the western division. This success was followed quickly by a series of locally produced original melodramas starting with the espionage serial "Lime House Fog," written and directed by Lyall E. Ullyet. By 1937, CHAB had become the exclusive broadcaster of programming in Moose Jaw for the newly organized CBC. The next year it increased its power to 250 watts.

CHAB rapidly became training ground for the main network and many of its on-air personalities went on to national prominence. Elwood Glover, who had been at CHAB since 1936, was sent to CBC Toronto in 1938. For thirty years he was one of the best loved broadcasters on CBC Radio and TV, and was named top announcer in both Canada and the US two years in a row. Earl Cameron also moved east and became the voice of the CBC news for years.

Meanwhile CJRM, which for a time had shared the rights to CRC shows, expanded as well. In 1934, it built a new state-of-the-art 1,000-watt transmitter at Belle Plaine, and had studios in both Moose Jaw and Regina. But in 1938, CJRM moved its studios to Regina, leaving CHAB as the only station in town.

The Most British City in the West
Just as the Depression couldn't destroy the cultural life of the city, it couldn't dampen its social life

Appearances were kept up and the social graces were still important. Elegance and formality counted for something. It was still a very British city and it showed.

"The ladies of the town had a lot of what they called in those days tea parties," Ted Joyner recalls. "They served tea, of course, and coffee. Sandwiches – I used to love when my mom had her tea parties because she made all these stupid little sandwiches with egg salad or whatever in them that you took a knife and trimmed all the crusts. A lot of people in those days lost their teeth earlier and they couldn't chew crusts, I guess.

"In those days it was a formal thing. You came properly attired.... When you went to your friends' home for the tea party, your invitation was from two to four. You got there at two; you left at four, and you were properly dressed. It was all very formal and you had to hold your little finger right. It's something known as élan, that's all."

Moose Jaw's "Britishness" was expressed in more than tea parties, of course. Despite the hard economic times, despite the dust, despite the grasshoppers, despite the widespread unemployment, despite the anger toward government, Moose Jaw's love affair with British royalty never wavered. When Lord and Lady Bessborough, the vice-regal couple, came to town in 1932, businesses closed and children were given the day off school. Most of the city showed up to greet them. Then, in the middle of the day, someone noticed that while Regina was on "fast time," Moose Jaw was not. The vice-regal couple had to cut their visit short to rush to Regina to get to the official reception on time.

Old Ladies Tea, June 26, 1930, Home

Moose Jaw Old Ladies Tea at the home of Mrs. A Benson in Wesley Park on June 26, 1930. Participants included: Mrs. Fisher, Mrs. Holdsworth, Mrs. Stauffer, Mrs. Jenner, Mrs. Headington, Mrs. Wilson, Mrs. Doney, Mrs. Green, Mrs. Warren, Mrs. Agar, Mrs. Stewart, Mrs. Staples, Mrs. Davies, Mrs. Brattan, Mrs. Greenhill, Mrs. Miller, Mrs. McColl, Mrs. Purdy, Mrs. Underhill, Mrs. Lee, Mrs. Wilkinson, Mrs. Williams, Mrs. Adkins, Mrs. Holden, Mrs. Hutton, Mrs. Foster, Mrs. Galey, Mrs. Saunders, Mrs. Shaw, Mrs. Ringle, Mrs. Carr, and Mrs. Black. The little girl is Marguerite Benson Gardner.

In 1935, the city celebrated the silver jubilee of King George and Queen Mary. The daylong celebration included the presentation of medals, the broadcasting of the royal address at the exhibition grounds, and a parade featuring veterans of the Northwest Rebellion. Peggy Johnson remembers that "everybody was so excited to think the royalty was coming." In the depths of the Depression, the royal visit was a morale booster, she says, "because so many of the prairie people at that time were of British heritage.... There was a great deal of pride in our Royal Family at that time."

The next year, the city mourned the death of its beloved king. The Governor General set January 28 as a National Day of Mourning. Memorial services were held in the city's schools and one thousand people crammed into St. John's Anglican Church to mourn and pay their respects.

In 1936, the new Governor General, Lord Tweedsmuir, came to town. Again large crowds greeted the special train with three coaches bearing the royal coat of arms. Lord Tweedsmuir visited the Robin Hood mill, the BA refinery and the Wild Animal Park. He rode a combine at a nearby farm, attended the funeral of a local doctor, and was suitably impressed by Crescent Park.

In May of 1939, with the Depression almost over and Europe on the brink of war, Moose Jaw went wild over another royal visit, this time of the King and Queen.

On the evening of May 25, thousands of people crowded the streets around the CPR station. It was estimated that the number of people on Main Street was forty thousand or so – double the population of the city.

After a holiday featuring parades and sports tournaments, people lined up for hours in a light rain to await the royal train, even though George and Elizabeth's stay would be brief. A roar sailed skyward from the crowd as the royal party emerged from the station. People at the back of the crowd – north of Fairford Street and more than three blocks from the station – strained to catch a glimpse of the King and Queen as their open limousine began its journey up Main Street. Young men hung by their fingertips from the walls of the Post Office and the bank buildings. As the rain fell harder, the motorcade sped up to prevent the royal couple from becoming drenched. The cars turned at Caribou Street, some eight blocks north of the station, and the procession raced back the way it came. At the station, the royal couple spent their last few minutes in the city talking to hospital patients brought there in a truck, "in a most charming manner," according to a report in the *Times-Herald*, before

> "Everybody was so excited to think the royalty was coming. Because so many of the prairie people at that time were of British heritage.... There was a great deal of pride in our Royal Family at that time."

A sign erected above a downtown shop welcoming King George VI and Queen Elizabeth during the Royal tour in 1939.

reboarding the train.

Despite the dampness, which fizzled the fireworks, despite the fourteen people who fainted in the crowd, despite the shortness of the stopover, the royal visit of 1939 was one of the high points of the decade. The exhausted, almost delirious crowd split up to go dance the rest of the night away.

Within months, those good times would seem long, long ago.

THE EFFECTS OF WAR

World War II Comes to Moose Jaw

Wings Over the Prairies

On September 1, 1939, as Hitler's Panzer divisions pushed into Poland, Moose Jaw sat on the verge of fundamental social, economic, and political change. Ten days later, after more than two decades of military isolationism and downsizing, the reality of war was brought into the living room of every Canadian household as the government of Prime Minister William Lyon Mackenzie King followed Britain into battle.

Moose Jaw wasn't just irrevocably altered by the dynamics of the war, it played an integral part in the Allied efforts toward a hard-won victory. Moose Jaw's servicemen were engaged in the heights of military action, her population contributed to the war effort from the home front, and the entire city shared in the communal hardships and sense of loss that was dealt by the conflict half a world away.

No manifestation of the war was more prominent in Moose Jaw than the construction of a British air force pilot training base just five miles south of the city. At No. 32 Service Flying Training School (32 SFTS) of the Royal Air Force, officially opened on January 1, 1941, hundreds of young pilots were trained for wartime service. Their presence in the city, their role in the war, and the longer-term effects of the base made an indelible impression in the

Opposite: A group of Royal Air Force airmen in training at the Moose Jaw Flying School in 1941.

A more relaxed group of airmen.

setting plaster of Moose Jaw's developing history.

The decision to train Royal Air Force personnel overseas was a direct result of the aerial assault levied on Great Britain by Germany's Luftwaffe from the onset of the war. With a determination to build an air force dominance, the British signed an agreement with the Canadian government in December, 1939, that established a series of training bases known as the British Commonwealth Air Training Program (BCATP) throughout Canada. Moose Jaw immediately sent a delegation to Ottawa to lobby for a

training site. By late June, 1940, construction on what would become the largest of the training sites began just outside the city.

Moose Jaw was selected as a flying training centre because it offered optimum flying conditions: a clear horizon, good flying weather, and thousands of miles of uncongested airspace. It was a place where young pilots, removed from the threats of combat and the distractions of England, could concentrate on their training. The school — one of several training facilities in Saskatchewan that included others in Mossbank, Caron, and Assiniboia — initially consisted of five double-sided hangars, a cramped headquarters and training area, and a series of hastily con-

WWII Flying School pilots posing on a Harvard Trainer.

Lads of 2 Group, 32 SFTS.

"A Long Way from Home"

With the opening of 32 SFTS, the social composition of the city underwent an instant and very noticeable transformation. From its earliest days, Moose Jaw had been the centre of a rural population and its inhabitants were raised from the stock of a farming culture. By-and-large, those who lived there had chosen Moose Jaw, and were intent on staying. Then, at the signing of a government contract, into this population of twenty thousand was injected an entirely new group numbering in the hundreds at any given time, in the thousands over the course of the war. All men, all young, many of them foreign, predominantly middle-class, and

structed tar-paper barracks. The first airplanes arrived in January, 1941, beginning with twin-engine Avro-Ansons, which were crated and shipped from England after the Battle of Britain. They were soon accompanied by twin-engine Oxfords, and the time-honoured Harvard single-engine trainer which had been in active service since 1934.

Over the course of the war, 32 SFTS trained some twelve hundred pilots from Canada, Britian, Norway, New Zealand, Poland, the United States, Free France, Czechoslovakia, Belgium, and the Netherlands. Col-

lectively, the air training program in Canada produced over 131,000 aircrew, of which more than 55 per cent were Canadian.

Ground crew at the Flying School preparing a bomber for flight.

each looking for adventure; it was a re-visitation of the demographic from the earliest days of Moose Jaw when the CPR wound through town bringing a group of adventure-seekers in its wake.

The two groups made for a strange brew, but they co-existed remarkably well considering the differences of cultural and personal background. Perhaps more than anything else, the value that tied the students of the new base to their Moose Javian hosts was the shared determination to serve the cause of Allied victory.

"Back then everybody lived-in," said Moose Javian Dale Cline, who remembered the base as a ten-year-old in 1941. "There was nowhere else to go."

Restricted to travel by foot, the first trainees were nonetheless eager to explore their new surroundings. Equally as enthusiastic was the reception awaiting the new foreigners by the residents of Moose Jaw. These men meant many things to many people: for the shop-owner, more money being spent; for the young women of town, new male faces to be found along Main Street; and for the average proud Moose Javian, that their city was doing its bit for the overall war effort.

Cline remembered Moose Javians meeting the westbound CPR trains, often filled with new trainees, with coffee or chocolates. Support for the servicemen often took more personal forms, with many people extending offers to attend parties or dinners. "It was perfectly normal in my home, every Sunday, to have one or two air force officers over for an evening meal," recalls Ted Joyner. Joyner's father, the proprietor of one of the city's main clothing stores, based much of his business on the new service personnel. It was this type of relationship, between business economics and social hospitality, that partly defined, and continues to define, the relationship between the military and civilian populations of Moose Jaw.

"I remember my Dad being down there (at the store) to provide overshoes to these poor guys that just arrived in the middle of a snowstorm at ten at night," Joyner recalls. But just as the people of Moose Jaw saw their new neighbours in terms of opportunity, the trainees appreciated the personal touch in the city's welcome. "I'm sure (the offers for dinner) would account for some of the lads being a little more eager to go to Sunday church," said Cline. As one serviceman recalled in the base newsletter, *The Prairie Flyer:*

"The people of Moose Jaw were, from the start, almost embarrassingly

Looking north on Main Street from the CPR Station in 1946.

hospitable. I remember on Christmas Day several kind people called on the chance of picking up some airmen to entertain, only to find that there were none left to take."

But the hospitality of the city, and assimilation of the foreign airmen into the local culture, had a far greater scope than merely invitations for dinner.

A CFB Moose Jaw history booklet recounts that "a former star of the Brighton Tigers hockey team taught the boys ice hockey, about which they are becoming enthusiastic."

The booklet, written in 1986, goes on:

"Regular bus service by the city takes the men into Moose Jaw when their busy schedule permits, where they enjoy the hospitality of the people, an elaborate war services club, Canadian ice cream, enormous steaks (even a small steak is the size of your plate), and where they teach Canadian girls, of whom they are very fond, the 'Bombs a Daisy.' Moose Jaw orchestras have fallen into line with their demands and include in their repertoire the 'bombs' dance, the Lambeth walk, and others."

The arrival of a new base com-

The RAF marching through Moose Jaw during WWII.

mander, British Group Captain E.J. George in the summer of 1943, changed the dynamics of the RAF presence in Moose Jaw. Until then, airmen could venture into town dressed in civilian attire, making for easier assimilation with the local townsfolk. George demanded that all service personnel wear their uniforms, and he elected to live on-base rather than in town as his predecessor had done. With his attention focused firmly on base issues,

George was seemingly blind to an increasingly hostile environment between his personnel and some of the city's young civilian men, a hostility which would climax in the city's infamous "Zoot Suit Riot."

Much of the resentment from local boys was founded in the attraction of Moose Jaw girls to the dashing young airmen, as this imagined anecdote, based on facts and circumstances of the time, illustrates.

"Well done, old boy," says the flying instructor as 21-year-old Flight-Lieutenant Patrick Hackett climbs from his Harvard trainer. It's September 12, 1944.

"Thank you sir," replies Hackett, with suppressed excitement. "720 Harvards in Canada when I went up; still 720 left."

Only a few weeks into his flying training program, Hackett has just logged the first of fifty solo hours he'll fly before being sent off to soar the volatile skies of Europe. His days are long, spent simulating coordinated flight in the Link trainer, attending classes on every aspect of flightcraft – especially navigation, in response to the RAF increased need for bomber pilots – and, the greatest thrill, flying the Harvard.

"Excellent, Hackett, excellent," his instructor says with a weary grin. He's seen that confidence a thousand times before. "Now log your flight, get together with your mates, or that young lady of yours. Take the evening off."

"Yes sir," Hackett responds, a broad smile sweeping his face before it regains its military composure. His oldest friend, Charles Boswell, soloed two days previously, but waited for Patrick's flight so they could

celebrate together. They were schoolmates in London, joined the air force on the same day, and were slated for the same training course in Moose Jaw. Now they're here, and for the last two months life has been extraordinary. Neither had known anything like a Canadian winter – permanent snow was unimaginable, frostbite unheard of. The miles of endless prairie are a stark contrast to the overpopulated suburbs of London, and the frontier farming attitudes of local Moose Javians a far cry from the "tea time" mentality in which they were raised.

But if there is one welcomed addition to Patrick's life, it's Sheilagh Wilson. Nineteen years old, just out of school, she helped him buy winter boots when he met her at Joyner's Department Store.

"These are useless," she said matter-of-factly, looking at his Royal Air Force flying boots. "You'll freeze." He loved her voice, her smile, her all-Canadian attitude. In days to come, they met for dinner at the Savoy Café and at the CP restaurant. She dropped her boyfriend Jimmy, and now she's Patrick's girl. He savours the thought.

"You'd better not crash, mate," Charlie joked that morning. "I've told Sheilagh you're the best student on course, and she believed it. Love is blind." The plan now is to debrief, link-up with Charlie at the stu-

dent mess, and take a taxi into town to pick up Sheilagh and Charlie's date, Ruby. Then it'll be steak dinner at the Harwood Hotel, a movie at the Capitol Theatre, and dancing at Temple Gardens.

The evening is perfect – laughter, high tales, soft talk, and eager hands. Then, walking south on Main Street, the foursome are approached by a group of shadows.

"Hey, ya' limey bastard." The words, spewed with venom, turn Patrick and Charlie in their tracks.

"That's right, ya' bastard, I'm talking to you." It's Jimmy Renaud, Sheilagh's ex. Illuminated by the half-light of a passing car, he stands tall and angry. "Been having a good time with my gal?" His eyes pierce Patrick, who has distanced himself from Sheilagh.

"Get lost, Jimmy," she says with nervous conviction. "This has nothing to do with you."

"Like hell it doesn't. I'm sick of these flyboys, these yellow-bellied cowards that need to escape from Europe and come waltzing in here like some kinda God's gift…like prima donnas in their fancy-boy uniforms."

"Give it a rest mate," Patrick finally says. His voice is measured, his tone taut. "We're going home, we want no bother with you and yours."

A WWII British airman at the Flying School.

"Bloody ignorant," Charlie mumbles under his breath.

"What's that, flyboy," says Jimmy, his head pivoting from Patrick.

"I said you're bloody ignorant," repeats Charlie. "Where's your uniform, when are you going overseas?" His anger is level and logical, taking Jimmy off guard.

"She wants nothing to do with you," adds Charlie, looking at Sheilagh. "Neither do we." He motions for the group to leave, and they turn cautiously to cross the street.

"We'll see about that flyboy…limey bastard…we'll see about that. Enjoy the dance."

That evening, a group of young Moose Jaw men, some of them dressed in the colourful "zoot suits" fashionable at the time, attacked several air force men as they left Temple Gardens.

The friction between airmen and locals was real enough, and so was the street-fighting on the nights of September 12 and 13, 1944. A police report explaining the incident noted that Moose Jaw's "feminine gender appear to favour men in uniform preferably to those in civilian dress." The Regina *Leader-Post* called the antagonists "irresponsible youth between 16 and 18." The evening following the altercation at Temple Gardens, the air force trainees returned, and another fight ensued, to which "thousands of people flocked to the downtown area hoping for a ringside seat," according to the paper. The police detained some local boys, read the riot act to the airmen, and Group Captain George confined his men to barracks until discipline had been restored and tempers soothed.

Following the second fight, which received national news coverage and gave Moose Jaw a black eye in terms of unwanted publicity, measures were taken on both sides to hold the contesting young men at bay. Deputy Mayor Robert West issued a plea through the *Times-Herald*:

> "They [the airmen] weren't really a bad problem, but sometimes I guess the guys would steal someone's girlfriend and then the fights began. But they were pretty good to deal with."

"The City of Moose Jaw has received some very unfavourable publicity over the radio and through the press, resulting from the unfortunate altercation between groups of our young boys and airmen stationed at 32 SFTS. I appeal to all citizens to use their influence at home and elsewhere to prevent any recurrence of these disturbances. Men stationed at 32 SFTS are good citizens of their own country, and desire nothing more than the good will of our people. They are, in a sense, our guests, and we should treat them with courtesy and respect. Undoubtedly, there has been some provocation on both sides, but we should remember that this provocation has been confined to a very few individuals."

Bad feelings between local men and men stationed at what would become Canadian Forces Base Moose Jaw continued for years after the war, usually focused around women, as Stan Montgomery, a former Moose Jaw policeman and mayor, acknowledges. "They [the airmen] weren't really a bad problem, but sometimes I guess the guys would steal someone's girlfriend and then the fights began. But they were pretty good to deal with." And, aside from occasional minor disagreements, there was never another "riot" like the ruckus of September, 1944.

The 77th Battery, the first troops to leave Moose Jaw for overseas. Stan Ingleby is in the middle row, third from the right, and his brother, Sgt. Tom Ingleby, is in the front row, second from the left.

Moose Jaw Pitches In

Moose Jaw contributed more than its fair share to the cause for Allied victory — nearly one in six of Moose Jaw's residents served in the army, navy, air force, or women's divisions of the services — 3,465 people in all. Almost immediately after the declaration of hostilities, recruitment began through Moose Jaw's standing militia unit, the King's Own Rifles of Canada.

Moose Javian Stan Ingleby, born in the city in 1920, joined the unit on September 16, 1939, a mere week into the war. "My brother was in, and I also figured it would make for a bit of extra money for Christmas," he recalls. A recruiting depot had been hastily established on Main Street, and Ingleby remembers that it was a popular place for the city's young men.

Recruitment in Moose Jaw immediately reached a high level and remained high throughout the war, as it did for Saskatchewan in general. By January of 1942, according to Military District #12 Headquarters in Regina, Saskatchewan recruits taken into the Canadian Active Army more than doubled the national quota expected by National Defence Headquarters.

Due to lack of proper facilities, plans were made to train many Moose Jaw recruits outside of the city. "We didn't get much training here," Ingleby recollects. "They didn't have the equipment; they didn't have the uniforms even." He was soon transferred to a new local unit, the first local battery fully recruited for overseas action, the 77th Battery, artillery. Some two hundred of the new soldiers were housed in a stately house on South Hill known as St. Anthony's Home. The first military tenants of the improvised barracks received a rudimentary basic training course of three months with the most minimal of equipment.

In 1989, the *Times-Herald* recollected: "Material was in short supply right across Canada in the fall of 1939, and the army couldn't even afford to issue real guns to many of the servicemen. Guards posted to walk the perimeter of St. Anthony's carried wooden cut-out replicas of the rifles and machine guns they would later tote in European theatres."

However lacking the training may have been, and however short, Moose Jaw's young men were soon off to war. Ingleby remembers the day he left Moose Jaw for Europe – December 10, 1939. In reflection, Ingleby acknowledges that he joined the service as much out of a young man's yearning for adventure as for reasons of patriotism. During the war, he saw service in England during the Battle of Britain in

1940, and was among the Canadians who pushed through Sicily and fought north through Italy in July, 1943.

Back home, the news nobody wanted but everyone expected arrived on July 19, 1940. The war in Europe was brought to the front step of every resident of Moose Jaw when it was reported that Rodney Woodward had become the city's first wartime casualty. Serving in a Royal Navy anti-submarine boat, Woodward was killed when his craft was strafed by a German ME-110 Messerschmidt. The death of Woodward was a poignant reminder to

Moose Jaw of the very real dangers to be faced overseas.

By this time, hundreds of Moose Javians were sharing in those dangers, at sea, on land, and in the air. Many others, like Fred Ansell, who had a job at the local refinery, did their part at home. Ansell tried to enlist, but was turned down. "They wouldn't take me because I was too important working the refinery to keep those Joe boys going," he recalls.

The stories of how the war touched each individual household, and people's commitment to the cause,

Employees at the CPR shop about 1945.

are uniquely different. Peggy Johnson, born in Moose Jaw in 1915, remembers that "We weren't going to avoid war, but we were young and you don't take things too serious...but then our young boys started to enlist and that was a different story...then the war was real for us." Johnson kept tabs on war news through the radio, through Lorne Greene's "voice of doom" on the CBC, and she says matter-of-factly that if there was a silver lining to the horrors and losses of the Second World War it was that, after the devastating effects of the Depression, the economy took a huge upturn. Overseas soldiers were sending home pay cheques, and for the first time in a long time "at least the mothers and fathers at home did have a steady income."

Jack Freidin recalls having to place his shoe business into storage in order to serve. As a boy, Freidin had only the flimsiest interest in world affairs, he recalls. "As a teenager, I was interested in having a good time." But when world affairs came to his doostep, he joined the army, not wanting to be known as a "zombie," the pejorative term often thrown at young men seen as not doing their bit for the wartime effort.

Once overseas, Moose Jaw's recruits quickly fell into the life of courage and sacrifice the war required. The list of wartime commendations is a credit to the city. Many were on the very front lines, in the heat of action. Of particular note was the Conspicuous Gallantry Medal awarded by the Queen at Buckingham Palace to Flight Sergeant K. Brown for his role with the RCAF in a critical dam-busting mission. Standing above and beyond all others was the extremely rare Victoria Cross won by Major David Vivian Currie, one of only a handful of Canadians awarded the Empire's highest military honour during the Second World War. Currie was cited for "coolness, inspired leadership, and skilful use of the limited weapons at his disposal" when he led a small mixed force of Canadian tanks, self-propelled anti-tank guns, and infantry which cut one of the main German escape routes at St. Lambert sur Dives during the Normandy invasion.

Other Moose Javians who received public recognition for their wartime heroics included Jack Elliot, Spud Elliot, and Doug Greene, who all served in the now renowned US-Canadian First Special Service Force. Made

Major David Currie, V.C.

famous by its portrayal in the movie *The Devil's Brigade,* but kept secret during the war and for many years after, the group later served as a model for the Americans' Green Berets. All three men were injured, but as Jack Elliot describes matter-of-factly about the group's many commando style conflicts: "We couldn't fail, or we had to die. We just had to make it."

Not everyone did. 228 Moose Javians were either killed or reported missing in

Mildred Davis, from Moose Jaw, working for the RCAF in England.

action during the hostilities. Another thirty-five were prisoners of war.

Beyond the few local servicemen who received medals or headlines, there were the thousands of Moose Javians whose equally important contribution to the war effort was not publicly recognized. They include Fred Jardine, who, as a firefighter with 425 Squadron in Tholthorpe, England, helped save the lives of crew members in a burning, fully armed bomber. They

include Johnnie Felt and Bert King, for their important work in the newly developed, and highly secretive, field of radar. It wasn't until 1996 that the Department of Veteran's Affairs recognized the crucial efforts of Felt, King and some five thousand other radar personnel. But it was not only Moose Jaw men who actively served the war effort overseas. Kay Lloyd was an ambulance driver in England, transporting wounded airmen to hospital in Cambridge – one of the many women from the city to serve overseas.

Hundreds of other Moose Jaw women were pressed into the forefront of the struggle at home. As men left Canada by the thousands to fight on Europe's battlefields, the economic, political, and social status for women altered drastically and immediately.

Jean Young was one of many local women catapulted into the hazardous and very demanding sector of wartime industry. In 1940, as a construction technician helping to build Cessna aircraft for wartime training, Young worked in the Prairie Airways factory on 600 Fairford West. She remembered the experience in an interview years later with the *Times-Herald*:

"We covered the frame with fabric, the fuselage, wings, and tail assembly, and we pinned it all together before rib stitching it together by hand. Over the seams a special tape was tightly fitted, then the fabric was 'doped' with an aircraft paint with spray guns. The fumes were terrible. It smelled like strong nail polish remover, and at the time we had no masks to protect our lungs and noses from the fumes."

The Red Cross room in Moose Jaw in 1943, packing medical supplies for the front and "care" packages for prisoners of war.

Other local women left Moose Jaw in order to contribute to the industrial war effort, often taking on dangerous jobs of necessity. Four dozen women from Moose Jaw, single or married with their husbands overseas, elected to work at the Ajax munitions factory in Ontario. They wore special clothing to reduce the possibility of generating sparks. The work was often tedious, and always volatile. "There was a sense of adventure to it, I suppose, and also a sense of patriotism," recalls one of the women. "It was really monotonous work, but it was a different way of life and you really couldn't help but feel you were making a meaningful contribution."

Other Moose Jaw women supported the nation economically or politically, many of them throwing themselves into the campaign to raise money for the war effort through the sale of bonds. In 1941, in a move to spur the hearts and minds of Moose Javians into a fuller appreciation for what defeat in the war could ultimately mean for Canadians, the Moose Jaw War Savings Committee staged a mock attack using smoke, sirens, planned power outages and bright simulated explosions.

The *Times-Herald* reported:

A Victory Loan parade on Main Street.

"As the 'anti-aircraft guns' barked the people on the street ran onto the road to see where the explosions were coming from. Those near the CPR depot had the best picture, for up Main Street could be seen the throngs of people converging around the cars with dim headlights, and at frequent intervals a loud explosion would echo between the confines of the buildings followed by a vivid flash. The 'bombs' were falling and the 'anti-aircraft guns' were roaring a reply.... Thus those on Main Street had a sample of what could happen during a sudden attack from the air. Things had been planned in advance for the occasion, but when the 'attack' came many of the carefully scheduled plans failed to materialize, and the street saw crowds asking 'What has happened, where are the soldiers?' – just as they must have done during the air raids over Finland and the early raids over London. And so the War Savings Committee unconsciously presented an even truer picture of a poorly defended city under attack from the air than it had intended to."

A year later, under the third national Victory Loan Drive, Moose

Jaw was the first city in Canada to reach its objective, and was the only city to more than double its quota.

After nearly six years of conflict on the battlefield, and hardship on the home front, victory in Europe was finally achieved on May 8, 1945. For Moose Javian Art Ogle, who had joined Moose Jaw's King's Own Rifles of Canada when war was declared and later transferred to the 27th Armoured Sherbrook Fusilier Regiment, the declaration of peace was hard to believe. Having landed with his regiment on D-Day in Normandy some eleven months earlier, Ogle had been hardened to the conditions of continuous field combat. He reminisced to a *Times-Herald* reporter on May 8, 1985: "It's hard to describe your feelings. Not a letdown, I don't think. It was just hard to believe. There was no noise. We hardly knew what to do next. It went like any other day, except we weren't fighting."

On the day of victory, a profusion of nationalism flowed from every corner of the country, from every citizen, large corporations, small businesses. Turner and Ellis Hardware, of 23 Main Street North, placed a prominent ad on page two of the *Times-Herald* on May 8, 1948:

"They've won for us a glorious victory! May peace bring them all the joy and happiness they deserve, back home in civilian life. We wish to express our special gratitude to the service men and women of Moose Jaw and district for the splendid part they have played in the great struggle."

Of the 3,465 Moose Javians who served in the armed services during the war, 2,089 were in the army, 1,000 the air force, and 367 the navy. Less than half of them – just 1,479 – went overseas, but all played their part.

A Distinguished Homecoming

As it did following the end of the First World War, Moose Jaw mobilized to greet the veterans. City Council voted to hold a series of welcome-home banquets, and, by February, 1946, eight separate such events for groups of returning veterans had been held. As for the returning servicemen themselves, their sights were set on establishing a new life in Moose Jaw.

To help settle veterans, the federal government sponsored a program to make affordable housing available. In Moose Jaw, some vets chose to settle as

farmers under the newly invoked Veteran's Land Act, but many more went for the new houses. The city's initial allotment was one hundred and fifty – the first fifty for workers of the Prairie Airways plant just beyond the city (and, when it closed, for workers of essential wartime industry), the next hundred for members of the armed services – many of them coming home with war-brides – or families of the dead. In January, 1946, the city requested another hundred houses to try and accommodate some 340 new applications – it got only fifty houses. Many returning veterans would be disappointed.

On average, a four-room wartime house cost $2,700, and a six-room $3,400. The homes were a hot commodity and construction was watched with great interest. On May 8, 1947, James Hunter, a wartime sergeant with the Royal Canadian Electrical Mechanical Engineers and later a mechanic with Patterson Motors, became the country's first recipient of a serviceman wartime house.

As veterans began to settle back into life in Moose Jaw, many of them had the new responsibility of introducing their young war brides, mostly from England, to life on the Canadian prairie. Peggy Johnson remembers the foreign women arriving with their servicemen husbands: "For them to learn to live like prairie people lived was hard – they struggled, they struggled – it was hard." But, Johnson says, Moose Jaw bent over backwards to make these women feel welcome. "They were well accepted because they were married to our boys, and they were made part of everything."

Originally from Manchester, England, Rose Sagal was twenty-two when she accompanied her new husband Gus to Saskatchewan immediately after the war. Like many wartime romances, circumstances were less than ideal for a normal courtship. First meeting Gus at a dinner party, Sagal recalls that they "probably dated for three weeks out of the whole year...a few weekends, and then D-Day came along and they got no leave for about three or four months, and meanwhile he proposed to me by letter. Of course I told him I couldn't answer his proposal until I saw him again."

Gus and Rose were married in 1944 and arrived in Saskatchewan in 1946. "When I first drove through

Looking north on Main Street from the CPR Station in 1946.

Moose Jaw from the train station I thought Main Street was beautiful with all those little lights they had...I liked everything about it." First moving to Eyebrow, then later to Marquis, Sagal eventually settled in Moose Jaw in 1954. "It was the prairie, and I had no idea what the prairie was. I had no idea it was so vast," she recalls. "My coming to Moose Jaw was heaven to me, absolutely. From Eyebrow and Marquis in a little wooden house that was unpainted and barren to here with running water and a big tub." Sagal admits that the loneliness of being away from England, and the initial bar-

riers to meeting people of a different culture, made adjusting to her new life difficult. However, she firmly maintains that she was well received by the people of Moose Jaw.

Stan Ingleby, who also returned from Europe with a war bride and settled in Moose Jaw, agrees that his new wife was warmly welcomed. "They were received with open arms," he recalls. With a war brides' association serving as a means of support and a social network, many of Moose Jaw's new residents were able to adapt to their lives with close friendships and understanding.

The Postwar Decades

The Rebirth of Hope

The end of the Second World War had a profound influence on Canadian society. In Moose Jaw, it ushered in a prolonged period of euphoria. Men were returning from the battlefields, new families were starting, and the collective anxiety which had shrouded the city for six years was lifted. Moose Jaw, with its central train station, was the hub of activity for servicemen from Southern Saskatchewan reuniting with their families and friends.

The city hosted a seemingly endless parade of visitors, who eagerly filled the CPR station, local bars, and hotels. Within one year of the war's end, Moose Jaw's population blossomed, and the value of building permits increased by as much as 500 per cent. By 1947, Moose Jaw's population was 23,000 – an increase of 10 per cent over two years earlier. Many city streets were repaved, and federal money was put into upgrades on the Trans-Canada Highway.

The immediate postwar frenzy of jubilation and relief buoyed the residents of the city. With the hardships of the Great Depression and the constraints of war finally behind them, they were ready to catch up on many lost years of enjoyable social life. It was a time to relax. Going to the movies became an increasingly popular activity, with the Orpheum, Royal, and local drive-in theatres regularly attracting large crowds. Dance halls were hugely popular, with Moose

Opposite: The 1949-50 Normal School graduating class at a Temple Gardens celebration.

Javians cramming the floors of such popular clubs as the Temple Gardens.

During the summer months, people enjoyed boating and swimming at the Moose Jaw Aquatic Club, and many attended regular baseball games at Ross Wells Ballpark. The ever-strong popularity of hockey was reflected in the decision to allocate funds toward the restoration of the city arena in 1947. Junior hockey thrived, with the Moose Jaw Canucks playing as a farm team of the Chicago Blackhawks.

In 1948, the city hosted its first music festival, beginning a tradition that would last more than half a century. There were calls for development of an art gallery and cultural centre, a cry that received further attention after a February 11, 1954, visit by film actor Charles Laughton that attracted a crowd of more than a thousand. But, inasmuch as people were exploring newfound avenues of social interaction, the mass advent of television made the home a center for entertainment. On February 13, 1954, Moose Jaw's first TV store, McCaslin Radio and TV, opened on High Street West, although it wasn't until five years later that the city got a television station in CHAB-TV. The station was a CBC affiliate until 1962, when it switched to the fledgling CTV network.

Although the experience of war was slowly fading in the minds of Canadians, and even though a new air of social positivism was eagerly alive, Moose Javians still had reasons for social concern. Immediately after the war, polio had claimed several victims, with seven people killed by the disease in the first eight months of 1947. And racism continued to play a role in the life of the city.

One of the key post-war political incidents in Moose Jaw centred around a group of Japanese wartime internees, who, to protest their treatment, refused to leave a relocation centre established at the former air base. The federal government had moved several "troublemakers" from other internment camps to the new "hostel." It was widely believed that the McKenzie King Liberals had chosen the Moose Jaw location out of spite because Saskatchewan, under its CCF government, was not only the sole province not to support the internment of Japanese Canadians, but actively to oppose it.

The intent of the government was to release the Japanese from the camp, leaving them to their own resources. But the internees, some of whom were in their seventies and in poor health, wanted to return to their homes in British Columbia, from which they were still barred, and demanded help with relocation.

Although press and public sentiment was still strongly anti-Japanese – the *Times-Herald* regularly using the term "Jap," for example, and several minor scuffles between the Japanese and local police drew attention to the issue – many in the city supported the internees. Ross Thatcher, a former alderman elected to Parliament as a member of the CCF in 1945, spoke up

Police and officials attempting to evict Japanese-Canadian internees from the "relocation centre" at the abandoned air base on August 19, 1947.

publicly for the internees.

The Moose Jaw MP's protests were ignored by Ottawa, which cut off heat and eventually food at the base. The protesters were aided with support and daily deliveries of food by local people, including Japanese-Canadian residents of the city who had escaped internment because they lived far from the "sensitive" Pacific coast. The "strike" continued for weeks, but slowly the protesters gave in and left, women and children first, dispirited by the cold and inhospitable conditions.

The social upturn that marked Moose Jaw for some fifteen years following the war was, in many respects, unparalleled. It was a time of positive thinking, initiative, hard work, and appreciation. But this buoyancy could not have existed without an accompanying and profound economic upswing.

The war had jump-started the city's economy, and the peace brought no slowdown. Work was abundant. Coincidentally, the disastrous ten-year drought had withered to an end, and agriculture was once more booming. With a rural trading area of some sixty thousand – more than double the population of Moose Jaw itself – farmers exercised great influence on the economic landscape of their host city. "The CPR man got paid if it rained or not, the school teacher got paid if it rained or not, but the farmer

A livestock show at the Exhibition Grounds about 1950.

never got paid if it didn't rain," explains Ted Joyner, who operated a prominent clothing store in Moose Jaw for three decades. "So every time it rained you had trickle-down economics; the farmer now has a positive approach and he buys his wife that new dress."

In the urban centre, many women remained in the workforce, meeting an unprecedented call for employment at several key industries including the CPR, Robin Hood Mills, Swift Canadian, and British-American oil. "Moose Jaw was pretty much a thriving place," recalls John Livingston. Stan Ingleby agrees: "Everyone just seemed to be in such a happy mood, a spending mood."

In pursuit of economic opportunities, hundreds of people were migrating to Moose Jaw. As the postwar decade marched on, a variety of companies set up. A new rapeseed extraction plant produced essential marine oil for international exports, and hired thirty people. In 1950, the Paul Edwards clothing manufacturers opened a plant with a staff of fifty, and in 1953 the Texas Refinery Company opened in a former wartime chemical plant.

The post-war revitalization of Moose Jaw was perhaps most firmly reflected in a 1954 federal government report which indicated that the city had the lowest unemployment rate in the country. As the 1950s progressed, and with the added economic influence of new industry and NATO pilot training, Moose Jaw firmly re-established its economic footing.

The CPR yards in the 1950s.

The Civic Reform Association

W.G. "Bill" Davies

Each year the Moose Jaw and District Labour Council suggested a slate of candidates for City Council likely to do more for wage-earners in Moose Jaw. There was, however, no organization through which unionists could work to select their own candidates. The Council was controlled by a Family-Compact type of group which sponsored candidates each year through a Voters' Committee. We were dissatisfied with the Council, to put it mildly.

In 1947, L.H. "Scoop" Lewry was head of the Regina *Leader-Post's* Moose Jaw Bureau, and reported on all the local happenings of any significance. He was a member of the CCF and quite sympathetic to labour's cause. One Saturday afternoon, we got to chatting about City Council. Scoop had run for Council the previous year, just scraping in by a few votes. He was coming up for re-election in the fall of 1948, and in light of the presence of the Family Compact, he faced a grim prospect at the polls.

I proposed that we launch an organization similar to the Regina Civic Labour Association, which had had a degree of success in electing candidates since 1935.

Time was short, so I proposed that we immediately get a membership card printed for twenty-five cents per member, calling the new body the "Moose Jaw Civic Reform Association." Because of the time element, I proposed that we arrange to sell as many memberships as possible, then call a meeting to elect officers, adopt a simple constitution and program, and make preparations to name candidates for the fall elections.

I prepared the cards, including a slogan of some appropriate wording, and drew up a list of general proposals for the other side of the card. Scoop and I then repaired to the printers, where we ordered five hundred copies of the card made. Thus began the Moose Jaw Civic Reform Association – it had only to be formalized by the first meeting of its members! This, however, proved no great difficulty.

Initially, I had no intention of becoming a candidate. In the result – we had quite a campaign! – I ended up with Scoop on Council. This was the beginning of my eight years as a city alderman, a period that was sometimes frantic and stormy.

In a year or so, Scoop was to become Moose Jaw's mayor (following Robert "Bobbie" West, who had been elected under the Civic Reform banner), and he was to remain mayor for the longest period that anyone held that office. Within three years, our association had elected several additional aldermen to Council and others to school boards. In one particular year, we actually controlled Council by the margin of one vote, although in most years we were in the minority by one or two votes. But even

when we were in the minority, our presence was strong and we got things done.

Among the more important matters where the Civic Reform Association was able to exert a positive influence were: the termination of the Local Government Board financial supervision, which had been brought about by the City's default on its payments to bondholders, and the subsequent arrangement to repay this in part over a number of years; the change to a Union Hospital district; the establishment of a reliable water supply; the building of the first tri-partite, low-cost government housing plan in Saskatchewan; the establishment of a publicly-owned bus system; the first tri-partite Land Assembly plan in Western Canada; the creation of the Moose Jaw Museum; the first city-wide reassessment project; the establishment of stable relations with city employees; the introduction of a fluoridated water supply; and the prevention of an ill-advised city merchants' plan to bring the Number One Highway right through the centre of the city.

The young Bill Davies with a daughter in 1944.

The Politics of Equality

Moose Jaw didn't escape the postwar political forces sweeping across Canada in general, and Saskatchewan in particular. The expression of a new political ideology emerging in Saskatchewan, especially around Moose Jaw, was embodied in the spectacular growth of the left-wing Co-operative Commonwealth Federation, or CCF, which had sprung onto the provincial stage a decade earlier when it became Official Opposition in 1935.

The CCF swept into power on June 16, 1944, overcoming a desperate, red-baiting smear campaign by the Liberals under Jimmy Patterson, to capture forty-seven of fifty-two seats in the legislature and establish a "beachhead of socialism on a continent of capitalism," as one newspaper put it.

Moose Jaw, strong union town that it was, elected the CCF candidates in

The executive and stewards of Local 177.

both of its ridings. J.W. Corman became attorney-general in the new government and D.H.R. Heming later became minister of public works. For more than twenty years, Moose Jaw continued to elect CCF candidates in every provincial election. Heming served until 1960, when Gordon Snyder was elected in his place, and Corman until 1956, when W.G. Davies, who later became the health minister and shepherded the controversial medicare bill, took his place.

Even in 1965, when the Liberals under Ross Thatcher put an end to twenty years of CCF rule, Moose Jaw stood firm and returned Davies and Snyder to their seats in the Legislature.

Under the dynamic leadership of Tommy Douglas, the CCF dramatically changed the face of the province, dragging it into the twentieth century, as some people said, and all the while paying off an enormous provincial debt accumulated by previous governments. Rural electrification, massive highway-building programs, and the nationalization of many key industries such as utilities were the trademarks of the era, as well as the introduction of numerous social programs, including health insurance and pensions. The sum of these advances had an indelible effect on Moose Jaw.

The introduction of government hospital insurance – Canada's first Medicare program – in 1947 went smoothly, but expansion to include doctor's visits was seen by many as a step too far toward rampant socialism. The issue divided the city, with many people supporting a provincewide

Local 177, led by Bill Davies, marching in the 1945 Labour Day parade.

The Women's Auxiliary of Local 177, meeting in 1945.

An Enduring Relationship

With the end of the war, the British Commonwealth Air Training Plan was wrapped up and the flying training facilities in Moose Jaw were shut down. What had, for the better part of half a decade, been a bustling aerodrome, was now left mostly to the elements. As a ten-year-old in 1947, Bob Currie remembers using the airbase, much of which was deserted, as a playground. "My first experience with the airbase was in the late 1940s when we used to ride our bikes over and there were these old planes," Currie recalls. "We used to climb the fence and play in them, Flying Catalinas and others...these planes were pretty great."

From 1945 to 1950, the former air force base saw little action, although, after its brief stint as a Japanese-Canadian detention centre, it did remain in service as a civilian aerodrome through the Department of Transport. Then, in 1951, RCAF pilot training resumed, to the delight of the Moose Jaw business community, and reconstruction and expansion of the site began. Construction of the new base consisted of digging sewage lines and erecting barracks, office complexes, and a family housing area.

doctors strike. Moose Jaw was always a strong union town, due to the large industrial base, but this was balanced by an equally large, more conservative faction from the mercantile sector.

Large caravans of protestors left the city for the legislature in Regina to participate in futile attempts to forestall the implementation of the new health legislation, but the doctors strike petered out after three weeks.

The rising fortunes of the CCF in the Moose Jaw area also, ironically, set in motion the political career of the man who would, twenty years later, bring the

CCF government down: Ross Thatcher. The son of a prominent Moose Jaw businessman, Thatcher was elected to Parliament in 1945 as a CCF member, but would eventually desert the party to lead the provincial Liberals and defeat the government of his former colleagues.

Thatcher shocked the CCF by joining the Liberal Party in 1959 and leading the campaign against Medicare. Five years later, riding on the anger generated by the doctors' strike, he led the provincial party to a narrow victory, becoming the third Saskatchewan premier to hail from Moose Jaw.

The Base

More than any other single institution or industry, the military base 5 kilometres south of Moose Jaw has had an indelible effect on the city. It has injected money into the local economy, created much needed jobs, shaped the social fabric, and put Moose Jaw on the international map. Opened on January 1, 1941, as the No. 32 Service Flying Training School of the British Commonwealth Air Training (BCATP), the base was constructed in response to the European air war and Britain's urgent need to train pilots quickly. The City of Moose Jaw had sent a delegation to Ottawa in 1939 to lobby for a BCATP site and the following spring it was announced that Moose Jaw had received the green light to begin construction work. Construction began on May 30, 1940. Moose Jaw was ideal as a flying training centre because it offered a clear horizon, a high degree of daylight hours, generally good weather, and, most importantly, literally thousands of square miles of unrestricted airspace. In its early years the base operated Avro-Anson and twin-engine Oxfords, and used as its primary trainer the legendary Harvard.

After the war, in 1945, the base was closed. Although the property remained open as a civilian aerodrome, it was essentially unattended until 1951 when the Royal Canadian Air Force (RCAF) decided to once again use the site for its pilot training. Following a hurried schedule of construction the new base, RCAF Station Moose Jaw, was officially opened in June 1952. The jet age came to Moose Jaw with the arrival of the T-33 Silver Star in the early 1950s, and an influx of foreign instructors gave the base an international flavor within a few years. By the late 1950s the base had grown into a town-within-a-town with its own sports centre, pool, theatre, and golf course.

The last Harvard flew from Moose Jaw on October 22, 1964, and the following year the new Canadair CT-114 Tutor jet trainer arrived, marking the transition of the base to a full jet system. The runways were lengthened to accommodate the faster aircraft and the base continued to conduct training for other NATO countries. The mainstay of the base was #2 Canadian Forces Flying Training School. With unifica-

Air Force Day in 1969.

tion of the three services, RCAF Moose Jaw was renamed Canadian Forces Base (CFB) Moose Jaw on May 1, 1966.

In 1971 the base hosted the first of the highly popular annual Saskatchewan Airshows. Drawing planes and pilots from across North America, the airshow has been a mainstay of Moose Jaw's tourism program since its inception, and in 1995 set a weekend attendance record of 110,000. In 1971 the base formed a flying demonstration team, who later grew to become the internationally renowned Snowbirds. The base also played sporadic host to the CF Flying Instructors School, which trained airforce pilot instructors and provided pilot upgrades to jet category flying.

In 1993 the name of the base was once again changed, this time from CFB Moose Jaw to 15 Wing. The Wing connotation, a traditional air force term, connected all airforce bases across the country with an exclusive identifier. In 1995, in a bid to save the base from closing, approval was given for industry giant Bombardier to begin a consortium with the Department of National Defence to market 15 Wing Moose Jaw as an international military pilot training centre. The program officially began on June 6, 2000 using Ray-theon Harvard II turboprop and BAE Hawk 115 jet training aircraft. Initial signatories to the program included Italy, Denmark, Britain, and Singapore. The opening of the new international NATO pilot training program (NFTC) marked the beginning of a new era for the base.

> Moose Jaw was ideal as a flying training centre because it offered a clear horizon, a high degree of daylight hours, and literally thousands of square miles of unrestricted airspace.

"That was a busy year," recalls Donald O'Hearne, who was in service with the RCAF from 1939 to 1965 and was one of the first men posted to the new base. "If there's one thing I remember, it's how filthy the place was...all the mud...it was an absolute quagmire." O'Hearne remembers moving into married quarters: "We had to get a bulldozer to push the moving van to the door because it couldn't get through the thick mud by itself."

In June, 1952, the freshly overhauled and greatly enlarged base was officially opened as Royal Canadian Air Force Station Moose Jaw. It was the fresh beginning of a long and healthy social and economic relationship with the city.

On the pure flying side of things, the base was home to instructors from England, France, and Italy. The new training school was initially called Ginjaw, in reference to the move of flight training to Moose Jaw from Gimli, Manitoba. Students did their basic training in the Harvard, and would then move up to the T-33 Silver Star jet for advance training. The T-33 ushered in a new era of training – the era of jets. "We went from being a cowboy type air force to a really professional bunch," explained Dale Cline. "We all felt that somehow flying had become a much more serious game."

Although the Korean War had no direct impact, the next ten years would see many changes for the base. Buildings were added, social functions grew, and the economic link to Moose Jaw was increased. In addition to the hundreds of base personnel and civilian support staff involved with running the base, more than two hundred students were trained annually. In essence, the base became a miniature town onto itself, complete with a full gymnasium, pool and sports centre, theatre, curling rink, even a nondescript nine-hole golf course.

But what seemed positive to some Moose Javians did not incite happiness in others. By 1956, after only a few years in service, some people were worrying aloud that, rather than acting as an economic stimulus to Moose Jaw, the base was actually drawing potential money out of the city's downtown core. Astounded at the premise, the station commander of the day pulled off a brilliant piece of public relations by

NATO pilot and instructor.

ordering all base staff paid in $2 bills. As the bill was unpopular in Moose Jaw because of its past association with the vices of prostitution, it was rarely found in the city. An almost instant proliferation of the currency throughout the city was a clear and ringing indication of the breadth and depth the air force presence had on the local economy.

The relationship between the expanding base and its host city continued to develop positively throughout the 1950s. Under a NATO agreement that began in 1954, student pilots began arriving in Moose Jaw from the United Kingdom, France, Italy, Denmark, the Netherlands, and Turkey.

But just as the city was basking in an upbeat period of prosperity, on April 8, 1954, a tragedy struck which caused some Moose Javians to deliberate deeply over the adverse aspects of having pilot training conducted so near the city. A student pilot was on a solo flight when something went terribly

An aerial view of the scene of the 1954 crash taken by a Regina *Leader-Post* photographer.

wrong and his Harvard trainer collided in mid-air with a passenger flight of Trans-Canada Airlines, precursor to Air Canada. The student pilot, four crew members on the airliner, and thirty-one passengers, as well as one Moose Javian on the ground, were killed as the two planes plummeted from the sky and crashed in a tangled fireball. It remains Saskatchewan's worst air disaster and one of the worst in Canada's aviation history.

W. G. "Bill" Davies, then an alderman, recalled hearing "the impact of the collision from my office window. I telephoned Mayor Lewry, who minutes later picked me up in his old car. We approached the scene with the wheels of the car straddling the hoses of the first city fire engine to arrive on the spot. One house had been struck by pieces of the wrecked North Star and was fiercely ablaze; another house was also on fire. Lewry and I spent the next hour or two with city employees, who quickly covered the many bodies that had been scattered down from the planes as they fell after the collision. This was a very shocking day."

Notwithstanding the 1954 disaster, the NATO training ran very successfully throughout the 1950s. From 1953 to 1964, when the base evolved to a full jet program, 2,047 pilots were trained in Moose Jaw. By this time, the NATO trainees had become a common sight, and people welcomed them warmly, although sometimes the suave jet jock-eys with their big money, their innocu-

The Joyner Department Store float, winner of the best commercial float in the 1955 Jubilee parade.

ous arrogance, and their continental accents would cause a little friction with the local boys.

On October 22, 1964, the last of the Harvard trainers lifted off from the airbase and made one final flight north to a storage facility in Saskatoon. The venerable old beast was slow, ugly, unwieldy, and noisy, but beloved by those who flew them and by hundreds of children who had grown up watching them buzzing through their childhood sky. The trainer, which had been the airborne classroom for thousands of pilots since WWII, was now being replaced by the new Tutor Jet. A new, more efficient course — training one pilot on one plane at one base — cut the student time from eighteen months to fifty-seven weeks. NATO pilots came from all over Europe to train at CFB Moose Jaw, incidentally pumping large amounts of money into the economy of the city.

Mayor Joseph Hampson breaks sod for the new Civic Centre in 1958.

The new Civic Centre.

The Sky's the Limit

With war's end, Moose Jaw's population had taken off. It had risen from less than twenty thousand before the war to twenty-three thousand immediately afterwards and to almost thirty thousand a decade later. By 1961, it stood at thirty-three thousand. A few years later, Earle Levin, the overly optimistic planning engineer for the city's municipal works department, predicted a population of fifty thousand by 1980. In fact, the city reached thirty-five thousand in 1966 and hovered at that level for the next twenty-five years.

Despite a construction boom, new housing could not keep pace with the increase in population. The situation was exacerbated by the ageing of much of the city's existing housing stock. Alderman E.J. Hemming reported to City Council in 1950 that 269 homes were not connected to the sewer and water mains. In one part of the city, a thirteen-block area had three "unmodern" houses in each block. By the 1960s, the problem was getting acute and starting to embarrass City Hall. A 1965 study concluded that of 8,794 houses in the city, 1,343 were not worth repairing and should be destroyed. Another eighteen hundred needed to be upgraded. The study also concluded that four thousand new houses would be needed in the next decade. The most disturbing conclusion was that more than four thousand people lived in overcrowded conditions. All kinds of rental units were in very short supply.

Still the construction boom continued unabated. In 1950, the number of building permits was the highest in twenty years, and the pace didn't cool. The city was quickly spreading into the hitherto vacant pastureland. In early 1959, the last house on Grace Street West was on the corner of 11th Avenue. A year later, houses extended past Thirteenth Avenue. When lots in that area – Palliser Heights – were offered for sale, people lined up early in the morning to apply for them. By 1964, the housing shortage had become so acute that a rumour circulated that armed forces personnel would be forced to live in Regina and commute by way of a special train service.

Housing was not the only construction. A second airport appeared north of the city just beyond the junction of highways 1 and 2. Six hotels, most of them on River Street, were renovated, and a new motel costing $150,000 went up across the street from Crescent Park.

Canada Packers expanded and modernised its operation. The Pla-More Booster Club built an $80,000 arena on South Hill. Excavation at the airbase began a $3 million project to lengthen and improve the runways in preparation for the arrival of new jet trainers — a project somewhat less satisfying to local pride because a Regina firm had won the contract.

The Civic Centre, a combination ice rink and general purpose arena on the edge of downtown just north of the Armoury on Main Street, was finished in late summer of 1959. Its radical design, with a "ski slope" roof, was at first scorned and derided, and scoffers felt vindicated when a major blizzard damaged the roof before the building was even completed. But spectators soon grew to love the unobstructed view of the ice provided by the roof supported by huge steel cables that obviated the need for pillars.

The Civic Centre was opened with much hoopla and fanfare on September 2. Jazz legend Louis Armstrong was the first performer to grace the new building, drawing an audience of 4,100.

The same year, the new Federal Building opened. Construction of the

Saskatchewan Technical Institute began at the old Teachers' College. St. John's Anglican Church, City Hall, the McCabe grain feed plant, the city-owned trailer court, and CanaDays' clothing factory all built additions.

Most of the schools in the city were renovated or expanded in anticipation of the demographic bulge that was approaching like a tidal wave. Palliser Heights School, the first in the city with its own gym, was built in 1959. The area grew so fast, and the little baby boomers arrived in such numbers, that in the first year children only attended classes for half a day. That way

the rooms could accommodate two separate classes in the same day. Riverview Collegiate, the first high school on South Hill, was built in 1963.

Boom Again

The Fifties morphed into the Sixties. Anything and everything seemed possible — growth, prosperity, enhancement of lifestyle — and technology was transforming modern life, even in Moose Jaw. Television had become commonplace since its arrival in 1954.

The CCF provincial government had succeeded in its ambitious plan to

Queen Elizabeth saluted by the Moose Jaw Boy Scouts leader during the Royal tour in 1959.

The Queen and Prince Phillip at the Tuxford farm of Carl and Olive Wells.

get electricity and improved roads to most rural communities: from 1949 to 1958, forty-seven thousand farmers were wired to the grid; by 1960, the major highways were paved (there'd been only 148 miles of blacktop highway when the CCF came to power in 1944), and an elaborate system of modern gravel and oiled roads criss-crossed the province.

As the surrounding rural areas came crashing into the twentieth century, Moose Jaw benefited, especially since agriculture was on an upward spiral. Good weather meant good crops; wheat sales to China and Russia combined with low fuel and input costs meant money in the pockets of farmers. With Moose Jaw still the most important rail centre in the province, it was the commercial centre for a large part of southern Saskatchewan, with more than fifteen farm implement dealers and innumerable hardware stores.

As Moose Jaw rushed headlong into the future, the past was all around it. Every day, you passed people on the street who had fought at Vimy, at Passchendale, at Dieppe, or at Normandy. Some of the people who had helped build the city out of the treeless immensity of the prairie were still around – the first white baby born in the area, Ethel Scott lived past mid-century.

The ten-year boom in the Canadian economy faltered a step in 1960, but Saskatchewan did not do so badly. Pushed by an excellent crop year and an increase in the production of gas, oil, and electricity, the provincial economy continued to grow. Personal incomes grew by 14 per cent, farm incomes by 5 per cent. Things were still looking good. Unemployment was so low that a shortage of skilled tradesmen, sales personnel, and domestic workers developed.

New industries moved to town. Mid West Steel opened in 1960. Pushed by the record construction of the previous year, two concrete plants opened in 1960, and Styrene Industries built a $500,000 plant to manufacture building materials. Trans-Canada Pipeline began a $1.7 million expansion at nearby Caron, injecting large amounts of money into the service industries of the city. Work began on the ambitious Diefenbaker Dam on the South Saskatchewan River.

Industrial expansion, the construction boom, and the buoyant agricultural sector sent ripples through the local economy. The service and retail sectors expanded and prospered. Loblaw's opened a supermarket in 1959 and greeted sixteen hundred customers the first day. The $1.25 million Co-op Shopping Centre opened in the summer of 1962. Retail sales skyrocketed and hit all-time record highs in 1965. Moose Javians enjoyed one of the highest average personal incomes in the province, exceeding the national average.

Opposite: A Lions Club banquet at Temple Gardens about 1958.

Life is good

When White Track Ski Resort, the first publicly owned winter resort in Saskatchewan, opened at nearby Buffalo Pound Lake, the excitement was palpable. Here in the middle of the great plains – true to stereotype, as flat as a tabletop – arose a ski hill. Oh sure, it was a small hill, no rival to Banff and the other great alpine runs of the Rockies. But it was no longer necessary to travel eight hundred kilometres for a weekend of skiing. White Track had all the conveniences – tow ropes, two chalets, everything. Moose Javians took to alpine sports with a remarkable enthusiasm.

People began to build winterized and cosy Alpine-style A-frames at nearby lakes. On winter weekends, a significant part of the population between the ages of twelve and thirty would disappear from the city.

Those who stayed in town could take their pick from more cafés than you could count, and more than a dozen hotels. From the CPR station six blocks north to Athabasca, the Saturday sidewalks were thick with people. Traffic clogged Main Street to the extent that City Council frequently debated the number of traffic lights needed to control the rush of traffic.

The city was prosperous and life was good.

BOOM AND BUST

"It Was the Best of Times..."

Coffee and Cruising Main Street

Until television changed the social habits of North Americans, visiting was an almost ritual activity in Moose Jaw. There "used to be a lot of socializing, visiting house to house, visit your neighbours and play cards, that sort of stuff," recalls Anne Ingleby. Around nine o'clock in the evening, she says, people would go to someone's house for "coffee." The host would have a table set with bread, tins of salmon, slices of tomato, pickles, sliced meat, cookies and cakes, and endless mugs of coffee perked in big glass percolators. A game of cards, a little lunch, some spirited conversation (likely to get a bit loud if football or hockey or the forbidden topics of politics and religion came up), a few more cups of coffee, and it would be time to go home. In those days, people either weren't bothered by large amounts of caffeine or didn't talk about it.

In the 1920s and '30s, the city was a collection of small communities centred on a few small shops. Each neighbourhood had a food store, maybe a hardware store, and a bakery. People would do their daily shopping in the neighbourhood, and go "downtown" only to shop for larger items. By the fifties, the commercial life of the city had shifted to the downtown area. Before the advent of the shopping mall, Main Street was the centre of everything.

And coffee was the fuel that kept Main Street moving.

Opposite: Massed bands at the Band Festival of 1978.

Coffee row in the 1950s, where the future of the city was discussed.

In "the most British city in Canada," coffee – not tea – was the focus of much of the social interaction in the Fifties. In the afternoon, "going for coffee" was a daily ritual. The "smoke-filled rooms" of Moose Jaw were likely to be the counter at Eaton's coffee shop or one of the many cafés that lined Main Street. In Moose Jaw in those days, Main Street was the centre of the universe.

John Livingston, future teacher and city councillor, was one of the high school kids who hung out downtown in the fifties. "You really did have the feeling that Main Street was the centre of things," he recalls. "It was 'the strip'. It was where people drove up and

down, and parked with the angle parking, and you just sat and parked and watched people go by. It really was the social centre."

Some cafés were the turf of specific high schools. Some were for jocks, some were for greasers, and some for the small community of Bohemians. Cafés would be almost empty between 2:00 p.m. – the end of the lunch hour – and 4:00 p.m., when the schools were out for the day.

"Our lives were lived on Main Street, in cars and at Temple Gardens," recalls artist and educator Rod Konopaki, who grew up in Moose Jaw during the following decade, the swinging sixties. "There was little else

to do in the city and these were the places where adults didn't intervene. It was up and down the Main drag, and if you didn't want to hang out on the street you went into one of the cafés." The two most popular, according to Konopaki, were the 722 (which the kids called "The Deuce"), at the north end of the downtown strip, and the Ambassador (called "The Ace" by the kids), towards the south. It was at those cafés "where we routinely met, talked, smoked, and made plans for the evening or weekends. The Uptown and the Astoria were also well liked."

At the 722, Konopaki remembers, kids tried to keep on the good side of the owner, "Mr. Mac," who usually "put up with our antics but would occasionally bounce a group for being overly boisterous or lingering too long without ordering anything." It was the Ambassador that had the jukebox "that provided the soundtrack for our lives," Konopaki says. The Stones, the Beatles, the Kinks were popular but the "oldies" – Roy Orbison, Patsy Cline, Brenda Lee – also got considerable play.

The lucky ones who owned cars or had access to their parents' would drive from Manitoba Street at the south end

Opposite: Looking north on Main Street in 1965.

of Main Street to Saskatchewan Street to the north. With enough gas money, they could cruise up and down the street from when school was let out until it was time for supper.

The bar was another important social locus, but the drinking culture was largely a male domain. The "wild west" lived on in Moose Jaw, and if there was liquor around there was sure to be a fight, or two, or three. Some men lived for the weekend when they could get enough to drink and take on the world. Stan Montgomery, who joined the police force in March, 1954, when he was twenty, recalls there were more fights, and dirtier fighting,

than there are today. "It kept us really busy, we were going all the time." It was tough on uniforms, he says with a laugh: "We...pretty well lost a shirt every Saturday night."

Montgomery recalls that, in the late fifties and early sixties, Moose Jaw was plagued by gun-carrying gangs. "They had to steal a car and drive it for so long to join. And go out and shoot a cow in somebody's farm. And break in to so many places."

Déja Vu all over again

By the Sixties, the infamous River Street had become a shadow of its formerly glamourous self. The better restaurants had disappeared. The bars and cafés were dingy and run down. The street was infested with hookers and drug dealers selling marijuana, hashish, and sometimes morphine and

cocaine. The understaffed cops — the police force was the same size as it had been in the 1920s, but the city was almost twice as big — had their hands full staying in control.

"People would come down to River Street to watch the activity," Montgomery recalls. "We had a lot of trouble down there." Most of it was minor, though: feuding between pimps, and streetfights.

The last hurrah of River Street came in the early Sixties when Ben

Cashman, a reporter for the *Times-Herald*, wrote an exposé of bootlegging and prostitution in the city.

At that time, there had not been an arrest for bootlegging since 1958 or one for prostitution since 1957. And, while the activities of River Street were, as Montgomery points out, out in the open for anyone to see, the good citizens of Moose Jaw – and the press – had chosen to look the other way. Cashman, who spent three months on the story, had no trouble documenting eight speakeasies, a dozen bootleggers, underage prostitutes, and a call-girl ring operating out of the downtown business district. Perhaps most shocking to the avid readers of his report in the *Times-Herald* was his claim of regular weekend beer bashes where hundreds of high schools students, drunk on bootleg beer, destroyed houses and girls passed out ravaged on the floor.

Two months later, an internal police report triggered by the newspaper story blamed the rampant teenagers on lax parental supervision, and praised the police as efficient, competent, and professional, albeit severely under-equipped and in need of a new building. As for the charges of bootlegging and prostitution, the police report found the newspaper

story's information was enough only to arouse suspicion. There was really nothing, the police said, they could do.

Just the same, over the next few days, city police and RCMP did conduct a number of scattered arrests, though Chief Mickey Mackey carped that the newspa-

In 1965, the force
was again rocked
by scandal.
There were charges
in City Council
and newspaper editorials
of inefficiency,
bad discipline,
and poor morale.

per reports had hampered the police investigation by making the culprits more wary. Mayor O.B. Fysh's only comment was, "I am happy to see the police are doing their duty and their usual good job."

Five years later, the whole issue resurfaced when Mayor "Scoop" Lewry (who

earned his nickname as a reporter for the *Leader-Post*), charged that the city was wide open for drinking and prostitution. The mayor's charges and then another story in the *Times-Herald* about prostitution on River Street caused a furor. The police once again cracked down. Lewry received threatening phone calls, but some hotel owners welcomed the chance to make their businesses respectable, and gradually the presence of prostitutes declined. In 1999, as Moose Jaw was establishing a reputation as a tourism destination point, a senior police officer could not remember the last prostitution-related arrest in the city.

Problems within the police department also continued to haunt Moose Jaw in the sixties. In 1965, the force was again rocked by scandal. There were charges in City Council and newspaper editorials of inefficiency, bad discipline, and poor morale. A special commission reported that discipline was lax, absenteeism was rife, and that twenty-six policemen had quit in the previous two years.

Mackey resigned as chief after it was revealed that he had removed confiscated weapons from the police station and taken them home, though he protested he had only taken the guns to repair and

restore them. Some people believed Mackey was made a scapegoat to divert attention from the department's problems. But others thought the chief's old-fashioned ideas as reported in the *Times-Herald* – he was against women officers, and said the most important attribute of a policeman was to be big and tough – contributed to the problem.

...and Everyone was an All-star

As always, sports played a big role in the life of the city in the Fifties. In some ways, the decade was the best ever for sports.

Hockey was, of course, king. The Moose Jaw Canucks won their league from 1945 through 1949, reaching the Memorial Cup finals in 1945 and 1947. They dominated the provincial junior hockey league in the late forties, but the championship always escaped them.

Although the Canucks were important and, as a farm team for the Chicago Back Hawks, garnered much attention and produced many NHL stars, the senior Pla-Mors (formerly the Moose Jaw Millers), were also major athletes in the city. The Pla-Mors, with players like the popular Harvey Stein, were local heroes,

and stories about them featured prominently in the newspaper. The arena was packed for both senior and junior games.

Women's hockey was also popular in the fifties, and Moose Jaw's Wildcats were the Western Canadian champions in 1954. The big story, however, was the game between the Wildcats and a "United Nations" team from the RCAF training school. The local girls won the game 8-1 despite, as the *Times-Herald* reported, "fighting an uphill battle in contending with prejudiced referees, score keepers, goal judges, and any other officials who happened to get into the act." It was, as might be suspected, not a very serious game. The UN team was made up of male fliers from five countries who had been playing hockey for a few months. The high point of the game was a ten-minute misconduct penalty awarded to goalie Helen Green for kissing referee Stoney Edmonds.

Women in team sports were not new to the city. Many Moose Jaw women went on to play in the All-American Girls' Professional Ball League, which had its heyday during World War II. Olive Bend pitched for five years. Sisters Ann Deyotte and Lee Delmonico are members of both the Saskatchewan Baseball

Hall of Fame and the Baseball Hall of Fame in Cooperstown, NY. Delmonico, who played in the "bigs" for four years, had been a member of the Moose Jaw Royals. Another Royal was Bertha "Bert" Podolski, also a Saskatchewan Hall of Famer, who also played for the Moose Jaw Jewels. From the time the Senior Girls Fastball League was organized in 1926, teams from Moose Jaw won many provincial championships.

The Arena Rink in mid-conflagration on August 27, 1955.

Disaster struck the sports scene in August of 1955 when the Arena rink burned down, leaving the Canucks and the Pla-Mors homeless. The Canucks folded for lack of a place to play and practice, and the Pla-Mors were forced to play in Weyburn.

The situation was unacceptable, there was no doubt. The city was booming and had a passion for sport. Enter Dr. Fred H. Wigmore. He was another in a long line of Moose Jaw residents who would not sit back when the city was faced with a problem. Like those who had built the Wild Animal Park, the big hotels, and CHAB, he sought a local solution to the problem. Four years of furious politicking and fundraising resulted in the construction in 1959 of the futuristic Civic

Centre and the return of serious hockey to the city.

Moose Jaw was also always a big baseball town. Bob Currie remembers sneaking into the Ross Wells ball park and cheering on the Mallards and later the Millers in the late forties and early fifties. His favourite player was Don Gillies – "a long, lanky first baseman who could hit" – whose son Clark later became an NHL hockey star.

In 1954 Bill Nutzhorn organized Scotty Kwan's Moose Jaw Lakers, which went on to win the provincial championship in their inaugural year with a record of 25-5. A young pitcher on that team, Mike Dayne, went on to pitch for the Washington Senators (which later became the Minnesota

Twins) for six years. He returned to Moose Jaw in 1961 and coached the Steelers to the Southern Saskatchewan Baseball League championship. That team included local great Wally Blaisdell, who had nine RBIS in the 15-8 win over the Swift Current Indians. In the same game George Hunchuk hit two home runs. Hunchuk was still catching at the age of sixty-six when the Moose Jaw Old Birds won the Provincial Twilight League championship for the fourth time in seven years in 1993. Pitcher Reggie Cleveland, another Moose Jaw alumnus, was 1971 National League rookie of the year.

Moose Jaw has had a long affinity for combative sports, as the sixties proved. Dave Pyle, a hand-to-hand combat instructor in the war, came back to Moose Jaw in 1950, and started the Moose Jaw Wrestling Club in the police gym. The club won eight championships the first year. Through three decades, the wrestlers he trained won twenty-seven gold medals in national competitions, and four internationally. In 1960, Ray Lougheed, a CPR brakeman, became the pride of the city when, as the Canadian lightweight wrestling champion at twenty-five, he was chosen to compete at the Rome Olympics. He was the first Moose Javian to compete in the Olympics since Phyllis Dewar in 1932.

Other Moose Jaw wrestlers coming out of Dave Pyle's gym included John Bozak, who dominated the Saskatchewan and Canadian heavyweight category for years. Frank Abdou was also a long-time champion and coach. Later, his son Justin followed in his footsteps all the way to the Summer Olympics (in 2000), as had Terry Price in 1976.

Pyle, who was later inducted into the Saskatchewan Sports Hall of Fame, was also the first judo instructor in the city. He continued a long tradition of martial arts training in the city that began at the YMCA as early as 1915. Pyle also tried his hand as a professional wrestling promoter and many of the biggest names in the game appeared on his cards at Temple Gardens and the Arena rink.

The Y had been an essential part of the culture and sports life of the city. However, in 1949, the women's organization found itself in a financial bind. Its old Ominica Street building, occupied since 1913, had become too expensive to maintain, so the building was sold and the YWCA rented space from the YMCA.

The two Ys formally merged in 1954, despite some strong opposition from people who claimed the courtship was insincere and the men were just after the $50,000 the women had realized from the old building. Ilse Scohay, the physical director for the YWCA, resigned over the marriage.

The new inclusive Y became an essential part of the educational and social life of the city. The organization, which was still strongly rooted in its Christian identity, developed programs such as Hi-Y for teenagers. No city schools except the Technical High School (later renamed the A.E. Peacock Technical High School) had gyms, so phys-ed classes and sports depended on the Y for space and coaching.

Words and Music by...

Music Festivals had been popular in the city since the 1920s. Even in the depths of the Depression, the Southern Musical Festival attracted three thousand musicians to the adjudications. In the postwar era, festivals moved to a new phase.

In 1950, E.J. Hemming, local bandmaster, alderman, and member of the chamber of commerce, had an idea. Interest in band work was not as strong as he would have liked and he knew how to improve it. He took his idea of a band festival from service club to service club. There was little interest. With a pioneer-like perseverance, Hemming continued to sell the idea until, finally, the Kinsmen club, somewhat reluctantly, started the Kinsmen International Band Festival.

The first festival was held on May 27

Another view of the burning Arena.

of that year, with a dozen or so bands from Saskatchewan and Montana vying in a Saturday morning parade down Main Street, solo and band competitions in venues such as the Studio and Orpheum theatres and downtown churches, and an evening concert at the Arena rink. It cost the Kinsmen a $1,300 loss on a $1,500 budget, but the club carried on.

The festival grew in size and in stature. In 1955, thirty bands took part; in 1956, the festival expanded to two days, in 1959 to three, with fifty bands from all over North America competing in what had grown to be the largest band festival in North America. More than that, the festival was unique. Most such festivals allowed only one kind of band – either military, community, youth, or high school – but the Kinsmen's embraced them all.

The Kinsmen International Band Festival soon became a signature event for Moose Jaw, which adopted the nickname "The Band City." Not only was the festival itself successful beyond anyone's imagining, but the band movement in the city exploded. The Moose Jaw Lions Junior Bands became immensely popular and internationally renowned under the direction of Scottish-born Frank Connell.

Similar festivals, such as the Moose Jaw Festival of Music and, especially, the Moose Jaw Festival of Dance, created an atmosphere of sophistication and accomplishment. They became a springboard for scores of professional musicians and dancers and music educators for decades to come.

While music thrived, theatre struggled. Television weakened live theatre in the city, but it was too well established to die outright. As late as 1961, an audience of more than six hundred watched the opening night of Gilbert and Sullivan's operetta *The Mikado* performed by students at Riverview Collegiate. The following year, more than eight hundred showed up for the Canadian Players travelling production of *St. Joan*. That same year, the Little Theatre group from the airbase won the first regional drama festival award in twenty-two years. The tradition was nurtured by people like Walter Mills, a Moose Jaw-born teacher who later went to the drama department at the University of Saskatchewan.

In the tradition of an earlier generation of poets and authors, the city continued to turn out nationally known writers, including novelist and playwright Ken Mitchell, and Robert Currie and Gary Hyland, the city's joint poet laureates.

The Moose Jaw Lions Junior A Band at the 1978 Band Festival.

The Safety of Trestles

Robert Currie

Growing up in Moose Jaw at mid-century, I was intrigued with the city's trestles.

I lived on South Hill, only a few blocks from the CN line that ran south of town. Beginning in Grade 3, my friends and I escaped the city for Round Hill, where we played cowboys, hiding in the valley's bushes to gun one another down. By Grade 6 we were camping there overnight, cooking beans in stained army surplus pots we'd bought for a song at the Army & Navy Store. The problem was that the route to Round Hill ran across the trestle.

Walking on the trestle always released a flight of magpies in my stomach. As I stepped out, my insides beating and flapping, my friends would say, "Don't look down," but I was a skinny kid and I knew that if I didn't look, I'd stumble and slip between the ties. I always crossed with slow, deliberate steps, worrying that a freight would trap me in mid-trestle – though I'd glued my ear to the track before starting across, straining to detect any hum that might signify an approaching train. We all knew that a boy had once

been caught out there by a long freight and had barely made it to the platform that hung with its rusty barrel over the river. He'd hung on while the platform quaked beneath him, shaking the barrel into the river. It was a true story. It had to be. Someone had heard about it once from someone else.

There was another way across the trestle. We boosted each other to the top of the cement pile on the north bank, then crawled along the steel girder that crossed the sluggish river far beneath the tracks. This was easy. There was something to hang on to. The problem came on the southern pile where the drop to earth was twice as tall as we were. How would we get down? Finally, someone with arms outstretched launched himself into the air, his arms reaching, encircling willows which swayed and dropped him lightly to the bank. We all dove behind him.

The city's other trestle was long and high. We crossed it by walking the tracks to the first cement pillar, then climbing over the edge, squeezing through an opening in the steel siding, perhaps six inches wide. There was nothing below it,

nothing behind it, but there was a metal railing at chest level. We grabbed the railing with both hands and sidestepped into space. Sometimes we stopped for a rest and a smoke on a pillar high above the river. We knew we were safe, for no adults would catch us there.

Once, we crossed to the north shore and clambered down the girders, ducking into the woods between the river and the CP tracks, into hobo jungle. We crept through the trees and discovered an old shack made of cardboard and tarpaper; before it, flames curled beneath a coffee can. Even as the doorway darkened with a shadow, we were running for the trestle.

"...It Was the Worst of Times"

The Boom Goes Bust

"Robin Hood Mills closed," Stan Ingleby remembers. So did Swift Canadian. And Canada Packers, though it opened again soon. "All the businesses seemed to just fold up at one time practically. CPR laid off lots of men. I don't know what caused it. It was just a general depression, I guess. But all the major industries...Pittsburgh Glass, Swift Canadian, Husky Oil...they just packed up and left."

Suddenly, things were not going so well in Moose Jaw. Modernization, economic rationalization, the rise of technology, and the decline of the railways conspired to cut out the legs of Moose Jaw's industrial base just as the rest of the western world was enjoying the biggest economic boom it had ever known. The completion of the Trans-Canada Highway, with its implicit subsidization of the trucking industry, started to erode the pre-eminence of the railways as the prime long-haul mover of goods. The rapid development of passenger aircraft and the decreasing cost of air travel all but eliminated cross-country passenger service on the railways by the mid-sixties. The newly completed system of safe and smooth grid roads meant that travelling locally by car was easier and cheaper than by train.

To anyone who grew up there, one sound defines Moose Jaw. One sound *is* Moose Jaw. It is a sound so pervasive, so ubiquitous, that most people who stick

Opposite: Cars buried on a Moose Jaw street on December 15, 1964.

around no longer hear it at all. It is the heartbeat of the city – the mournful cry of a train whistle. Now the cry seemed to be mourning the city itself.

Railroads had built Moose Jaw. Now, as the railroad shrank, the city weakened.

The CPR station was the busiest rail passenger terminal in western Canada in the mid-fifties, seeing more than fifty trains a day. John Livingston was eleven as that decade began. He used to go down to the CPR station to pick up the Regina papers that he delivered and remembers it as "just the busiest place in town."

Many of the hotels were clustered around the station and catered to business travellers. Salesmen, sample cases in tow, made their rounds of the province by train. Tourists, both on the transcontinental and spur lines, came to the city as a destination, or as a place to wait for their connecting train.

"The trains were so busy – comin' and goin' all the time," Stan Montgomery says. And that meant there were "so many people down there on Main Street at night. All night long."

Now things were changing dramatically.

The Post Office crowed in 1960 about the improvement of mail service after the switch from trains to trucks. The last passenger run on the Soo line pulled into the CPR station on May 31, 1961. The following March, the CPR announced it would be discontinuing the 480-kilometre Moose Jaw-to-Macklin service. In 1965, despite the vigorous protests of the colourful and energetic Mayor Scoop Lewry, the CPR cut one of the two remaining cross-country trains, leaving one westbound train in the small hours of the morning, and one eastbound every evening.

The elegant station dining room, once the most prestigious restaurant in the city, with its linen tablecloths, fine silver, and French service, had long been closed. The beautiful station itself was an empty, echoing, all-but-deserted shell. (The final blow would come in 1989 when VIA, the Crown corporation that took over passenger service in 1977, closed the southern route through Moose Jaw and Calgary in favour of the old secondary route through Saskatoon and Edmonton.)

The unions fought to preserve jobs,

"Red Joe" Kossick at the front of one of the last steam engines in Moose Jaw.

Cow's Tails

Jim McLean

It snowed in Moose Jaw the night of May 1, 1956.

I started my career with the CPR Car Department the next morning and I was grateful for that snow. It gave me something I could do, and I shovelled ferociously all that day in the bright sunshine – a simple job for a green kid. That was 45 years ago, and it was yesterday.

The Rip – the Repair Track. Row upon row of freight car wheels, brasses locked together in intricate piles, draft gears, couplers, air brake components in wooden boxes. The bolts they gave us were so crudely machined we had to tighten them in the vise and run the nuts on a couple of times to make them usable.

There wasn't a single automobile on the entire Division when I started, unless you counted the big old maroon Buick with its steel wheels that the Superintendent drove to tour his territory by rail. We went by train or push car or by foot because it was, after all, a railway.

We lined up at the Freight Sheds every two weeks to sign for our pay cheques and then lined up at Joyner's Department Store to cash them – the banks opened only from 10 am to 3 pm, closed on weekends – and in return bought overalls from Joyner's or maybe from the Army & Navy, along with those striped caps and four-dollar boots.

Funny, how often the senses will trigger the mind to recall something or someone from the distant past: the smell of steamer smoke; a cinder in the eye and the sure hand of the first-aid man as he picked it out with a cigarette paper; the hammering of the rivet gun; the absolute beauty of a smooth clean weld; nicknames – Tin Ribs, Putty Eyes, Doc, Black Magic, Magpie, Tom the Bomb; tying hoses at 40 below, the rubber like steel; water fights with stinking creek water; cutting through the yards at dawn, heading home to pick up lunch and go to work; everybody drinking from the same water pail, using the lid for a cup; pulling boxes and singing up a storm in the racket of the dope room; the indescribable stench of rotting grain; sitting in the cab of a locomotive on a frozen midnight, watching the flames from a River Street hotel on fire; arguing politics in the lumber shed; the fur-lined piss pot they made up for me when Chicago lost in

the Stanley Cup play-offs, and how hearing "Don't Be Cruel" always reminds me of chopping out those six-foot blocks high up in the darkness of the ice-house.

And we apprentices, rooting through the cattle cars for cow's tails, pinning them to the overalls of the old-timers as they stood in line at the punch clock, following them up the hill to Home Street as they trudged along, their lunch pails under their arms, their tails swaying....

but no new firemen were hired. A second, and more important, effect was the result of the superior reliability of the new engines. They needed fewer repairs and much less maintenance. By the mid-sixties, the huge, famous roundhouse was closed down and dismantled. The ultimate result was the loss of four thousand jobs. The CPR was still the largest single employer in the city, but it was rapidly becoming a wraith.

As the railroad became less important, industry in general no longer found the city as attractive.

As late as 1990, Moose Jaw still had more people per capita employed in industry than any other city in the province. But its grip on the title of Saskatchewan's industrial capital was badly slipping.

By the sixties, many firms were getting old and were ready to adopt the rapidly developing new technologies. In the past, industrial strategy had been to build plants near the source of the raw materials, and ship finished products to market. It now seemed more rational to build the plants closer to large markets and ship the raw materials. Robin Hood Mills, a major

employer in the city since 1911, closed its doors in 1966, transferring a few workers but treating ninety of the hundred or so at the plant to an early and unwanted retirement. The city lost, in one day, millions of dollars a year from its economy. Within a year, the Prairie Bag Company, less than a block away, closed. Without its biggest customer, it had no reason to exist. People on the prairies now had to have the flour made from their own grain shipped to them from Montreal.

Successive city councils tried to attract new industry. Castle Wines of Kelowna, British Columbia, built a winery on the eastern edge of the city. The land near the river was suitable for growing raspberries good enough to make into wine, but, in the days when wheat was indisputably king, few farmers were willing to grow berries. Finally, using grapes shipped in from the Okanagan Valley, it produced wine for about three years before it too closed its doors.

The three major refineries were also affected by the changes in the world economy. BA was taken over by Gulf Oil, which was in turn taken over by PetroCan. Increasing rationalization

of the industry saw the three refineries dwindle to two, then one. Eventually, the only refining done in the city was at the asphalt plant, which was a mere remnant of the once huge BA refinery.

As industry fled, joblessness grew.

A study by the Civic Reform Association in 1971, reported that a full third of Moose Jaw's families had no one employed, a figure even worse than the darkest days of the Great Depression. It "was a time when it seemed like nothing good was happening," Bob Currie recalls, summing up the general feeling in the city.

But, although things slowed down, they did not immediately grind to a halt. Even as the industrial base shrank, the retail trade did well as long as the farm economy was steady. The 1970s saw new records for building permits set regularly. The continued expansion of residential areas and large projects like the Town and Country Mall in 1974 and an expansion in 1979 drove up the value of construction.

In the early part of the century, the city had seen itself as a leader in the world and capable of unlimited growth. But something had happened. Once the province's largest city, Moose

Jaw had long since been overtaken by Regina and Saskatoon. Now Moose Jaw seemed destined to be a small town forever, always on the margins, always slightly behind the rest of the world, It had become a place to come from, not a destination. All the building and expansion could not shake the sense that the city was in decline.

Yet despite that decline, people weren't leaving.

"They built all these new houses and still the population stays the same – amazing!" Currie says with a puzzled shake of his head.

It was true. Moose Jaw's residential areas spread inexorably, consuming prairie and farmland, but the population never seemed to change, staying around 33,000 for years. What did change was the composition of the city. The downtown core, which had once been a lively residential area with apartments on the second and third floors of many secondary streets and many private houses, hollowed out as the middle class moved to larger and more luxurious houses on the edge of the city. Main Street, which had once seen crowds of people "all night long," was now deserted at night.

In 1983 the city suffered a major blow. On October 7, the last Dutch student pilots at the airbase graduated and the NATO pilot training program ended. This closure was another in the "death by a thousand cuts" as the economic base of the city was again reduced incrementally.

> As the worst drought
> since the Dirty Thirties
> tightened its grip
> on the countryside
> through the eighties,
> farmers were
> going broke again.

To fight the slide, the Business Improvement District was formed as an offshoot of the Downtown Business Association in 1984. Its mandate was be a "self-help program for downtown business." The first projects were parking enhancement and the installation of street furniture, including cedar benches and new trees and light standards. It was the beginning of a long and arduous process of rejuvenation that would come to fruition nearly a decade later.

Before that, though, things were to get worse.

Out in the rural areas surrounding the city, things were changing. As the worst drought since the Dirty Thirties tightened its grip on the countryside through the eighties, farmers were going broke again. There were bigger farms, fewer farmers, buying larger equipment but less of it. The number of farm implement dealers in the city dropped from eleven, in 1980, to three by the late Nineties. Six full-service hardware stores once serviced the city; by the 1990s, they were gone, reduced to hardware departments in lumberyards and department stores.

The impact of the farm economy's decline went further than hardware, though.

When the Town and Country Mall was built in 1974, many people expected it to be the harbinger of some sort of economic rebirth. There was little thought given to where the cus-

Looking north on Main Street in 1970.

Despite cheerful and soothing and optimistic words by boosters like Lewry, the 1980s saw many historic businesses close. The Harwood Hotel went into receivership in 1986. That same year, Eaton's, Zeller's, and McLeod's all closed their downtown stores. In 1987, the future of the Wild Animal Park, by then losing over a quarter of a million dollars a year, became doubtful. The provincial government finally decided to privatize it.

The haemorrhage continued for years. When the national recession hit in 1989, it got worse, though that had once seemed impossible. When Via Rail closed its southern route, bypassing Moose Jaw, it was estimated that it cost the city $1 million a year in lost revenue. Businesses in the city were now closing at a rate of eight per month. It seemed the city would soon be a ghost town.

tomers of the new mall were going to come from. There were no new shoppers, so there was only one place for them to come from: downtown. As businesses moved up to the top of the hill, Main Street started to look deserted. Eventually, on some blocks, almost half the buildings were empty and boarded up. Even on traditionally busy Saturday afternoon, the street was all but empty.

Meanwhile, national chains were taking over more of the retail trade.

The economic effects of "foreign" ownership were subtle but increasingly significant. Lou Pate, a manager at Eaton's, recalled receiving stock in the women's wear department that, while suitable for the Toronto market, was obviously not going to sell in more conservative Moose Jaw. She complained frequently to head office, to no avail. Stock sat on the shelves, and the store in Moose Jaw was one of the first unprofitable Eaton's outlets to be closed.

Deck Chairs on the Titanic

"I didn't like what was happening here," Stan Montgomery remembers. "Everything was so negative." The city, he felt, was heading "down, down, down."

The rest of the country was enjoying the optimism of Centennial year and the beginning of Trudeaumania. But in Moose Jaw, still caught in the economic doldrums, the mid-sixties saw the beginning of a long period of self-destructive bickering at city council that continued for decades. Fear of change, fear of spending, and, it seemed, a sheer love of arguing sometimes led the council to endless stalemates.

The Liberal government of Ross Thatcher was building highways and one of the priorities was Highway 2, which ran from the North Portal border crossing with the US, through Moose Jaw and north to Prince Albert. The road was being repaved, widened, and generally improved. It was a good deal for Moose Jaw. If the highway went through the centre of the city, downtown merchants, gas stations, and restaurants would all benefit. But where to put it?

The provincial government wanted the highway, at the city's south end, to split into two one-way arteries: northbound on 1st Avenue S.E., and southbound on Main Street. The only problem with this was that King Edward School sat between the two streets. Council worried about the childrens' safety and, after a month of furious debate, countered with a route through River Park. But, apart from the potential environmental impact, the circuitous River Park route would

> The rest of the country was enjoying the optimism of Centennial year and the beginning of Trudeaumania. But in Moose Jaw...the mid-sixties saw the beginning of a long period of self-destructive bickering at city council that continued for decades.

add significantly to the length of the road and add to the cost.

The province, with the support of the chamber of commerce, rejected the park route. The premier was not a man to take opposition lightly. His relationship with Mayor Lewry, his erstwhile CCF colleague, had been fractious ever since Thatcher had deserted that party to lead the Liberals. Scoop had further exacerbated the hostility by running against him for his seat in the legislature. Thatcher gave his hometown an ultimatum: take the route though the city or the highway would go elsewhere.

The highway went through the city.

Since the beginning of the decade, City Council sometimes seemed incapable of being decisive. The city had been negotiating with the federal government for years to take over the post office building as municipal headquarters. The old city hall was deteriorating rapidly; its bell tower had long ago been destroyed by a heavy windstorm. In 1960, the federal services, including the Post Office, Customs, and Canada Manpower, moved into a new building, and the old building sat vacant. Council first decided to buy it, then not to, then to put it to a referendum. An exasperated Mayor O.B. Fysh called his colleagues "a no backbone council," and voters put salt in the wound by rejecting the deal. A couple of months later, though, council switched gears

The Phyllis Dewar pool.

and went ahead with the purchase anyway.

The approach of Centennial celebrations brought out similar indecisiveness. Council fought about possible projects for years. At one point, it looked as though a combined YM-YWCA and civic auditorium would go through, but doubts about the compatibility of two such different uses killed the project. The next idea was an expansion of the Wild Animal Park, but voters overwhelmingly said no in a referendum.

Finally, with time running out and faced with the loss of federal grants, council turned its attention to Crescent Park, deciding to build a much-needed art museum attached to the library and an outdoor pool (dedicated to the "Moose Jaw Mermaid" Phyllis Dewar) at the Natatorium.

As the economic situation worsened, successive councils became more desperate. Revenues shrank, and there was a growing unwillingness to spend money to encourage new business. Increasingly the city looked to outside sources for new growth.

By 1988, the city was becoming desperate for new economic blood. Council began to lobby the province to permit a large downtown casino. The plan revived memories of River Street in its notorious heyday and opposition erupted almost immediately. Lewry, in his nineteenth year as mayor since first being elected in 1950, tried to reassure people council didn't want to turn the city into a "playboy of the prairies" or a "hotbed of crime and scandal." At a CBC debate on the casino plans, the format had to be changed when no one could be found to speak for the casino.

Council vacillated, first ordering a referendum on the casino proposal, then cancelling it. The proposal died a whimpering death when the provincial government said no.

In 1989, the city was treated to the spectacle of the Great Battle of the Library. A new facility was sorely needed and council put it at the top of the capital works list for the year. In April, the city was invited by the new owners to build on the Grant Hall hotel parking lot – the old Temple Gardens site. But many people were afraid that the historic old building would be lost if the library moved and a grassroots movement was organized to fight the plan, which was soundly defeated in a public vote. The old library, once spurned by Carnegie, was instead enlarged and restored.

The front desk at the Moose Jaw Public Library in 1964. Pictured are Ida Cook (at rear), Mary Jefferson assisting an unidentified patron, and John Mansbridge at the table.

Anger, Angst, and Alienation

Peace, Love, and Burn Baby Burn.

The youth culture of the 1960s came to Moose Jaw just as it did to the rest of North America. Drugs had always been part of the life of the city, as far back as the turn of the century. Cocaine and morphine and opium were common in the twenties. Former policeman and mayor Stan Montgomery says the city's strategic location on the rail line helped make it "the drug capital of Canada."

The railways, with easy access to the West Coast and the large cities of the US midwest, were as good a conduit for drugs as they had been for alcohol. In the sixties, though, the drug culture spread beyond the confines of River Street, and found its way into the high schools. A survey done in 1971 by the Moose Jaw and District Medical Authority found that 17 per cent of students aged sixteen to eighteen and 20 per cent over the age of eighteen used marijuana and/or LSD. Mayor James E. Pascoe, speaking for a large proportion of the city, was sceptical of the numbers and argued against funding a drug-counselling centre. His argument was that the kids who did not get into trouble deserved the money more than those who did.

Meanwhile, the faltering economy, especially the difficulty that young people had in finding decent jobs, and a growing pessimism for the future led to a

Opposite: Main Street at night in 1970.

sense of anomie among the youth of the city. The combination of disaffected kids and drugs culminated in what Montgomery laughingly calls a "riot" in the summer of 1971, when a large group of teenagers "stormed the police station" after a few arrests at a raucous party.

By some accounts, the riot was more about youthful exuberance than sixties counterculture beliefs. The fracas grew not out of a demonstration, a picket line, or a sit-in, but out of a house party that drew a couple of hundred beer-soaked teens.

One participant (who prefers to remain unnamed) in the fighting recalled in 1999 that the trouble began when a drunken girl threw a whiskey bottle at a policeman who'd come to warn the kids to break up the party. The police responded with reinforcements in riot gear.

A fight erupted outside the house and several youths were arrested. Then the crowd moved downtown to the police station on Fairford Street, where police recruited a group of pipeline workers to strengthen their lines. Fists flew and police hurled tear gas grenades while making arrests. In the

The Technical High School, "Tech," now Peacock Collegiate.

end, twenty-six people were charged with forty-four offences, including one young man accused of stealing a police cruiser.

By 3:30 a.m., the fighting was over, but half an hour later a fire erupted during a break-in at Vanier Collegiate, destroying the library and severely damaging the newly constructed wing. Police believed the fire was somehow connected to the riot, but never managed to track down the culprits.

In the aftermath of the incident, police were accused of denying the

youths their civil rights, a charge which Chief M.G. Crawford rejected. He also denied that a special session of court was held in secret, as parents of some defendants claimed, or that some parents were not notified until after their children had already been sentenced.

Despite this high-profile incident, the majority of young people of the city were not violent. Peaceful antiwar protests had been seen for years. And two weeks before the riot, more than a hundred young people demonstrated peacefully in front of City Hall to protest the closing of a youth drop-in centre.

Our Biggest Export Is People

Thanks to federal employment programs, some of the youth of the city were able to channel their desire for social activism into organized programs, like the Moose Jaw Civic Reform Association, which dealt with the city's housing crisis. The Moose Jaw Transient Youth Hostel Society ran a hostel for the thousands of young people who were hitchhiking across the continent, many of whom had almost no money and often slept on the ground at the side of the road. Every night, workers from "Band Aid" (the

name was a play on the city's slogan, "Moose Jaw: the Band Capital of North America") would drive out to the highway and round up people stuck in the dark. The Committee for Crisis and Youth Centres ran a coffee house and crisis centre in the abandoned and soon-to-be demolished Exchange Café.

But mostly, the city's youth were intent on leaving.

The more advances in transportation and communication technologies shrank the world, the smaller Moose Jaw seemed. Fashions hit "the Jaw" two

years after they surfaced in New York, or Carnaby Street, or San Francisco. Movies often got to Moose Jaw screens long after they'd disappeared from the screens of larger cities. Even Regina seemed more hip, more advanced, more in tune.

Of course, the idea of Moose Jaw inferiority was nothing new.

Shoe store owner Jack Freidin recalls how the rise of teenager culture in the 1950s killed the Aquatic Club, once one of the many sources of civic pride for the people of Moose Jaw. At its official opening in 1913, W.B. Willoughby, the local MLA, had boasted that no other city in the province had such a beautiful facility. "On the weekends you couldn't move over there for young teenagers," Freidin recalls. But by the fifties, lots of teenagers had cars and wanted to use them. "And where'd they all go? Regina Beach. And so Regina Beach used to have all the kids from Moose Jaw and Regina and surrounding area go there." The Aquatic Club went into receivership.

It wasn't just kids in their jalopies. Moose Javians went to Regina to shop. Trendy clothes, furniture, even groceries were better if you got them in

The old Aquatic Club being moved up the hill in 1958 to its present location.

Regina, or so it seemed. Even hick border towns in North Dakota had more allure than home. Its confidence shaken, Moose Jaw began to believe that it wasn't as good, as progressive, as interesting as just about anywhere else in the world.

For young people, Moose Jaw was a place to come from, but not a place to come back to. Most of the jobs that still existed were low paid, manual, and semiskilled. It was now a given that the future existed elsewhere. Moose Jaw's biggest export was its youth.

"We had these brilliant kids, great kids, and they'd grow up here, get through high school and they'd have to leave," Stan Montgomery laments. "There was not a damn thing to bring them back."

Over the decades Moose Jaw had provided the rest of the world with a wealth of talent. It was once said that Central Collegiate provided more Rhodes Scholars than any other school in the empire. There were, in fact, five: Neil Hosie, who became a Vancouver lawyer; George F. Curtis, once dean of law at the University of British Columbia; Ken Hamilton (son of the redoubtable Sam), who became a physician in Edmonton; Russel Hopkins, a lawyer who served as parliamentary law clerk and counsel in Ottawa; and Robin Boadway, who went on to a career in the armed forces.

As the post-war era progressed, the demographics of the city changed. The number of seniors grew, and, with the birth-rate in decline, the number of children in school dropped. Many retirement residences went up in the seventies and eighties, including Victoria Place on the site of the long-gone Victoria School. Reacting to these changes, the city directed more of its resources toward the elderly and City Council was ever more reluctant to spend money on projects aimed at youth.

The perception that the city had nothing but indifference for its youth climaxed in 1996 with the airing of *The Last Word From Moose Jaw*, made by local film-maker Jeff Beesley. The young people interviewed in the film expressed an extreme sense of alienation from their own city.

Who Do You Think You Are, Anyway?

With its tradition of amateur theatre, music festivals, youth bands, community concerts, and art exhibits, Moose Jaw has long provided artists with excellent basic training. For most artists, though, Moose Jaw, like any other small city, was also a place to come from, not a place to stay and work. Artists, musicians, and actors were forced by a combination of reality and perception to leave home. You had to go to New York to paint, to Los Angeles or New York to make music or act. If you wanted to stay in Canada, it was Vancouver or Toronto. Even writers who stayed couldn't count on much of a career. The perception was that nothing ever happened in Moose Jaw, or Saskatchewan, for that matter.

Shan Lawrence had been known since high school as an actor and monologist. She made her way to London, England, to study at the Royal Academy of Dramatic Arts and went on to play roles in major international films. Back in Canada she starred in several CBC dramas. Danny Tait, tenor and violinist, went east to join the Canadian Opera Company and the Festival Opera Company in 1959. Classical singer Marilyn Duffus studied in Berlin and went on to a career of TV and concert performances. Singer

Karen Jensen had a successful career in England before returning to Canada to teach.

Although there was a general sentiment that you had to leave to make it big, there were those who flourished in Moose Jaw.

The city exploded with rock 'n' roll bands. Groups like "Mozart and the Wolfgang," sometime house band at Temple Gardens (billed as both the "most popular band in Saskatchewan" and the "most repulsive band in Canada"), played every weekend to large crowds. Many had troops of fans who followed them from venue to venue, and even fan clubs, though none became hit recording artists. Rod Konopaki, drummer for "Mozart and the Wolfgang," recalls, "We dedicated every waking hour outside of school to the progress of the band. At first, it was learning our instruments, selecting material and practicing. But very quickly opportunities presented themselves and we were eager."

The band's initial gig was at the Oddfellows Hall, where they took over from the previously popular house-band The McCoys. Soon, they were playing at Temple Gardens and it became their home. "For two years we played most Friday and Saturday nights – that is, when we were not out in the country playing at small community dances. Frequently we also played on Sundays at Temples for roller-skating."

The band attracted a large group of hangers-on, who became known as the Funseekers. "They ranged from other musicians, poets, youthful mystics, loners, fighters, girlfriends, more girls, and always the partygoers," Konopaki remembers. "We counted on them all for advice, support, and friendship. In our lives, one thing was a constant, the necessity to have a good time, to live hard and fast. But it never seemed trivial. Every one of us was looking for something, asking questions. I suppose we were establishing the ground rules for all that was to happen as we stepped into the mid-sixties."

Many Moose Jaw painters managed to carve out reputations without leaving. Bart Pragnell and Alice Macreadie were known across the country. Vaughan Grayson Man, who eventually moved to British Columbia, was shown all over Canada, as well as in England and New York. Joan Rankin,

Moose Jaw native and international opera singer Marilyn Duffus is presented with flowers by Patti Johnson after a concert at Zion Church on October 16, 1964.

who moved to Moose Jaw "temporarily" in the sixties, has works in the National Gallery and the Moose Jaw Art Museum, which she was instrumental in building.

Over the years, many people dreamed that the city would become a centre of the arts. Many thought the

In Moose Jaw

Joy Kogawa

We lived at 104 Winston in the valley end of Moose Jaw in a little green two-bedroom bungalow, my husband David, our two children, and I. David was a psychiatric social worker at the hospital. Our friends were mainly from his professional circle and almost all of them were, like us, transients.

Nature surrounded our house – the slow moving river and the bridge over it, trees changing colours, leaves falling. We raked them. The children romped in them. We built snowmen in the winters.

It was while we were in Moose Jaw that my first short story saw daylight and the poems began leaping out of the dream world. This was one of the first:

Communication

You
Are swathed
In layers of silly chains
Which I may not cut
Or burn or wrench away from you
Because you love them.
To reach you I must first say

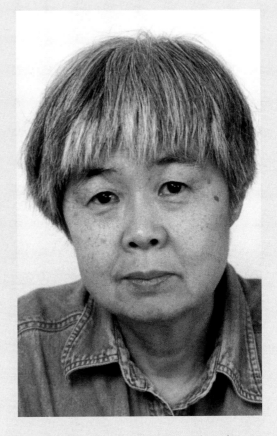

"How beautiful are your chains today."
Then I must kneel
And tap my message on your chains
And hope
That you will hear.

And this was another – both published in my first collection called *The Splintered Moon*.

In Moose Jaw

In compact Moose Jaw, a person
Can stand in a park
And see the library, a funeral home,
A stone shell of a church which burned
One winter night. A short block away
He can see Main street
And the lights which say
"Go" and "caution" and "stop."
If not myopic he might also see
The shadowy sign that says "Pause."

Probably the most significant year of my life was in Moose Jaw, 1964, not just because the publishing began, but because my sense of life as a journey of trust took shape and deepened and continues to this day.

I'm grateful for my short pause in Moose Jaw and sorry that I've lost touch with some of the friends I had – especially Lilian Loney Spals who went off to New York. My daughter still remembers the little Carpendale girls who lived next door. And my son remembers throwing spear grass at the other kids on his way up the steep hill to school.

Kinsmen Band Festival was a step in that direction. In 1965, a committee that included Mayor Scoop Lewry and dance instructor and impresario Helen Tait worked to establish the city as a theatrical centre. Walter Mills, expatriate Moose Jaw teacher and professor of drama at the University of Saskatchewan, did a study that concluded that the city was a suitable home for a touring theatre company. Eventually, the Globe Theatre in Regina took on that role, and in the late sixties and seventies, in a reversal of the committee's dream, brought each of their shows to Moose Jaw to perform for two nights at the Union Centre until rising costs and falling subsidies made it unfeasible. Although the YMCA/Civic Auditorium Centennial Project came to nothing, the theatre community was given a fresh injection of energy.

Bob Currie recalls that, when he arrived in Moose Jaw in 1966, there hadn't been a theatre group in the city for a while, but the following year Theatre '67, named in honour of the Canadian centennial, got going, and he got involved. After a few years, that group became Chocolate Moose, which is

"It's Gonna Happen," a song about a bright future for the city performed by Harley Wolowski, Gary Hyland (kneeling), Sophie Hasapis (now Yanitsos), and others.

still going strong. Amateur theatre thrived for the next few years. At one point, there were more than three theatre groups in the city.

In 1975, Ken Mitchell, already an established novelist and playwright, came home with an idea. Moose Jaw, he said, had a wealth of talent and a treasure of wide open spaces, like the Wild Animal Park, that would make a natural outdoor theatre. The city also had great need of attracting tourists. He had just the play, *The Medicine Line*,

about Sitting Bull's sojourn near Moose Jaw following the Battle of the Little Big Horn. All that was needed was a little operating capital and some courage.

The Moose Jaw Outdoor Players performed the play for three summers. Critics praised it, the production values were high, and constantly improved, but the city ignored it. Tourists came by the thousands, but few Moose Javians attended.

Mitchell didn't give up on Moose

Is There Anybody Here from Moose Jaw?

from the play *Year of the Moose.* **Music and lyrics by Ken Mitchell, Barbara Sapergia, and Geoffrey Ursell**

Oh, once I was in Australia, in the Great Outback
I was out of gas, out of water, no food in my pack
When bounding through the desert what did I behold
But a digger on a kangaroo covered all in gold

"Oh, is there anybody here from Moose Jaw?"
Is what he said to me
"Is there anybody here from Moose Jaw?"
Waltzin' Maltilda-ly!
"If there's anybody here from Moose Jaw
I'll take the bloke along
And if there's anybody here from Moose Jaw
We'll find a billabong! (Bonza idea, eh mate?)"

Oh, I was in the Himalayas, up on the highest peak
When the sherpas all threw down their packs and vanished in a wink
I turned back up the mountain, and what to my surprise
The Abominabable Snowman stood right before my eyes!

"Is there anybody here from Moose Jaw?"
Is what he said to me
"Is there anybody here from Moose Jaw?
I get lonely here you see
Is there anybody here from Moose Jaw
Who knows that old be-bop?
Cause if there's anybody here from Moose Jaw
I'll take them to the top!"

In the Elephant and Castle we were drinking Watney's Ale
The bombs were falling thick and fast, the streets were living hell
When through a secret tunnel, Winston Churchill did appear
"The Mother Country needs your blood, your sweat, your tears!"

"Is there anybody here from Moose Jaw?"
We stood up as one man
"Is there anybody here from Moose Jaw?
If you can't do it, no-one can!
We will fight them on the beaches,
We will fight them on the shores,
But we need someone from Moose Jaw
To even up the score!"

I'm planning a vacation for two thousand twenty two
I'll travel on a spaceship to the craters of the moon
And I know that when I get there, I'll never be alone
Cause the Man in the Moon is a Moose Jaw boy
who's wandered far from home

"Is there anybody here from Moose Jaw?
I thought you'd never come
Is there anybody here from Moose Jaw?
Some old Moose Javian
If there's anybody here from Moose Jaw
Let me hear you yell! (Moose Jaw!)
Cause if there's anybody here from Moose Jaw
It's time we raised some hell!"

"Oh, is there anybody here from Moose Jaw?
I thought you'd never come
Is there anybody here from Moose Jaw?
Some old Moose Javian
If there's anybody here from Moose Jaw
Let me hear you yell! (Moose Jaw!)
Cause if there's anybody here from Moose Jaw
It's time we raised some hell!"

"Shutdown," a song about the closing of industries in the 1950s and 1960s.

Jaw. In 1982, he returned with *Year of The Moose,* a musical drama about Moose Jaw's hundred-year history, co-written with Barbara Sapergia and Geoffrey Ursell, expat Moose Javians then living in Regina. The musical spectacular debuted with a cast of eighty-two, playing to sold-out houses. It was revived the following two summers by The Moose Jaw Thing, and in 1989 with a much smaller cast by Golden West Summer Theatre Productions.

Amateur theatre plugged on with great artistic success, and the Community Players ended the decade by win-ning awards for best play, best director, best supporting actor, and nominations for most of the other awards at the Nova Scotia Drama League's festival in 1989.

Tear the Damn Thing Down

The face of the city was changing. In the space of a few years on the cusp of the seventies, many buildings fell, vic-tims of a peculiar notion of progress. More than half the buildings on the first block of High Street West disap-peared. Quirky and distinctive build-ings were replaced by modern, faceless, characterless squares and rectangles. On High and Main, three banks on three corners — all examples of the pseudo Gothic style of architecture once pop-ular for banks — were torn down and replaced by the slab-sided boxes.

Having once developed a distinc-tive architectural presence, Moose Jaw was now devouring itself. When the historic Royal Theatre was repossessed, city council saw it as an eyesore and could hardly wait to tear it down.

The city had lost its confidence. After the heyday of the postwar boom, when the sky had seemed the limit, Moose Jaw had now hit a wall. The city looked outside for solutions and models. Anything from Moose Jaw was no good, old stuff was just old stuff, and direction must be taken from Toronto, or Vancou-ver or Calgary. As the decades passed, and economic troubles deepened and desperation grew, the city seemed to turn toward a kind of self-flagellation.

Dave Smith, Moose Jaw's city plan-ner, devised a plan to rejuvenate the downtown core by encouraging the renovation and restoration of the city's historic buildings. The architecture of the city was, he said, an asset that should be nurtured and even exploited.

Temple Gardens in November of 1977, just before it was torn down.

But no one was ready to listen. Within a few years, both Smith and many of the buildings he had championed were gone, and it would be fifteen years before his ideas would be put into practice. By then, many of the historical structures had been reduced to rubble and nostalgic postcards.

In 1978, Temple Gardens, where several generations of Moose Javians had danced the night away, and one of the emotional and economic lifelines of the city, was purchased by the owners of the Grant Hall Hotel and demolished to make way for a parking lot. The same year, the public school board put Victoria School up for sale. Safe-

way, the supermarket chain, offered to buy it if the land could be rezoned for commercial development. Council okayed the rezoning, but the controversy that followed resulted in a public vote. The issue was not so much the fate of the school but that of Crescent Park, which was right across the street. Developers wanted the whole area rezoned as commercial so they could construct a large mall. Residents feared the historic and beloved park was about to be destroyed. Voters nixed the plan.

The park was safe, but the school was still in danger. The Moose Jaw District Labour Council and the quickly

formed Protect Crescent Park Committee asked the school board to transfer the school to the city. The board rebuffed an offer from the city by putting the school up for public tender. Many people seemed determined to destroy it. The conflict seemed to be about more than just an historic building.

Two uncompromising camps emerged. On one side were those who saw progress as an absolute: growth and pure market economics were all that mattered. As Jack Freidin, by now on City Council, put it: "No matter what way [the public vote] goes, Victoria School is going to go."

On the other side were those who saw the past as a legacy to be cherished and lovingly passed on to the next generations. To them, the relics of the past were a source of the collective identity, to be protected, cherished, and preserved. Many voices joined in the fight to save the old building, including Heritage Canada, which called the school an "architectural masterpiece." Its vice-chairman, writer and historian Pierre Berton, wrote a letter to City Council pleading for it to save the building:

"It will be a sad day indeed, not only for Moose Jaw, but for all of

Opposite: Victoria School in 1907, the first multi-room school to be built in the West.

Canada if this building is destroyed," he wrote in his open letter published in the *Times-Herald*. "For if that happens, Moose Jaw will have lost some of its identity and we will all suffer as Canadians. Moose Jaw will have lost a part of its physical and historical character. If the process continues, eventually Moose Jaw will be indistinguishable from other public places. Only an unusual name attached to a thoroughly usual place will remain."

Letters to the editor pleaded, begged, demanded that the school be saved. The Moose Jaw District Labour Council and the arts community worked hard to raise public attention. The provincial government said the building was worthy of being desig-

nated an historical site, but stopped short of actually doing that. The pleas fell on deaf ears.

Ultimately the school was razed to make way for an apartment house for the elderly. The saga of the oldest multiroom school in the province ended in the early morning of December 1, 1978, as one lonely protester, Marion Tolley, marched up and down the street in front of the school trying to stop the wrecking ball.

The Mitchell house on High Street East, with its unique mirror image design, followed on the school's

heels, to be replaced by an undistinguished apartment building by developer Sam Klein. The fight to save the house was an early failure of the fledgling Moose Jaw Historical Society, which was distinguished more by enthusiasm than experience.

The demolition of the house, the loss of the Royal Theatre, and especially the destruction of Temple Gardens and Victoria School were collectively a trauma for a large segment of the population. It galvanized people, and a movement began to do something effective to preserve the history and architecture of the city. Eventually many old buildings were designated heritage buildings, and more effectively protected, though many more were lost in the process.

Emblematic of this struggle was the historic Russell block, which was obtained by the city for tax default. City Council was unwilling to spend money on maintenance while it searched for a buyer and, rather than repair the roof, which was badly deteriorating, had it covered with plastic sheeting. Woefully inadequate, the plastic did not keep out the rain, or the snow, or the pigeons, while deal after deal to save the building fell through. Ultimately, in 1999, exposure to the elements had damaged the beautiful old building beyond repair. The hardwood floor of the once-elegant third-storey ballroom was warped, rotted, and covered with several inches of pigeon dung, the magnificent circular staircase was destroyed, and the beautiful tin ceiling corroded beyond recognition. The inevitable demolition cost the city more than repairs on the roof would have a decade earlier.

A River Runs Through It: Rebirth

Even more fundamental to the city's history than its downtown is the river.

The sixties had seen the rise of environmental awareness throughout North America. In Moose Jaw, people were becoming increasingly aware that the environmental promises made when British American took over the refinery in the thirties — including returning only pure water to the river — had not been kept. Complaints about the smell had begun shortly after the company took over, and in 1960 neighbourhood housewives again complained, this time about the BA waste pit disposal method. Eventually, the refineries began to feel the need to reassure the public and the politicians that the river was not being polluted.

Percy Hill, then a member of the district labour council's environmental committee, recounts the measures that were taken to hide polluting practices. "We got a phone call that they were spreading white sand on the shores of the river because City Council was coming down and gonna make a tour of the river, and that was the result of all the shit we were raising."

The next morning, Hill and Jerry

Churchill Park during the flood, April 12, 1948.

Hudson joined the politicians' flotilla in a canoe near the High Pressure Dam. As they'd been tipped off, white sand had been spread on both the shores of the river to cover up oil residue they knew was there.

Hill recalls "So we went in. I pulled the canoe up and called over [Mayor Herb Taylor], and he pulled in. I took the paddle and shoved the paddle without any resistance right down into this muck that the canoe beached itself on. Shoved it right down to the end of the handle, and pulled it out and it was just dripping with this black goop that was being dumped in the river. And Herb Taylor actually stood up in this boat he was in and said, 'My God! What's that!'"

The decline in the quality of the city's drinking water was getting even harder to ignore. Blue-green algae was poisoning dogs and causing serious concern for the health of children at Buffalo Pound, the reservoir to the north that supplied the city. Large, out-of-control blooms resulted from phosphates that poured into the river in the runoff from neighbouring farms and from the city's

Opposite: The unique architecture of the Mitchell house on High Street was not enough to save it from the wrecker's ball.

Unidentified canoers at Churchill Park on April 12, 1948.

partially treated wastewater.

The river was a mess. The once beautiful beach at the General Hospital (long since renamed Union Hospital) had turned into a garbage dump. Where trees and grass and flowers once drew crowds for a relaxing day of swimming or sunbathing now sat piles of discarded refrigerators, medical equipment, bedpans, broken surgical tools, used syringes, bloody bandages, and other surgical waste. Neighbourhood children rummaged through the detritus hoping to find some particularly disgusting cast-off.

Elsewhere things were just as bad. Pollution from the CPR and the refiner-

ies had killed off most of the wildlife, both in and out of the water. Derelict cars, unwanted household appliances, boxes of trash, even bags of dead kittens littered the shore. Silt from the eroding banks was threatening to change the course of the river. Untreated sewage and agricultural runoff had driven people from the water, and the beaches that once attracted thousands of summer revellers were just a memory. Some said the beaches should have been closed ten years earlier, but no one was willing to say out loud just how bad it was. After all, all the stuff that poured into the rivers was a sign of the health of the economy.

In 1962 the city's waste disposal sys-

tem was creaking under the weight of rapid population growth. When the city built a new million-dollar, sixty-hectare sewage lagoon, a powerful explosion, apparently caused by seeping hydrocarbons buried in river sludge, did more than $140,000 damage.

"It wasn't just that the park was run down," Hill recalls with indignation. "The whole river system was a bloody mess."

Not many people seemed to care.

Among the first environmentalists, ironically, were members of the labour council committee Hill belonged to. Although few listened at first, they talked to anyone who would, invited reporters to view the damage, and railed against the indifference that was killing the river. The federal and provincial governments were uninterested and City Council, having been persuaded to allocate $10,000 for a cleanup, then cancelled the project. Hill took reporter Dennis Hegland of the *Times-Herald* on a tour of the river in the summer of 1971. The rusting car bodies and the bags of garbage on the bank made good copy. A few days later an editorial spoke about the need to clean up the mess.

"People don't like to see garbage

lying around," Hill says, but he and his cohorts found it was harder to get the public to understand the invisible damage done by chemicals put on the land.

The city's first attempts to clean up the river would be aesthetic only – dealing with the car bodies and dead kittens. City Commissioner Gordon Botting pointed out that water purity was beyond the power of local authorities when environmental legislation was so weak that anyone could dump anything into the river without fear of legal consequences. Indeed, it wasn't until 1981 that the CPR stopped dumping oily waste into Thunder Creek.

Concern about the river's deterioration was sharpened by spring flooding which devastated low-lying residential areas in 1960, 1969, and 1974, causing people to think seriously about flood control and, by extension, the environment in general. After the "one-in-five-hundred-year" 1974 flood, which caused over $9 million in damage and temporarily displaced over 1,500 people in Moose Jaw, the city began to buy out people whose houses had been destroyed, then changed the zoning to prevent additions and new structures in the flood plain. The city eventually bought most of the property in the flood plain and later passed it on to the Wakamow Valley Authority.

More than merely making noise in the media, environmental committee members amassed data, taking photos and collecting soil and water samples.

When the provincial health department refused to give them sample jars, they collected samples in jam and mayonnaise jars. They lobbied City Hall, driving council almost crazy with their avalanche of data.

Gradually, their efforts bore fruit. The community was becoming more environmentally sensitive. Awareness was growing of the potential economic boost that tourism represented – but what tourist wanted to see a garbage dump? The idea that pollution was a symbol of prosperity was losing its currency. The tide of public opinion was turning in favour of conservation and restoration. The pressure politicians were feeling led directly to creation of the Wakamow Valley Authority, Hill says.

In 1978 the province and the city began to develop an extensive plan to

Thunder Creek overflows onto Manitoba Street in 1974.

Mayor Louis "Scoop" Lewry at flooded Kingsway Park on April 13, 1969.

protect and rejuvenate the river, involving almost five hundred hectares of parkland within the city limits stretching from the CPR station to the Wild Animal Park. The two primary projects were to be development of Plaxton Lake – the artificial lake created behind the CPR's high-pressure dam at the confluence of the Moose Jaw River and Thunder Creek – and a wildlife interpretative centre at The Turn, as a dramatic bend of the river was known.

Enabling legislation was passed in March, 1981, creating the authority, a partnership of the province and city, with the city to be responsible for 60 per cent of the budget, the province 40 per cent. In 1983, the Progressive Conservative government of Grant Devine cut its share to 20 per cent, and the city was forced to form a non-profit corporation to raise funds both locally and nationally. In 1992, the new NDP government restored the province's share of the funding.

The first projects started in 1982, with the resurrection of Plaxton Lake. The former home of the Aquatic Club, long the epicentre of activity on the river, had become an eyesore, although the weeds choking the lake were only half the problem – it was badly polluted by mercury, residue of runoff from the CPR. In 1984, the Devonian Foundation of Calgary contributed $200,000 of the $400,000 needed for the construction of a 4.5 kilometre bicycle/pedestrian trail that runs from Crescent Park to Wellesley Park.

The city turned over 10 hectares of land across the river from the Wild Animal Park and an old dance pavilion was rebuilt as a covered barbecue and picnic area for up to 150 people. A 5.6 hectare site north of the Wild Animal Park and east of Seventh Avenue was developed as an ecological zone to preserve the last natural area in the valley. The patch of land had remained unchanged from at least the 1920s. With four vegetation zones within forty metres, the area has many species of plants that are now rare in this part of the province. One hundred-year-old trees and innumerable species of birds, amphibians, reptiles, and mammals make their homes there.

More elaborate and costly plans for a ski hill and golf course were rejected, and the bulk of the Wakamow park is devoted to preservation and nature trails. A walk through the parts of the park reclaimed from flood-ravaged former residential tracts can be a trip through the nostalgic remnants of other peoples' broken dreams. Wide expanses of native, naturalized meadows are interrupted by once-neat rows of overgrown caragana windbreak, lilac bushes, and the occasional concrete slab - all that remains of the foundation of a long-gone house. Walking through the fields of tall prairie grass, you occasionally stumble upon a patch of chrysanthemum like a slightly faded, but still beautiful debutante fallen on hard times.

Home: *mōsocāpiskin*

Standing on the outskirts of this small city, you might think you were at the top of the world – for only the full circle of the open sky surrounds *mōsocāpiskin*, as my Cree ancestors called it. From any of its vantage points Moose Jaw's vast southern Saskatchewan landscape stretches as far as the eye can see.

mōsocāpiskin – the literal Cree translation for Moose Jaw – is layered with a rich history now being retold because of the city's redevelopment. The Moose Jaw ecomony, in fact, is being fuelled, at least in part, by the First Nation stories of this place that are being brought back from the past.

Moose Jaw is known throughout Canada as *the friendly city*. In Cree that spirit of friendliness is evoked in the words *tawā, pē-pīhtokwē* which is as close an approximation as is possible to make in my mother tongue. In fact, the literal translation of these words is more inviting still for in Cree we would welcome visitors by saying *there is room, come in.*

Those of us who are First Nation residents of Moose Jaw are proud of this place. It was here, we remember, that the famed Chief Big Bear, one of our ancestral chiefs, sought refuge and set up his encampment in the valley on the south end of the city. That knowledge – that Big Bear sought this area for protection and peace – gives us a tangible connection with our cultural history, and it enables us to share the sense of peace that Big Bear and his people found when they sought refuge during those troubled times.

Being "named" is an honour in first Nation cultures and so we are honoured that the city's crest bears the Cree translation of its name: Moose Jaw. We are particularly honoured that the beautiful Wakamow Valley is best known by its Cree name, *wākāmo* valley. And the Wakamow Valley itself almost seems to celebrate creation in that its prolific and wild vegetation has been protected through the sound care shown to it by civic officials who have ensured the balanced integration of man-made gifts to the place the Creator shaped for his children to enjoy.

I was born a member of the Ahrahkakoop First Nation in northern Saskatchewan. It is my northern *spiritual* home because I was raised there and because my maternal ancestors rest there. Moose Jaw, however, has been my home for more than three decades so my family and my professional life have taken root here too. The city has become my anchor and my earthly home.

I have travelled extensively and have lived all over the land my ancestors called Turtle Island; I have experienced the beauty and the temperate climates of other places. But these are places to visit. When it comes time to kick off my shoes I want to be where my heart is allowed to be still and is given time to regenerate in the beauty of the familiar and the warm climate of belonging. There is nowhere else I can travel to seek and find the intangible human needs I find here in Moose Jaw.

nahtawīnān, ninanāskomanān ōma ē-miyikawaiyahk ōta mōsocāpiskin ka-wīkiyahk (We thank you Creator for this place given to us to live in.)

ēkosi
C.W. "Willy" Hodgson, Cree Elder, SOM

*Spellings of the Cree words were generously provided by Jean Okimāsis and Arok Wolvengrey of the Saskatchewan Indian Federated College.

MARCH TO THE MILLENNIUM

Like a Phoenix From the Ashes

New Life for the Airbase

As the 1990s began, the economic vitality of Moose Jaw grew increasingly positive. This upsurge was due to a variety of factors among the business, tourism, and political entities of the city. But the upturn was not a constant progression or easy transformation. There were many moments of doubt, many periods of setback. Would the spa become reality? Would the base close? Would NATO come back to town? Would the downtown core re-emerge? How would all these things happen? When?

"Full Steam Ahead" read the headline of the 1997 *Times-Herald* Community Pride edition. "Building on tourism, courting NATO pilots, and filling vacant shops, Moose Jaw is stepping down the road of economic recovery," the paper boasted. "No question. Moose Jaw is on a roll these days. Tourists are flocking to our spa, shoppers have replaced dust and boards in many downtown shops, and foreign leaders are eyeing our military base as a potential location to train our top guns. It's a dramatic turnaround from just a few years ago."

Dramatic indeed, but it hadn't happened overnight.

Although the business cycles of Moose Jaw throughout the nineties were affected by a number of factors, they were always overshadowed by considerations

Opposite: The new Temple Gardens Mineral Spa.

The Air Show in 1978.

regarding the city's biggest economic stimulus, the military base. Whether known as 32 Flying Training School, as it was during the war; RCAF Station Moose Jaw, in the postwar period; CFB Moose Jaw, after unification of the services in 1966; or 15 Wing, as of 1993, the parcel of federal government land five kilometres south of the city has been and remains an economic spark-plug for Moose Jaw. But, in the early years of the decade, the economic vitality that flowed from the base was increasingly threatened.

A number of military budget cuts throughout the 1980s had seen bases closed across the country and deep reductions in the overall numbers of armed forces personnel and civilian staff. New concerns were focused on rumors that the Snowbirds aerobatic team, based at Moose Jaw since 1971 and the stars of the city's increasingly famous annual air show, would be shuffled north to Cold Lake, Alberta, and that, as the aged CT-114 Tutor jet training fleet – which had just logged 1.5 million flying hours – reached the end of its days, the base would close.

The 1994 federal budget and defence white paper brought news that 15 Wing would remain open, for the time being, while the future of pilot training was considered. A local group known as the Friends of 15 Wing was soon organized and, in conjunction with City Hall and the chamber of commerce, began an extensive lobby-ing effort to save the base.

After many anxious months, the federal government finally announced the conversion of 15 Wing into an international pilot training centre to be used by NATO partners and other foreign air forces. It was to be run privately by industrial giant Bombardier, which would redevelop the base and provide new training aircraft – Raytheon turboprop trainers and British Aerospace Hawk 115 advanced tactical training jets. The establishment of the new program, known as NFTC (NATO Flying Training in Canada), meant new

The Snowbirds in formation at the Canadian Forces Base in 1978.

The Snowbirds

One of Canada's most recognized icons of national identity, the Canadian Forces 431 Air Demonstration Squadron – popularly known as the Snowbirds – has called Moose Jaw home since the team first flew in 1971. With their premiere performance at the Saskatchewan Homecoming Airshow that July, the team began a new chapter in the history of Canadian air force aerobatics excellence that began with the Siskins, a biplane team of the 1930s. Other notable antecedents were the Golden Hawks, flying F-86 Sabre jets in the 1950s, and the Golden Centennaires, in CT-114 Tutors during Canada's centennial year of 1967.

The Golden Centennaires were disbanded after one show season, but the team's commanding officer, Col. O.B. Philp, established an unofficial, non-aerobatic formation team in 1971 while he was Base Commander of Canadian Forces Base Moose Jaw. Flying the Tutor jet trainer, the original pilots and groundcrew of the team were volunteers, who flew after hours and on weekends. The team was named the Snowbirds, after a student at a local elementary school suggested the name in a contest.

In their first year, the Snowbirds flew in twenty-seven airshows to tremendous public response. In 1973, pilots were attached to the team for a one-year period, and in 1974 official try-outs were held for the coveted flying positions. That same year the team was cleared to fly full aerobatic routines. The team performed in Philadelphia in 1976 as part of the US bicentennial celebrations, and the following year the Snowbirds were formally designated the Canadian Forces Air Demonstration Team.

As with every other aerobatics team that preceded them, the Snowbirds' biggest challenge was their struggle for existence. Financial pressures saw the team operate on a year-to-year basis until 1978, when it was granted full squadron status as 431 (Air Demonstration) Squadron. 431 Squadron possessed a proud history: it was originally created as a bomber unit during the Second World War, and in 1954 as 431 Fighter Squadron at RCAF Station, Bagotville, Quebec.

The team expanded its formation in 1979 to include nine aircraft. It is that formation that millions of Canadians have come to recognize and revere. For three decades, the Snowbirds have performed

before more than ninety million viewers and have established themselves as an enduring testament to the skill, professionalism, and teamwork of the Canadian Forces.

In the Saskatchewan imagination, the Snowbirds are inextricably linked to the highly popular annual Moose Jaw Airshow, which began in 1971, the same year as the team. Drawing planes and pilots from across North America, the airshow has been a mainstay of Moose Jaw's tourism program since its inception, and in 1995 set a weekend attendance record of 110,000.

money and a long lease on hope for Moose Jaw.

Rod McLean, former executive director of the chamber of commerce, has fond memories of school children lining the streets with banners, residents adorning their houses with "Welcome NATO" banners, and wartime veterans at Providence Centre meeting a delegation of foreign generals as the city wooed NATO participation. "It was the nature of the community that impressed them," McLean says, "the friendliness of the community, the oneness of the community, the genuine nature of the community. They were most interested in 'Can we get affordable housing? Is it a safe community? What are the qualities of your schools? Will our families be happy here?'"

George Adamson, a Bombardier manager, agrees. "The city pulled out all the stops. It offered everything in terms of the total domestic waterfront. The visitors were amazed and delighted; nowhere in Europe would this happen."

Bombardier then moved ahead with plans to establish an international NATO pilot training centre at 15 Wing. It was "back to the future," as the base reverted to a role it played so proudly some forty years earlier. In a gesture to wartime years past, Bombardier named its Raytheon T-6A turboprop primary flight trainer the Harvard II. The initial contract runs at $250 million per year for ten years with Bombardier spending $35 million by 2005 on new headquarters, a ground school training facility, upgraded hangars, and new housing.

The NATO Flying Training Program in Canada was officially opened on July 6, 2000. Pilot trainees from Canada, Britain, Italy, Denmark, and Singapore were the first to make use of the program, with active efforts continuing to entice more countries. And people involved in the program agree Moose Jaw's welcoming nature is their biggest selling point. Although foreign air force generals are attracted to the base because it boasts an unrestricted air space larger than the entire area of Germany, Poland, Belgium, and the Netherlands combined, it's the city's unparalleled hospitality that can be counted on to close the deal.

With the base back on track, and a new turn to tourism as an economic engine, Moose Jaw had clearly turned a corner.

If You Rebuild It. . .

When one thinks of small towns, thoughts often turn to stereotypes; old buildings, locally owned independent shops, and narrow streets. Moose Jaw has plenty of that; character to spare. But over the past decade the city has also developed a robust and economically thriving industrial sector on its northern periphery. Originally developed to either side of Main Street North, an array of hotels, new restaurants, and major chain department stores have invigorated and diversified the city's economy.

In the early 1990s, as Moose Jaw's economy began to recover from far too many years of stagnation, the first signs of growth developed in the city's north end. Doug Marr, former executive director of the Moose Jaw Economic Development Commission, can't say "one way or the other whether one company or industry provided that impetus, but people got on a real high with the upswing of the city."

Expansion of the city had been examined closely by a number of studies. Plenty of available land, easy access, and proximity to the highway were ideal conditions for the establishment

The Spa

Moose Jaw's Temple Gardens Mineral Spa may be less than a decade old, but the history of the waters that make the tourist hotspot possible goes back literally millions of years.

Moose Jaw is located on the prehistoric site of Lake Agassiz, a vast ancient seabed created with the retreat of a glacial icecap some fifteen thousand years ago. As the ice melted, it left in its place a giant inland lake covering much of southern Saskatchewan. Below this lake, lay a foundation of porous rock, and it is within this rock, heated from beneath by the Earth's molten core, that the mineral-rich waters of the spa have for hundreds of millennia been generated.

Fast forward to the early part of the twentieth century. Early settlers soon discovered the 45-degree water that bubbled up in some mineral springs that had been natural luxuries for native Indians for generations before. Drilling into the formations began as early as 1910, and using a cable tool rig, it took some four years to drill to a depth of one thousand metres.

The Natatorium – a hot springs and pool – was opened in 1932 in Crescent Park and was highly popular until rotting wooden shafts delivering the water forced a closure of the facility in 1957. In 1988, fuelled by public interest to once again re-open the source of natural water, SaskWater, the provincial agency, agreed to drill an exploratory well for the new potential development of a mineral waters locale. The successful well was capped in 1989, and the debate of the decade began in earnest.

One school of thought was that a new spa should be the keystone of a revitalized downtown tourism trade, and should be built on the Natatorium site. Others argued that the spa should serve primarily as a "wellness" retreat and should be located away from the urban core in the Wakamow Valley. An independent development advisory team strongly supported another downtown option, and in 1993 public shares for a new spa went on sale. The city backed the project with an interest-free loan, and some fourteen hundred investors bought in. On May 10, 1995, the $9-million, 69-room hotel spa and conference centre opened. Its success made a 1998 expansion to 96 rooms possible and heralded a new era of tourism and economic revival for the city. In 2002, the Spa is slated to expand by another 84 rooms.

of new facilities catering to a slowly increasing tourist trade, fuelled by stories of Al Capone, a new spa, revitalized attractions and tours, and a newly established provincial tourism program that directly marketed south-central Saskatchewan as a "Great Trails" getaway.

"Moose Jaw was really looking at a lot of ways to be progressive," recalls Bill Kalbfleisch, former 15 Wing commander. "This was a period when a lot of energy went into searching for ways to improve its economic foundation."

Opening of the Temple Gardens Mineral Spa, a resort hotel, and the Tunnels of Little Chicago, a fledgling tourist attraction, both downtown, had a reverberating effect, and caused an explosive growth along Main Street north. The grocery chain Superstore opened an outlet in 1995, and Moose Javians – by and large – were delighted when the American Wal-Mart chain opened a sprawling building in 1999.

The area in the north served as an antithesis to its downtown predecessor – big versus small, franchise versus independent, modern versus old. It was a combination many old-timers feared. But it seemed to do the trick. It kept Moose Javians from wandering farther afield in their shopping habits, it brought in the buying dollar from farming families that might otherwise have spent the

> Opening of the Temple Gardens Mineral Spa and the Tunnels of Little Chicago had a reverberating effect, and caused an explosive growth along Main Street north.

day in Regina, and it brought tourists off the highway who were seduced by the lure of a new hotel or familiar restaurant. "Moose Jaw always competes with Regina in the sense of people spending their dollar," says John Livingston. "But, that is changing too. The people who used to drive through Moose Jaw will stop here now, and that means a few more dollars."

Ray Boughen, the previous mayor, says the city wanted the whole Main Street north part of Moose Jaw dedicated to commercial and retail development. "I think Superstore helped turn the corner for the city, so that people said, 'If this city can support a Superstore, we can support other things.'" He disagrees with those who contend that the quickly growing area will spell doom for the newly invigorated downtown core, claiming that they both serve different needs: upper Main Street caters to Moose Javians who need the offerings of Superstore and Wal-Mart; lower Main Street to tourists taking in the increasing number of activities and attractions of the downtown core.

And in the years since many of the new businesses opened on Main Street North, others have survived elsewhere in the city. Hotels throughout have maintained high occupancy rates, the Co-op supermarket has renovated in spite of the arrival of Superstore, and Safeway consolidated its two locations at an expanded downtown store.

The Tunnels

Mention history and Moose Jaw in a single breath and there's no escaping the most vibrant, mysterious, and alluring aspect of the city's past: the infamous tunnels. Rumours of darkened passageways, and all the wild lore of illegal migrants, illicit booze dealing, opium smoking, quick-fold gambling dens, rampant prostitution, and corrupt cops have fuelled the fires of intrigue for decades.

But it wasn't until the mid-1980's that a concerted effort was launched to get to the bottom of the story. In 1986 *Alberta Report* magazine ran a feature story on the supposed tunnels, and cited the new discovery of a mysterious doorway in the basement of the Cornerstone Inn leading across Main Street to the former Exchange Café.

Later that year, the Mayor's Task Force on Downtown Revitalization recommended that, "the Tourism Committee examine all available data and conduct whatever studies are required to delineate the extent of any tunnels between buildings in the downtown area." The report suggested tunnels did exist, but it couldn't define the nature of their use or the extent of their development. In 1989 the *Times-Herald*

suggested a more comprehensive effort should be made to turn the tunnels into a tourism attraction, and that "all that is needed is the political will and a few high-spirited people to spearhead the project."

That effort arrived some five years later and coincided with the opening of the new Temple Gardens Mineral Spa. The former Charlotte's Restaurant had already converted a small passageway into a mini tunnel display, and with the opening of the new spa, local Moose Javian businessman Brent Boechler launched the "Tunnels of Little Chicago." "There was something here

that was marketable," recalls Boechler. "People want to see the big picture, and the emotion and the romance; that's the stuff that works for the majority and that's how you have to gear your activity." With the first tour in June, 1996, the project was modest in nature, but the proverbial seed of tourist interest had been sown.

Following a fire in the summer of 1999 that destroyed an extension to the tunnels expansion, the operation was taken over by a Vancouver businessman – who had family links to Moose Jaw. Danny Guillaume, whose brother John runs the

Suntree Café on lower Main Street, injected a little entrepreneurial spirit and a lot of showbiz glitz into the tunnels program.

The tunnels were redesigned and expanded. Professional actors were hired as tour guides and given polished scripts. The tours were turned into interactive dramatic presentations, with the guides playing roles as gangsters, madams, and other Prohibition-era stereotypes recognizable from period movies and TV shows. Animatronic robot characters such as Joe the Bartender play pivotal roles, conversing with the guides and even addressing the audience directly. The tour branched out from the tunnels themselves to include set pieces such as the speakeasy and Al Capone's hotel room on the second floor of

the Suntree, and a sweatshop in the basement of the old Woolworth's building at the corner of Main and River streets.

The first phase of the project consisted

of two separate tours: The Chicago Connection, which presents a semi-comic version of the story of Al Capone's supposed influence on the city. Participants take a trip through a Moose Jaw speakeasy, guided by madams, gangsters, and bootleggers. The second tour, Passage to Fortune, tells the story of the Chinese in western Canada.

After only four years in operation, the tunnels have seen well over a hundred thousand visitors. When a third tunnel, called Bootlegger's Run, is completed, Guillaume expects more than a hundred and fifty thousand tourists will file through the venue yearly.

A Firm Hand on the Wheel

Having once again secured the economic stability associated with the airbase, and with the heightened economic activity related directly to the opening of Temple Gardens and Tunnels of Little Chicago, the financial situation in Moose Jaw began turning around nicely by the middle of the decade. Tourists were arriving, new business was moving in, condominium sales were brisk, housing starts were up, and the downtown core was being quickly regenerated.

City council gave generous tax breaks to new businesses, often as much as a complete tax holiday for the first year, with gradual phasing in, for certain industries. Council held the attitude that it was better to get something into a vacant building and have it benefit the city and the community than continue to have it sit empty.

As the industrial base strengthened, so did consumer confidence, as expressed in purchases of new property. Throughout the 1990s, housing starts had increased by 23 per cent, while overall provincial housing starts actually declined by 3.5 per cent. But, while the average home in Saskatchewan cost $77,396, fuelled by higher rates in Regina and Saskatoon, the average home in Moose Jaw stood at $58,469, making the city a very attractive place to which to move. In addition to houses, the decade saw the market include the relatively new phenomenon of condo-

> Beyond the explosion of...growth along the city's northern periphery, new attention was also being focused upon an economic revival of the city's downtown core.

minium sales. Designed largely for retirement-age buyers, many of whom have begun to move back to Moose Jaw from other areas of the country, modern condo units were hot sellers at the Regency on Athabasca Street, the Andross on Saskatchewan Drive and First Avenue N.W., the Rutherford on Hochelega, and the Manhattan on Athabasca Street and Third Avenue N.E.

Beyond the explosion of commercial and retail growth along the city's northern periphery, new attention was also being focused upon an economic revival of the city's downtown core. The antecedents of this rebirth lay in recommendations from the 1986 Mayor's Task Force on Downtown Revitalization which led to the establishment of a strategic plan from which the nineties' growth was generated.

"People had become accepting of nothing," Boughen remembers. "If I constantly see nothing, and I constantly do nothing, then 'nothing' becomes the norm." A perception had developed, the former mayor says, "that the city is kind of a retirement home for people, and that's good enough, rather than saying, 'Retirement is fine and there's lots of room for people to retire in this city, but there's also a vibrant kind of opportunity for business if we get the right kind of business going.'"

The most important impetus to downtown development lay in the burgeoning tourist trade, and this was hooked directly to the opening of Temple Gardens Mineral Spa and the

Tunnels of Little Chicago. A new bus terminal was built in January, 1995, and soon other business began to fill the southern two blocks of Main Street. Joyner's, which had sat derelict since its closure in 1994, was occupied by three new tenants. An ice cream shop opened, followed by the trendy Suntree Café, a sophisticated coffee bar, art gallery, and gift shop in the sensitively renovated Masonic Hall on the historic first block of Main Street. As the cap to this trend, the old CPR station was converted into several shops, including, in an ironic gesture to the past, the province's largest liquor store.

Farther along Main Street, the old Capitol Theatre awaits possible restoration, and the former Army and Navy Store has been turned over to "Arts in Motion." A $3 million dollar grant from the federal government's Western Economic Diversification program, provided to the city as an offset to 15 Wing transferring to a civilian flight operation, was distributed to a variety of community organizations, many of them dedicated to the revival of the city's downtown core.

The tourism-focused activity could reach its zenith with the much larger development being planned for the near future. Project Moose Jaw will include a four hundred-seat amphitheatre on River Street, where an interactive theatre piece will explore the storied past

"When I consider where we have come from in the past ten years, I have every bit of hope and optimism for the next ten years."

of "The Street." As part of the project, River Street itself is slated for a facelift, including a pedestrian mall and restoration of the historic buildings.

The Rural/Urban Design Assistance Team study commissioned by the chamber of commerce in 1992 stated in no uncertain terms that "a city without a strong downtown is a city with a heart condition." The study recommended that business development of the River Street area should be a priority and that tax breaks be used to encourage economic growth.

"Economic development isn't the retail merchant's problem, or the city's problem – it's everyone's problem," the study pointed out. "The community is in this together."

The call to arms was heeded by many businesses who welcomed the new economic opportunities. In the middle of the decade, the Spa opened, tunnel tours began, CHAB radio moved to new facilities, Lasting Impressions – the province's largest craft mall – moved into the former Lions Hall, the Heritage Pavilion expanded, Raider Industries relocated to Moose Jaw, Doepker Industries renewed its lease and expanded operations, and the city welcomed more than a dozen new enterprises.

Then-MLA Lorne Calvert, a long-time Moose Jaw clergyman, told the *Times-Herald* in 1997 he found more optimism and community pride "on the streets and in the coffee shops in our city...than I have felt in the past ten years." Moose Jaw had dramatically changed, Calvert said, and "many dreams have been accomplished." The future premier added, "When I consider where we have come from in the past ten years, I have every bit of hope and optimism for the next ten years."

Big Dreams

Pamela Wallin

Some of my earliest memories are of the bright lights and big city bustle of the streets of Moose Jaw, the Dairy Queen on Caribou Street, The Army and Navy on Main, and the trampoline near the Swing Inn down by the river. We would all pile into the '56 Pontiac and set out once a month to visit my grandparents, who lived on Third Avenue in a little house nestled next to a huge wall of caraganas that made for wonderful forts and hiding places. I was actually born in Moose Jaw, at the Union Hospital, but I have no recollection of the friendly nurses or the adoring coos of my grandmother – just the knowledge that comes from hearing stories retold.

As a teenager I returned to Moose Jaw to live with my grandmother, who by that time had moved to Grace Street, which was almost on the outskirts of town. I was terrified by the sheer size of Central Collegiate Institute, a school that housed almost as many people as the town I grew up in. I felt like a bit of a hick, sitting next to all those citified girls with their store-bought outfits. So I took a job at

the Co-op, to earn enough cash to buy some of the latest fashions.

Many years later, drawn by nostalgia and intrigued by a high school reunion, I drove back to the heartland of my youth, and was stunned to discover just how small it had become. The next trip was work – a television programme to mark the end of the era of passenger trains that had, for a century, criss-crossed this great country. We chose the historic Moose Jaw train station as our venue because the railway had been so crucial to the opening of the west. Notables, such as longtime mayor Scoop Lewry, recalled the heydays of the forties and fifties when the station had been jammed with travellers and loved ones sharing a parting kiss or a hello hug. At the time, the restaurant at the station had been "the place to eat" in town. Despite the memories, there was a sadness all around, and the once lively hub seemed a pale imitation of itself.

Then, in the summer of 2000, I made yet another foray back to my "home" to participate in a literary festival, and I found a city reborn. Like an aging lady whose memory has been sparked by a child's curiosity, Moose Jaw was alive again, proudly telling stories of her own amazing past, the writers and poets confi-

dently using her as both inspiration and backdrop. Everywhere, workmen were busy performing surgical facelifts and the once shrouded-in-secret tunnels were unearthed, dramatically capturing an earlier time.

I checked into the Temple Gardens Mineral Spa and couldn't resist a print of artist Yvette Moore's stunning interpretation of the life and times of the Gardens in an earlier era. As a girl, my mother danced there, as did I, three decades later. When I glance at the painting, I remember fondly a little city that lived big dreams, and is now, once again, becoming a grand canvas for a new generation.

New Hopes from Old Dreams

Painting the Town, or Visions of Change

Perhaps more than any other component of growth in the revitalization of Moose Jaw throughout the 1990s, the drive to market the city as a tourist destination stands above all else. But the vision of tourism was not one that sprang into focus overnight, nor was it a vision that was tied together by common agreement and goals. In fact, the phenomenal growth of the tourism industry began through piecemeal efforts, and nowhere is this more apparent than in the creation of the Murals of Moose Jaw project.

In 1986, the Mayor's Task Force on Downtown Redevelopment forecast that the city's future lay in a heightened promotion of its past, but, other than urging that more effort go into an already existing historic walking tour of the downtown, had no specific suggestions. Two years later, Moose Jaw resident Gail Fenwick thought up the idea of decorating downtown buildings with vignettes of Moose Jaw's past. As she explained in a letter to City Hall, Fenwick wanted "to paint large murals on all existing downtown buildings. Murals of quality and colour depicting our heritage, Saskatchewan scenery, modern themes, etc. The canvasses are just there waiting to be used." The project, she believed, would be a natural way of enticing travelers off the Trans-Canada Highway and into the city.

City council liked the idea and put together a group to spearhead it. The

Opposite: At the signing of the "Sunday Outing" mural. Left to right are Glenda James, the artist Wee Lee, Doug Cole, and Karen Mossing.

"Remember Old 80," with the artist, Don Sawatsky, in a bucket lift at the centre.

murals initiative was initially led by Dale Cline, an artist with family roots in the city dating back to 1882. Drawing on the highly popular example of murals in Chemainus, British Columbia, Cline and his group set to work organizing the first painting, the 1,500-square-metre "Remember old 80" – a reference to a CPR engine housed in Moose Jaw – on the side of the Royal Hotel. "It was a real clutch and grab operation," Cline remembered. "We got the artist in, but we didn't have a clue how to prepare a wall." Although Cline was an artist, the concept of large-scale painting on outdoor buildings was an entirely new venture for him.

The success of the first mural, ceremonially unveiled on August 30, 1990, soon led to numerous other projects, and within the first year ten murals were done in the downtown core, portraying spectacular spectrums of colour and local moments of history. Funding for new murals was raised from tours and through local tourism grants. Soon there were murals depicting many aspects of Moose Jaw growth specifically, and the surrounding agricultural lifestyle in general.

The murals committee had no expectations of realizing Fenwick's original hope of pulling people off the highway into town. "What we needed to do was get the people who come to the city anyway," Cline explains, "and we needed them to stay that extra afternoon. The longer you can get people to stay in your town, the more money they will spend."

Over eleven years, the project has grown to include thirty-three murals, including eight by Gus Froese. It's estimated they attract nearly ten thousand viewers per year. In 1999, the project

got a boost with the introduction of the Moose Jaw Trolley Car Co. The trolley, purchased with a federal grant, conducts regular tours from the Temple Garden Mineral Spa to most mural sites and has done a great deal to tie the murals tour into the overall thematic structure of Moose Jaw's history. "I think the murals project has made a lot of people proud of the city," says writer Bob Currie.

In the Glare of the Spotlight

The popularity of tourism, and especially the murals, has put a new spotlight on the city's arts scene. Accomplished

Dale Cline signing his mural "Storming Main Street – 1883."

The interior of Yvette Moore's Gallery and tea room.

artists have not been foreign to Moose Jaw, but the development of an active and community-supported arts community has been a long struggle. "It's like trying to grow a garden with one bucket of water," says local poet and arts organizer Gary Hyland. In many respects, Moose Jaw is a sports town, bred in the tradition of conquering, overcoming, and winning. "In a town where sport is a religion, literary culture is a tough sell," says film-maker Jeff Beesley, who produced the controversial *Last Word From Moose Jaw.*

The fostering of art, the allocation of civic space for artist endeavour, and public support beyond the level of amateur theatre and student bands needs specialized attention. Various travelling exhibitions at the Moose Art Museum, heritage displays, and the continued proliferation of local galleries and artists such as Yvette Moore have done a great deal to put "the friendly city" on the arts map.

In the summer of 1999, Moore opened a newly expanded gallery in the city's former Land Titles building. A spectacular showspace of five-and-a-half-metre ceilings, plaster cornice trim and beams, and historic and modern display cases, the gallery is home to an ever-changing collection of paintings, pottery, and crafts. "Interest is growing," says Moore. The revitalization of the arts scene "has helped in people recognizing art as a serious profession, not just a hobby. Finally we're standing back and saying we do have something to be proud of, we do have a story to tell."

People going to the library, taking in a concert, or attending a play don't necessarily realize they're participating in the arts, observes Hyland, instigator of Moose Jaw's Festival of Words, which, since its inception in 1997, has attracted some of Canada's most prominent literary figures. Hyland is spearheading the effort to revive the city's arts community. Raised in Moose Jaw, the retired high school English teacher and prolific writer believes that continuing support for an arts scene will evolve through education and exposure.

He's not against the sports tradition that Moose Jaw has proudly fostered, but believes that there is an equally strong role for arts. "There's great infrastructure for sports in Moose Jaw, but there's nothing beyond the library for culture." Hyland argues that artists "really commit to your community. They come from your community, they stay in your community, they celebrate your community, and they convey your community to the rest of the world."

The renovated Land Titles building.

Hyland is one of the key organizers of Arts in Motion (AIM), a collective representing some fifty-nine local arts organizations and businesses which is working to promote the Moose Jaw arts scene. One of AIM's biggest initiatives is to procure space for a downtown cultural arts centre, a project that got a real shot in the arm when it won a $300,000 federal grant. The group secured title in 2000-2001 to the former Army and Navy store and the Capitol Theatre. "Why shouldn't Canadian cultural products come out of the hinterland, out of Moose Jaw?" he asks. "Why can't they? The more it seems like a challenge, and the more stupid it seems to the people in Toronto, the more I want to make it happen."

No discussion of Moose Jaw's arts scene can omit mention of Beesley's 1998 film, which raised the city's national profile and caused a lot of Moose Javians to take a long, hard look at their home town. "When the film aired, it attracted a lot of attention and controversy throughout the city," Beesley acknowledged in a *Times-Herald* interview. "But it also attracted some much-needed attention to what there is in the city for arts and culture." Focusing on the dissatisfaction many young people have with their hometown, the film – which serves as a microcosm of small towns generally – implores viewers to discover the value of contributing to the arts.

Beesley admits there was much in his film "that people were going to take offense to" – and, in fact, many people were offended by it. But he insists it was not intended to be negative. His hope was that "the average viewer would say 'My God, we've got a whole generation of kids who are looking for something, and I think that culture is the answer.'" The film ends with the comment, by one young Moose Javian, that "We'd like to stay in Moose Jaw but, you know, it's a long time to wait for things to change." Says Beesley: "I think it's up to us to change it, it was my sort of call to my generation to let's get something going."

Ray Boughen agrees that the film was meant to be positive, portraying the opportunities lying untapped beneath Moose Jaw's cultural surface, but fears the message got lost.

Not on everyone. The *Times-Herald* boasted about the city's artistic potential in a 1998 editorial. "Moose Jaw has had many well kept secrets during its history," the paper wrote. "While the city's tourism industry is dusting off the past and putting it on open display, the spotlight is also starting to shine on the city's arts and culture community. Though a cloud has hovered over the arts scene for years, more people are taking a good look at what there is here for art, culture, and entertainment. While local sports have garnered a lot of attention in recent years, the arts have been quietly building a solid base. In fact, Moose Jaw is emerging as a hotbed of talent. Our singers, dancers, and musicians are performing across the country. Our authors and playwrights are earning national attention. Our painters and sculptors are producing some of the most intriguing work found anywhere. And great films are being made and produced right here in our own backyard."

Still Taking the Field

Beesley's film sparked a sports/arts debate that almost overshadowed the real athletic achievements of the nineties. The junior hockey Moose Jaw Warriors, moved to the city from Winnipeg in 1984, had their best season ever in 1998. The Warriors can boast of their

Browsing the book table at the Festival of Words.

top NHL draft selections: thirty-seven picks in fourteen years – among the recent top players are Curtis Brown (Buffalo Sabres '94), Ryan Smith (Edmonton Oilers '94), Darryl Laplante (Detroit Red Wings '95), Matt Higgins (Montreal Canadiens '96), Chad Hinz (Edmonton Oilers '96), and Jamie Lundmark (New York Rangers '99) plus Theoren Fleury and Mike Keane.

For a couple of years in the late nineties, the Moose Jaw Diamond Dogs, the city's first professional baseball team in many decades, made a daring dash for glory before succumbing to poor financial management and folding at the end of the 1998 season. On a brighter baseball note, the Miller Express, Moose Jaw's team in the Saskatchewan Major Baseball League, won the championship for the first time in twenty-five years in 1999.

On the level of individual achievement in sports, among the brightest lights were Susan Humphreys, the 1997 Canadian women's figure skating champion, who first began developing her talents at the age of three through the Prairie Royal Figure Skating Club, and Wayne Cormier, who in 1999 captured his 5th Canadian powerlifting championship.

The Place Everyone Has Heard Of

For a city of only slightly over thirty thousand, Moose Jaw has had a disproportionate amount of attention. Sure, much of it is by brief mention only, and more often than not is a putdown. As columnist Don McGillivray wrote in the *Ottawa Citizen:*

"More and more writers and broadcasters use Moose Jaw when they need a symbol of small-town Canada. They choose it because of what Moose Jaw is really like. Probably the name has a lot to do with it, just as Podunk has been used because it sounds like a backward stick-in-the-mud kind of place." To people who grew up in big-ger cities, McGillivray wrote, "Moose Jaw must seem typical of the flat, boring prairie. Even the main street is called Main Street. And then, there's the name."

Comics, movies, and TV shows have all capitalized on the comical name. The character of Joe Farrell in the hit TV comedy series *Ellen* was from Moose Jaw. In a 1999 episode of *The Simpsons,* a cartoon-charactered baseball team team threatened to move to Moose Jaw after a bad season, and, in the pilot episode of the *Due South* series, Constable Fraser is assigned to the RCMP detachment in Moose Jaw. The CBC comedy series *Royal Canadian Air Farce* none-too-politely referred to the chin of former Prime Minister Brian Mulroney as "Moose Jaw." One of the wacky hockey heroes playing beside Paul Newman's character in the 1970s comedy *Slap Shot* was billed as a proud Moose Javian. Even halfway across the world, in a 1997 comic strip that runs in the *Australian* newspaper, a garage in the middle of the barren outback sports a sign announcing "Moose Jaw Garage."

Mark Powers, who writes the popular Wolverine strip for Marvel Comics, used the city as a setting for one episode. "It may sound goofy, but we really just wanted a location with a cool name," he told the *Times-Herald.* "To an American audience, it's evocative, it sounds like a Canadian name. It gives them a feeling of a town on the edge of civilization."

For all the ridicule the city has received, though, sometimes it's evoked in a positive way. Peter Gzowski chose Moose Jaw as the location for the last episode of his long-running *Morningside* CBC radio show. And when CBC's *Midday* TV show broadcast from Moose Jaw one day in 1998, a press release characterized the visit as "a celebration of living in a small Canadian prairie city." Added executive producer Julie Bristow: *"Midday* and Moose Jaw are both quintessential Canadiana."

Attitudes

For Moose Jaw to sustain its economic growth it will need to draw deeply on the same positive attitude that turned the city around over the past decade. It may be the butt of comedians' jokes (impressionist Rich Little once quipped that "Moose Jaw is too small

Ode to Scoop Lewry: A Funeral Oration

Ken Mitchell

This is the final farewell, Scoop,
no coming back after this one
with your wooden nickels
and right-hand sidewalk lanes.
You're off to mayor heaven
and may you have a long tenure there.
We hope you will erect a statue
of the world's biggest bull moose
outside those white pearly gates,
complete to every anatomical detail.

Remember the square inches of Moose Jaw
you hustled on the stock market?
Kekoarama, Plamore Bucks, donkey
races in the Moose Jaw Arena?
The campaign for casinos on River Street
to siphon off a poke of that Vegas gold?

Scoop, will you relive the Canucks
hockey game, the time you dared
the Western mayors to a race
across the ice on high heels?
You and Juba and Harry Veiner,
falling on your asses for charity.
Our howling mob of kids
in the pig pen loved it
but the adults shook
their heads and muttered,
"What a fool, what a fool."

But you just kept coming back for more,
each defeat merely enhancing the victories,
whether a politician or a collision
or the big C waiting on the next corner.
Full of braggery and outrage,
you hurled more gauntlets
than Don Quixote could imagine
challenging the CBC and the feds
the newspapers and the Thatchers,
gopher-clubbing any smartass critic
or stuffy bureaucrat who dared
to lift a snout from his musty hole.

For you, Moose Jaw always progressed,
ever-advancing to greater horizons,
a future forged in the crucible
of adversity – and to hell
with the writing on the wall.

The mayor who succeeds you
will struggle to fill
those size twelve wingbacks
flatter than platters of warm spit,
the arches busted by the decades
you stood in line at receptions
for the Royal Family and turkey
buffets, grinning at the lame jokes,
your pockets crammed with wooden nickels
and Moose Javian credit cards.

Ponder this, electors of Moose Jaw,
as you write your history down,
and applaud the final comic blow
of our world-class political clown.

to have weather"), but from the most general of perspectives, the city is greatly enjoyed by its population. A 1999 survey indicated that some 87 per cent of Moose Javians believe the quality of life in the city to be "good" or "very good." With its family-oriented values, respect for the elderly, renewed economic environment, and progressive tourism trends, Moose Jaw is a city on the go, a work in progress.

"Moose Jaw is without a doubt the friendliest city we have every lived in," remembers retired Brigadier-General Bill Kalbfleisch, 15 Wing commander in the early '90s. "This was at a period of change, very good change, and you could feel how the city was reaching out to people. That spirit, that warmth, was a huge marketing factor for Moose Jaw."

The collective energy of Moose Javians and the desire to work together on economic, tourism, and arts projects will be critical to continued growth in the years ahead.

As former Alderman John Livingston says: "Moose Jaw has gone through its ups and downs, but it has survived and will continue to survive." But for the city to flourish, it must go beyond a mere "survival" mentality,

allowing itself to embrace new possibilities. Moose Javians have become more concerned about the future.

"We've finally got something positive down here, long overdue," says John Guillaume, Moose Jaw entrepreneur and manager of the Suntree Café. "It took a long time for this town to figure out what it could be good at: tourism is it. We need people to embrace tourism and be part of it." Rod McLean, former executive director of the chamber of commerce, believes that a positive attitude is being strongly fostered within the city, and will continue to fuel the fires of development and economic expansion.

In July, 2001, after a provincial moratorium on casino operations was lifted, an $8 million casino project in downtown Moose Jaw received approval. The casino will be the showcase, but an additional $12 million redevelopment of River Street, including a 400 seat amphitheatre, will also proceed. This ambitious project – simply called "Project Moose Jaw" – heralds a rebirth of the city's historic core. It ensures that Moose Jaw's past will have a strong role in helping secure the city's future.

"For a lot of people, especially smaller businesses, seeing is believing and they're not in the position to make the economic investment before it happens," a chamber report noted. "Once you see your neighbour do it, it becomes fashionable; it becomes necessary. Opportunities need to be systematically identified and pursued and social issues need to be openly and honestly dealt with. After all, what's it all about? No matter where one goes, the pursuit is the same – quality of life."

The Future

There is a new vision for Moose Jaw these days, one linking past to present. Moose Jaw's rich heritage is providing a way to reach beyond the present. The ancient waters that supply the spa may be a symbol of how that past – both distant and not so distant – can be a source of renewal.

Moose Jaw has been a frontier town, a boom town, a railway centre, an industrial city.

Now it may finally be able to make use of all these aspects of its past as it forges a new and vibrant identity for the future.

The Executive of the 1913-14 Literary Society.

Contributor Biographies

John Larsen – Raised in Europe, and later Edmonton, John Larsen obtained a BA in History from the University of Victoria, and worked for Parks Canada doing historical research and interpretation before enrolling as an officer in the Canadian Forces. He was stationed at the air base in Moose Jaw for three years in the early 1990s, and quickly realized that the rich history of the city had yet to be fully recorded. John lives, teaches, and works in Calgary.

Maurice Libby – Maurice Libby moved from small-town Saskatchewan to Moose Jaw when he was five, and grew up there. He returned to "the Friendly City" to live at the turn of the Millennium, after a twenty-year absence. Maurice obtained an anthropology degree from the University of Toronto, and worked there as a writer and artist until his return to Saskatchewan.

Robert Currie – Born in Lloydminster, Bob Currie spent his teen years in Moose Jaw before attending the University of Saskatchewan, then returning to Moose Jaw. He taught at Central Collegiate in Moose Jaw for thirty years before retiring in 1996 to pursue his writing career full time. He is a founding member of Coteau Books, started his own literary magazine called *Salt,* and was an early president of the Saskatchewan Writers Guild. Named one of the city's two poet laureates in 1991, Bob Currie began publishing poetry in 1967. His stories and poems have appeared in over forty magazines and anthologies, and he has served as either editor or co-editor for nine books. An award-winning poet, Bob Currie has published four books of poetry: *Diving Into Fire* (1977), *Yarrow* (1980), *Learning on the Job* (1986) and *Klondike Fever* (1992), as well as two collections of short stories, *Night Games* (1983) and *Things You Don't Forget* (1999).

W.G. "Bill" Davies – Bill Davies was born in Indian Head in 1916 and lived in Saskatchewan all his life. After marrying Rose Sapergia, he found work at the Swift Canadian packing plant in Moose Jaw, and was involved with the creation of the union there. Bill Davies' political career included eight years as a Moose Jaw alderman and fifteen years as MLA for the city. He served as Minister of Health in the W. S. Lloyd government during the province's Medicare dispute. A founder of the Saskatchewan Federation of Labour, Bill served in many capacities in the Saskatchewan and Canadian labour movements, including twenty-five years as the executive secretary of the SFL. He was a member of the Labour Relations Board for twelve years, and served terms on the Saskatchewan Educational Council, the Saskatchewan Arts Board, and other provincial bodies. He was a member of the Order of Canada and received an Honorary Doctorate of Law from the University of Saskatchewan. Bill died in 1999.

H.S. "Hub" Elkin – Hub Elkin was born in Moose Jaw in 1916, and raised in that city. His distinguished career in the service of the labour movement in Saskatchewan, Canada and beyond was inspired, he says, by the ideals of T.C. Douglas. After school, and a stint at the Kent and Brooksbank men's store in Moose Jaw, he started on the loading dock at Swift Packers in 1934. In 1942, Hub was the Local President of the union which negotiated its first collective agreement with Swift. He worked as a union organizer across Canada, for several different unions and was the founding president of the Saskatchewan Federation of Labour in 1944.

For a time a labour conciliator for the CCF government, he served as Deputy Minister of Labour from 1949 until 1965. After working for several labour organizations provincially and internationally, he landed a job at the Workers' Compensation Board, from which he retired in 1981. He lives in Regina.

Ethel Kirk Grayson – Ethel Kirk Grayson was born in Moose Jaw, in 1890. Educated in Moose Jaw schools, she received degrees from the University of Toronto and the University of Manitoba, then attended the School of Expression in Boston. She lectured in English Literature at Alberta College, Edmonton; at Mount Allison Ladies' College, Sackville, New Brunswick; and at the McMurray College for Women in Jacksonville, Illinois. She was a Charter member of the University Women's Club, Moose Jaw, and its first president. In 1938 she was one of the speakers on the eastern circuit of the Women's Canadian Club. Her published work includes the novels *Willow Smoke* (1928), *Apples of the Moon* (1933), and *Fires in the Vine* (1942), and a collection of poetry, *Beggar's Velvet* (1948). She also published a memoir, *Unbind the Sheaves* (1964), and her second book of poetry was published posthumously. She died in Moose Jaw in 1980.

Peter Gzowski – Peter Gzowski, the CBC Radio host of *Morningside* from 1982 to 1997, hosted the last edition of that popular radio show from Moose Jaw. The reason was that, after finishing university in 1957, he was the city editor of the Moose Jaw *Times-Herald* for a year. He was the youngest managing editor of *Maclean's* at the age of 28, when he was hired there the following year. Gzowski began his radio career in 1969 and hosted *This Country in the Morning, Morningside's* predecessor, in

1971. Peter Gzowski has won seven ACTRA awards, published nine books, is a member of the Canadian News Hall of Fame, and received an honorary degree from Trent University in 1987 for public service and broadcasting. A 1995 recipient of the Governor General's Performing Arts Award for Lifetime Achievement in Broadcasting, he was invested in 1999 as a Companion of the Order of Canada.

C.W. "Willy" Hodgson – Christine Wilna (Willy) Hodgson was born at Ahtahkakoop (Sandy Lake) in northern Saskatchewan. After forty-five years in the public service (nursing, social work, and human resources), she retired in October of 2000. A Plains Cree speaker and elder, Hodgson has received numerous awards for her work in Cree culture, language, and community development. Named Citizen of the Year in 1997 and Woman of Distinction in 1998 by the City of Moose Jaw, she was awarded a Saskatchewan Order of Merit in 1994. In 2000 Hodgson was presented the Bill Hanson award by the International association for Native Employment because of her outstanding contribution to native employment. She is married to Bill Hodgson, and has two sons, two daughters, and two grandchildren. She and Bill live in Moose Jaw.

Gary Hyland – Born and raised in Moose Jaw, Gary Hyland taught high school English there for thirty years before retiring in 1994 to pursue his writing full-time. He has published four poetry collections –

White Crane Spreads Wings (1996), *After Atlantis* (1991), *Street of Dreams* (1984), and *Just Off Main* (1982) – and two chapbooks. Not only has his work appeared in numerous anthologies, he has also co-edited four of them – *A Sudden Radiance, 100% Cracked Wheat, 200% Cracked Wheat*, and *Number One Northern*. Named co-poet laureate of Moose Jaw in 1991, Gary Hyland was a founding member of Thunder Creek Co-operative (Coteau Books) and Sage Hill Writing Experience. He has served on the executive of the Saskatchewan Writers Guild, as a Board member on SaskFilm, and taught creative writing at the Saskatchewan Summer School of the Arts. Co-ordinator of the Saskatchewan Festival of Words, Gary Hyland still makes his home in Moose Jaw.

Joy Kogawa – Joy Kogawa is known for her novels, poetry, essays, and activism. She was born in Vancouver in 1935, a second-generation Japanese Canadian or nisei. She and her family were evacuated to Slocan, British Columbia and later to Coaldale, Alberta during the Second World War. She pursued studies in education at the University of Alberta, studied music at the University of Toronto, and also attended the Anglican Women's Training College and the University of Saskatchewan. Joy Kogawa lived in Moose Jaw briefly with her husband and children in the 1960s, and published her first poems and stories while living there. She has

published several collections of poetry, essays, and children's literature, and the novels *Obasan, Istuka,* and *The Rain Ascends. Obasan,* which focuses on Japanese Canadians and the injustices they experienced during and after the Second World War, has received several national book awards. Joy Kogawa has been made a Member of the Order of Canada for her accomplishments.

Don Kossick – Born and raised in Moose Jaw, Don Kossick is now Director of the Community Outreach and Education Centre in Saskatoon. His experience in community education and social activism extends to over thirty years of involvement in local and international organizations, including the National Farmers' Union, SGEU, the Saskatchewan Human Rights Commission, and CUSO. Among his current projects are the Saskatoon Communities for Children and the Canada-Mozambique Health Renewal Project. One of Don's major interests is arts and the media. He is an award-winning photographer whose portfolio includes many audio-visual documentary productions. He is currently producer of Making the Links, a weekly community radio program on CFCR-FM.

Jim McLean – Although he now lives in Calgary, Jim McLean was born and raised in Moose Jaw. He joined the Canadian Pacific Railway in 1956 and worked in a number of locations throughout the country before retiring in October, 1995. He then worked for four years with Transport Canada in Calgary, retiring (again) in early 2001. Jim started writing while in Moose Jaw. He has published short stories, plays, and poetry in numerous anthologies and had them broadcast on radio. His book of poetry *The Secret Life of Railroaders* was published in 1982. He is an accomplished illustrator as well, publishing his work in many books, book covers, and scientific papers. His best-known work is in the book *Wildflowers Across the Prairies*. He recently completed a series of drawings for a field guide for the Grasslands National Park in southwest Saskatchewan, and is working on a collection of poems about Beethoven.

Ken Mitchell — Ken Mitchell was born and raised in Moose Jaw and now lives in Regina. The author or editor of over twenty books, he has been teaching at the English Department of the University of Regina for more than thirty years. He is also the author of several dozen screenplays, stage dramas, and radio dramas, most notably *The Hounds of Notre Dame* (Genie nomination for Best Screenplay) and *The Shipbuilder. Cruel Tears,*

his country music opera, has gone on to international acclaim. His dramatic tribute to Dr. Norman Bethune, *Gone the Burning Sun,* has toured all over North America and China. In 1999 Ken Mitchell received the Order of Canada for his work as a "literary ambassador," teaching and promoting Canadian literature in India, Russia, Greece, and, most notably, for two years in China.

Lewis Rice — The creator of many early twentieth-century photographs, Lewis Rice was born in Cape Breton around 1865. He moved to Moose Jaw in 1907 and established himself as a successful businessman and photographer. He was in the city during its greatest period of economic growth and physical expansion, which he documented with his camera. He was interested in architecture, and many of his photographs preserve unusual, even unique, buildings. He was also a master at capturing the energy of the city in its early days with dynamic and exciting street scenes. A lover of nature who did many

idyllic studies of the river, Lewis Rice also photo-documented the changing face of agriculture, as human labour gave way to mechanization. He was also the Commodore of the Aquatic Club, which was his brain child. He had his photographs featured in many prestigious exhibitions, chief of which was the Dominion Fair (the precursor of the CNE) in Toronto.

Pamela Wallin — Pamela Wallin was born in Moose Jaw, but grew up in Wadena. She returned to Moose Jaw as a teenager to attend Central Collegiate. After graduating from the University of Regina, she began a career as a social worker at the Prince Albert Penitentiary before switching to radio and television. Pamela Wallin was the first woman in Canadian network television history to be appointed an Ottawa bureau chief. Her career as a broadcaster and journalist has now spanned more than 25 years, several continents, and all forms of media. In 1998, she published her best-selling memoir, *Since You Asked.*

Acknowledgements

About two months before this manuscript was completed, I spent a few days in Ottawa. Flipping through the Saturday edition of the Ottawa *Citizen,* I noticed that Guy Vanderhaeghe was speak-

ing at a writer's festival. "Perfect," I thought. A writer, a "Saskatchewanite," a dose of inspiration. Vanderhaeghe said many things; some reflective, some matter-of-fact, and some amusing. One of his

phrases stayed with me: "I think in many ways, the decision of what to write about is often made for you."

And there it was — the absolute reason for why I had written everything I had for this book – the decision was made for me. I had arrived in Moose Jaw and marvelled at the history of the place. I had spoken at length about the uniqueness of the city. I had responded with restrained politeness as Haligonians, Edmontonians, Torontonians, or Vancouverites questioned the very concept of an interesting Moose Jaw. I worked with your city, lived in your city, left, and now continually return to your city. By embracing and living your story, it was the story I had to tell. The decision had been made for me.

My sincere thanks to everyone in Moose Jaw who contributed to making this book possible. By phone, letters, chats in the street, references – you are literally too many to be mentioned – my sincere appreciation. But I feel that a few names do need to be noted. To the whole crew at the Moose Jaw Times-Herald, for your public support and wealth of information. To the folks at the Moose Jaw Chamber of Commerce, for your assistance in everything from taking inter-provincial phone messages to letting me break your photocopier. To Rod McLean, a friend, confidante, and one of this city's most progressive thinkers. To Vanese Grant, for your constant support and guidance. To Dan Gottselig, for the insiders perspective. To Colonel (later Brigadier-General) Bill Kalbfleisch, for making Moose Jaw a highlight of my career. To The Festival of Words, for your support and exposure. And, of course most importantly, to all the many people that have made this book possible by giving of their time, the memory and their honesty. Some of those people are regrettably no longer with us; this book is for them.

Four other very special notes of thanks are also in order. The first is to my writing partner Maurice, for his dedication to and continued passion for the very difficult process of co-producing a book over a 3,000 mile distance. The second is to that special group of friends – Wade, Colin, Steve, and Conor – who fed my literary soul. The third is to my Mother, Sheilagh, who taught me how many great things there are to learn, and how many great people there are to meet in this amazing world. And lastly, to my fantastic wife Denise, for her unwavering support to this project and her complete faith in me. I couldn't have done it without her.

– John Larsen

They say that writing is a solitary pursuit. If that's true, why are there so many people to thank at a time like this? Of course there is my writing partner, John Larsen, which goes without saying. There are my parents, Harvey and Ruby Libby, who put me (and the ridgebacks) up through most of the research and had the patience of the saints they surely are. My brother Michael, for his encouragement and photographs. There was Joanne Foot, who helped in innumerable ways, and Larry Gusaas, especially his patience and sympathy in enduring many rants and tantrums.

Bob Currie for his support and for putting us onto Coteau.

Rod McLean, and everyone at the Chamber of Commerce for the office supplies and photocopier.

Geordie Telfer for everything.

The staff at the Moose Jaw public library were supportive and helpful in so many ways, especially Anne and Karon, and the staff of the Moose Jaw Archives, most especially Joyce (above and beyond the call of duty), Ken (ditto), and Dorothy (yes, the microfilm did ruin my eyes).

Robert and Stephanie for all the coffee and a place to scribble (I'm sorry to see you both go).

There are many people (too many to list, unfortunately) who gave us so much help: those who consented to be interviewed, those who let us use pictures and mementoes, and all those who gave us encouragement and support. I'm sure I'm forgetting a lot of people, and for that I'm truly sorry.

The Times-Herald for everything including a lot of good publicity. Thanks Carl and Leslie. CBC radio and CHAB, ditto.

And finally, Laura Lee Jones, who kept me sane and focused though the final stages, and whom I owe more than she'll ever know.

To you all, thank you.

– Maurice Richard Libby

Photo Credits

Photographs on the front cover (bottom) and pages iv, 2, 3, 4, 6, 7, 8, 9, 13, 14, 15, 16, 17, 18, 19, 21, 22, 26, 28, 29, 31, 32 (top), 33 (top), 34, 35, 36, 38, 39, 40, 42, 43, 44, 45, 49, 50, 53, 54, 55, 56 (top), 59, 60, 61, 63 (bottom), 64, 66, 67, 68, 69, 70, 71, 72, 73, 74, 75, 77, 80, 81, 83, 84, 87, 93, 100, 102, 104, 105, 106, 107, 111, 112, 113, 124, 125, 126, 127, 130, 133, 135, 136, 140, 141, 143, 146, 147, 148 (bottom), 149, 151, 152, 154, 155, 156, 164 (bottom), 165, 168, 169, 170, 172, 173, 176, 177, 178, 180, 186, 189, 190, 193, 195, 200, 201, 202, 205, 206, and 210, are courtesy of the Moose Jaw Public Library Archives.

Photographs on pages 23, 24, 62, 63 (top), 76, 85, 90, 91, 94, 97, 99, 116, 117, 119, 120, 157, 158, 159, 160, 167, 203, and 204 are courtesy of the Saskatchewan Archives Board.

The photograph on page 164 (top) is courtesy of the *Leader-Post* Collection, Saskatchewan Archives Board.

Photographs on pages 5, 20, 33 (bottom), 121, 166, and 192 are courtesy of the University of Saskatchewan, Special Collections Department.

Photographs on pages 32 (bottom), 110 top, 188, are courtesy of the Moose Jaw YM-YWCA.

Photographs on pages 138, 139, 142, 148, 161, 163, 210, and 211 are courtesy of 15 Wing Moose Jaw.

Photographs on pages 122 and 175 are courtesy of the Saskatchewan Sports Hall of Fame Museum.

The photograph on page 47 is courtesy of the Moose Jaw *Times-Herald*.

Photographs on page 56 (bottom), and on pages 114, 115, and 182 are courtesy of Don Kossick.

Photograph of Allen G. Hawkes on page 80 is reproduced by permission from *The Story of Saskatchewan and Its People,* by John Hawkes, 1924, S.J. Clarke Publishing Co.

The photograph on the bottom of page 110 is courtesy of Gregory and Marilyn Ursell.

The photograph on page 129 is courtesy of Bill McWilliams.

The photograph on page 145 is courtesy of Stan Ingleby.

The photographs on pages 197 and 199 are courtesy of Lyle Johnson.

The photograph on page 208 (also on the cover) is courtesy of and © Danny and Judy Boyer.

The photographs on pages 215 and 216 are courtesy of the Tunnels of Moose Jaw.

The photographs on pages 220 and 222 are courtesy of the Murals of Moose Jaw.

The photographs on pages 223 and 224 are courtesy of Yvette Moore.

The photograph on page 225 is courtesy of the Festival of Words.

The photograph on page 226 is courtesy of Maurice Libby.

The photograph on page 231 is courtesy of Geoffrey Ursell and Barbara Sapergia.

The photograph of Willy Hodgson on page 207 is courtesy of the Moose Jaw *Times-Herald*.

The photograph of Lorne Calvert on page 25 is courtesy of Digney Photographics Ltd.